Power Tools for PEAK PRO

A Complete Guide to the Mac's Most Powerful Audio Editor

BY DAVID M. RUBIN

Backbeat Books
San Francisco

Published by Backbeat Books
600 Harrison Street, San Francisco, CA 94107
www.backbeatbooks.com
email: books@musicplayer.com

An imprint of the Music Player Network
Publishers of *Guitar Player*, *Bass Player*, *Keyboard*, and *EQ*, and other magazines

United Entertainment Media, Inc.
A CMP Information company

CMP
United Business Media

Distributed to the book trade in the US and Canada by
Publishers Group West, 1700 Fourth Street, Berkeley, CA 94710

Distributed to the music trade in the US and Canada by
Hal Leonard Publishing, P.O. Box 13819, Milwaukee, WI 53213

Cover and text design by Doug Gordon
Composition by Maureen Forys, Happenstance Type-O-Rama

Library of Congress Cataloging-in-Publication Data

Rubin, David M., 1945–
Power tools for Peak : a complete guide to the Mac's most powerful audio editor / by David M. Rubin.
p. cm.
Includes index.
ISBN-13: 978-0-87930-847-6
ISBN-10: 0-87930-847-8 (pbk. : alk. paper)
1. Peak (Computer file) 2. Digital audio editors. I. Title.

ML74.4.P43R83 2005
006.5—dc22

2005028885

Printed in the United States of America

05 06 07 08 09 5 4 3 2 1

For Kata and Aaron

I've read, that things inanimate have mov'd,
And, as with living Souls, have been inform'd,
By Magick Numbers and persuasive Sound.

—William Congreve (1697)

Acknowledgments

Writing a book that explores Peak Pro's many capabilities has been like putting together a puzzle with thousands of pieces. I couldn't possibly have assembled a complete picture without the generous help of many on the BIAS staff.

In particular, I'd like to thank Christine Berkley for her enthusiastic support and for graciously providing me with the resources that I needed to get this project off the ground. I'd also like to thank Steve Berkley for creating Peak Pro in the first place and for helping to elucidate some of the more arcane technical issues that I encountered.

Thanks also go to Dan Spirlock and Zac Wheatcroft for lending their technical expertise and for helping me to better understand the program's myriad features. And finally, I owe my greatest debt of gratitude to Jason Davies. His upbeat spirit, unflagging support, endless patience, and overall knowledge of the software made him truly invaluable to me during the many months that I devoted to the writing of this book.

To all of these people and to the many others at BIAS whose work behind the scenes has benefited me during this endeavor: my heartfelt thanks.

—David M. Rubin

Contents

Chapter 1

First Look: The Power of Peak Pro

Back in the 1980s, when the Macintosh took the computer world by storm, the Mac's graphical user interface made it a natural platform for artists and musicians. It wasn't long before the first audio editing programs began to appear. Soon the audio-software landscape was dotted with powerful yet user-friendly editing programs like Sound Designer, Alchemy, and SoundEdit.

During the ensuing years, however, these and other stereo editing programs fell by the wayside, the victims of neglect and changing priorities in the companies that created them. Fortunately, a newer program arose to fill the vacuum. Peak from Berkley Integrated Audio Systems (BIAS) was the brainchild of Steve Berkley, the company's founder and president. For nearly a decade, Peak has thrived as it has evolved into the powerhouse audio editing program that it is today.

Peak's straightforward and intuitive user interface has become more refined as the program has grown into a professional-level application with an array of cutting-edge features and a raft of deep and detailed editing capabilities. It is now unquestionably the premier stereo editing program in a number of professional audio and video fields. With the introduction of Peak Pro 5 (see **Figure 1-1**) and in view of the program's current level of complexity, the time seemed ripe for a book to describe and explain in full what Peak's many tools and commands really do and how to use them most effectively.

Figure 1-1
Peak Pro's many powerful audio-manipulation tools let you tackle an impressive range of editing tasks.

Peak's Approach

Many people may wonder, "What does Peak Pro bring to the table that other audio applications don't?" And "How is Peak Pro different from those other programs?" To answer those questions, it's important to understand Peak Pro's approach to editing. Peak Pro is a stereo (or 2-track) audio editing program, which right away makes it quite different from multitrack DAW (digital audio workstation) programs, such as MOTU Digital Performer, Digidesign Pro Tools, and Apple Logic Audio.

Except when being used to assemble a playlist (see Chapter 11), Peak Pro always operates on one audio file at a time. Even if you have numerous files open at the same time, you can only listen to one of them. By comparison, audio/MIDI sequencers and other DAW applications are based on the concept of a *session* or *project.* These multitrack programs can play back numerous audio files at the same time, and derive their great appeal from being able to create a virtual onscreen studio complete with mixing boards, busses, and effects.

Peak Pro's approach is much simpler. To start work on an audio file, you just open the file, examine the waveform, and get right down to business. You don't have to create a new project or session and import an audio file before you can get started. Peak Pro's file-based approach is efficient and intuitive. But don't let the program's easy-to-use interface fool you. Peak Pro's editing tools and processing capabilities are amazingly powerful and surprisingly sophisticated, which is why many professionals use it for specialized audio editing tasks, even though their primary music software is a DAW.

Getting up close and personal with your audio files is what Peak Pro is all about. The program is designed to let you carefully scrutinize every nook and cranny of a recording and fix it if it needs fixing, adjust it if it's a little out of whack, or just twist it and distort it mercilessly if you happen to be in a creative mood. That's one reason why many sample-library developers and loop creators favor Peak and why Mac-based sound designers consider Peak to be an indispensable tool in the quest for new material.

But samplemongers and loopmeisters aren't the only ones who flock to Peak. Composers, mastering engineers, dialog editors, video producers, multimedia developers, remix editors, and project-studio owners rely on Peak for its comprehensive set of recording, editing, looping, processing, and CD mastering tools. And as most audio professionals have learned, Peak's file-based approach to editing perfectly complements the more elaborate project-based capabilities found in most DAWs, thereby providing the best of both worlds when the two are used together.

Of necessity, *Power Tools for Peak Pro* covers a lot of ground as it explores the program's multifarious audio editing and processing options. The book also covers a lot of ground in addressing a wide target audience. It provides a close-up look at Peak Pro's most sophisticated tools for professionals, but also offers full descriptions of the program's basic editing capabilities for relative newcomers. Tool Tips throughout the book provide additional insight into using Peak Pro, and keyboard shortcuts are supplied throughout the text to help you speed up your workflow.

Unlike the typical owner's manual, *Power Tools for Peak Pro* is organized according to the types of tasks that audio software users are likely to perform: sound designing, working with video, repairing audio files, editing loops, processing audio, and so forth. To give you a taste of what lies ahead, here's a brief description of the topics covered.

Up Ahead

To get the most out of Peak Pro, you must have a solid grounding in the physics of sound. So Chapter 2 delves into that subject and then goes on to explain (with a minimum of technical mumbo-jumbo) the often mysterious process by which sound gets transformed into computer data.

Chapter 3 offers a detailed look at Peak Pro's user interface, including many of its more arcane features. Even advanced users are likely to discover a few tips that can speed up their workflow and make their editing tasks easier. Beginners will find some little-known tricks to help them navigate the program.

In Chapter 4, you'll see how to record and play back audio with various options, and you'll learn how to import and export files of different types.

Chapter 5 covers the standard bread-and-butter editing operations that most users perform on a daily basis. Chapter 6 explores Peak Pro's many tools and commands for fixing audio problems and repairing damaged recordings.

Chapter 7 focuses on tools that are particularly well suited to working with music and dialog. Chapter 8 takes a look at Peak Pro's more exotic processing tools, which sound designers and sound effects editors especially appreciate.

Chapter 9 explains how to use plug-ins in Peak Pro and explores the program's highly flexible Vbox plug-in matrix. Chapter 10 describes the different types of markers and how to use them and also looks at Peak Pro's many looping tools.

Chapter 11 is dedicated to Peak Pro's powerful Playlist window and its capabilities for mastering and directly burning CDs. Chapter 12 looks at QuickTime movies and how to use them with Peak Pro for soundtrack editing. And Chapter 13 describes how to expand Peak Pro's processing and management capabilities through batch processing and the use of Apple Events.

Appendix I provides a handy list of keyboard shortcuts, and Appendix II lists and describes the audio formats that Peak Pro supports.

Features

Peak Pro's full set of tools, processors, and other features would be impossible to condense into a short list (which is why I wrote this book). However, to give you a sense of Peak Pro's editing versatility and its wide-ranging creative capabilities, here are just a few of the program's highlights:

- Hard-disk recording and playback at any of the standard sampling rates, using the Mac's built-in audio hardware or any third-party Core Audio-compatible hardware
- Support for 8-, 16-, 24-, and 32-bit audio files
- Support for a long list of audio file formats, including AIFF, Sound Designer II, WAV, QuickTime, MP3, and MP4
- Non-destructive editing with unlimited undo and redo
- Customizable waveform display
- Customizable Toolbar and keyboard shortcuts
- Support for third-party VST and Audio Units plug-ins
- Powerful looping and loop-editing tools
- Support for several popular hardware samplers
- QuickTime movie soundtrack editing with audio/video scrubbing and sync
- Sophisticated playlist editing and mastering

- Built-in Vbox effects-routing matrix lets you hot-swap plug-ins and create complex parallel and serial processing combinations
- High-end envelope-controlled fades, panning, amplitude, and other processing

New in Version 4

With the introduction of Version 4.0 and the later improvements in Version 4.1, Peak acquired several new features, including the following:

- ImpulseVerb high-quality convolution-based reverb
- Bit Usage meter
- Harmonic Rotate DSP tool
- BIAS Sqweez compressor/limiter plug-in
- Vbox Matrix support for both VST and Audio Units plug-ins
- Magic Pencil tool to smooth out clicks and pops
- Grid-based Markers From Tempo command
- Envelope-based Dynamic Tempo Change command
- Extended MP3 encoding rates up to 320 kbps
- Multithreading and multiprocessor support
- OS X-style brushed-metal user interface
- Improved VU meters
- New slide-out Contents Drawer for the Audio Document window
- Transparent Cursor Info Overlay
- Resizable Toolbar buttons with reconfigurable Toolbar window
- Red Book standard CD burning directly from an Audio Document or Playlist window

New in Version 5

In mid-2005, BIAS debuted Version 5 of Peak and christened it *Peak Pro.* This latest incarnation of the program added several sophisticated enhancements and some powerful professional-level features, including:

- A completely redesigned Playlist window with graphic waveform and list views
- Direct replication-ready CD burning
- ISRC support
- PQ subcode editing
- Track indexes and CD-Text support
- Unlimited undo/redo in the Playlist window
- Snap To CD Frames command
- Support for file names longer than 32 characters

- VSTi and Audio Units Instrument plug-in support
- MIDI support and onscreen keyboard for plug-in instruments
- Automatic plug-in latency compensation
- Envelope from Audio command
- Strip Silence tool
- Auto Define Tracks command
- New Change Duration algorithm
- New Change Pitch algorithm
- New Sample Rate Conversion algorithm
- New ImpulseVerb appearance and controls
- RMS Normalize command

Peak Pro XT 5

With the announcement of Peak Pro 5, BIAS also introduced a new software bundle called Peak Pro XT (Extended Technology). It combines Peak Pro 5 with the popular SoundSoap and SoundSoap Pro noise-reduction and audio-restoration plug-ins.

The rest of the XT package consists of BIAS's new professional-quality Master Perfection Suite (see **Figure 1-2**):

- SuperFreq (4-, 6-, 8-, and 10-band paragraphic equalizer)
- Repli-Q (EQ matching)
- Sqweez-3/Sqweez-5 (multiband compressor/limiter)
- PitchCraft (real-time pitch correction/transposition)
- Reveal (audio analysis displays)
- GateEx (noise gate/expander)

You can learn more about the XT bundle at: www.bias-inc.com/products/peak5.

What You Need

This book is designed to cover all of the most important features in Peak Pro 5. If you're using an earlier version of the program or one of the "lite" versions (such as LE or DV), you should seriously consider upgrading, because the lite versions are lacking most of the processing and many of the editing features found in the full Pro version.

Peak 4 has many similarities to Peak Pro 5, so much of the book can be useful even if you don't want to or can't upgrade. Keep in mind, however, that some of the details, such as available options, button positions, and editing tools, may be different than those presented in the book. In addition, the Playlist window and CD-burning features differ considerably between versions. If you're willing to take those differences into account, much of this book may still be of value in learning your way around the program.

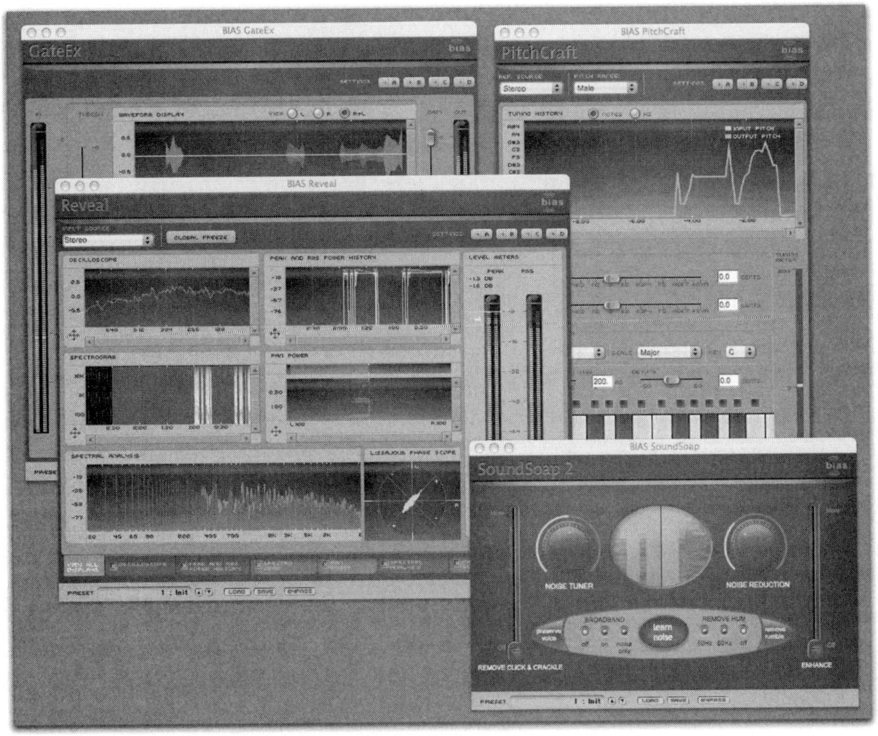

Figure 1-2
BIAS's XT bundle adds several high-end proprietary plug-ins to Peak Pro.

It's a good idea to keep your hardware system up to date as well. Technically speaking, you could run Peak Pro on a 400MHz G3 Mac with 256MB of RAM, but you might not get the very best results, and some of the features might not work properly. For example, Peak Pro 5's new sample-rate conversion algorithm won't work on a G3 CPU. (The program defaults to the earlier Peak 4 algorithm.) And the wonderful ImpulseVerb convolution-based reverb won't work in Peak Pro 5 on a G3 Mac.

As you might expect, you'll get the best results if you run Peak on a fast G4 or G5 processor. You can reasonably get by with a 500MHz G4 with 512MB of RAM, but a faster CPU with more RAM would be better. I'd recommend having at least 1GB of RAM.

I'd also recommend getting a top-notch color monitor with good resolution. It will save you a great deal of eye-strain in the long run. The resolution must be at least 640 × 480 to properly display the windows, but bigger is much better. Peak Pro works great with a dual-monitor system.

Although you can run Peak Pro from a single hard drive, you'll get better performance if you use a *separate,* fast (better than 18ms access time) hard drive to handle your audio data. This is especially true if you do a lot of complex processing and real-time editing. A dedicated hard drive affords the needed space while taking much of the read/write workload off the main system drive. Simply partitioning a single drive is not the same thing; you need a separate drive to handle the audio-data flow while the main drive is performing the program and system tasks.

Peak Pro works fine with the Mac's built-in audio hardware, but you can get better specs if you run your audio through a high-quality, third-party Core Audio interface. Be sure to install the appropriate updated drivers.

Fast Forward

Peak Pro is a fun and fascinating program to use. As I dug deeper into it while writing this book, I discovered many unfamiliar yet powerful features that changed my way of working with audio files. Whether you're an experienced old-timer like me or an audio-editing neophyte, I hope this book will unlock many of Peak Pro's secrets and bring to you a new appreciation for this amazing application.

Chapter 2
Sound Up Close: Analog and Digital Audio Basics

Sound is so thoroughly woven into our existence that most people take it pretty much for granted. After all, we've been listening to sounds since before we were born. But the seemingly mundane nature of sound belies its many arcane subtleties and complexities, and it's those same subtleties and complexities that most interest the people who work in audio-related fields. They recognize that the phenomenon of sound is no one-trick pony: it provides spatial cues and aids in orientation, establishes moods and settings, delivers warnings and alerts, carries music and dialog, and provides many of the subliminal cues that give us information about our environment.

The arrival of computers and audio-editing software has caused a sea change in the way that audio engineers and editors treat sound. Of course, sound is still the same as it's always been, but now we view it through the prism of the digital revolution. And for many people, that brings a raft of new terms and concepts to grapple with.

Many intermediate and advanced audio-software users have a somewhat fuzzy understanding of sound even though they are quite adept at navigating elaborate menus and detailed dialog boxes. So before we jump into Peak Pro and its inner workings, let's take a close look at sound and how it becomes digital audio. We can then use those concepts and terms as we explore the amazing capabilities of Peak Pro.

What Is Sound?

Reduced to its simplest description, sound consists of waves of compression and rarefaction passing through an elastic medium. (We'll take a closer look at those waves in a moment.) The elastic medium is typically air, but it doesn't have to be; we can hear underwater, and we could hear in a room filled with any of a variety of gases or gaseous mixtures other than air. Sound also travels through solid objects such as brick walls. There is no sound in outer space, however, because the molecules in space are too far apart for waves of compression and rarefaction to be propagated.

Did You Know? SPEED OF SOUND

How fast does sound travel? Well, that depends. At room temperature, sound zips along at approximately 1,129 feet per second (344 meters per second). The speed of sound, however, is not just a static number. For example, at the freezing temperature of water, the speed slows down to around 1,088 ft/sec (331.7 m/sec). At room temperature through sea water, the speed goes way up to 4,900 ft/sec (1,500 m/sec). That might seem pretty fast until you realize that the speed of light is 186,000 miles per second. That's why you often see things happen in the distance slightly before you hear them (a kind of audio-visual latency).

The speed of sound is just slow enough that it can cause problems in large auditoriums and arenas. (In room-temperature air, a sound wave travels only 113 feet in 0.1 seconds, or roughly one foot per millisecond.) This is something to keep in mind when developing or working with high-end reverb algorithms: The *predelay* parameter gives the ear important cues about the size of the reverberant space.

The air is set into motion by being in contact with a vibrating object: a playing card flipping against the spokes of a bike, the spinning teeth of a table saw, chalk rubbing against a blackboard, the shimmering body of a brass cymbal, the vibrating reed in a clarinet, the buzzing lips of a trumpet player, the stretched membrane on top of a conga drum, a plucked guitar string, or a speaker cone moving in and out. It doesn't matter what the source is, the basic concept is always the same: something sets up a pattern of movement that is transferred to the surrounding air. To understand how that occurs, let's look at what happens when you strike a tuning fork.

When a tuning fork is struck, its tines are displaced slightly in the direction of the blow. Because the metal tines are somewhat flexible but not extremely flexible, they travel only a short distance before quickly springing back in the other direction. That back-and-forth motion repeats as the tuning fork gradually transfers the energy that was imparted to it by the original impact to the surrounding air molecules.

Each time the tuning fork flexes forward, it crunches together (compresses) the neighboring air molecules, creating an area of higher-than-normal pressure (relative to the current ambient air pressure). When the tuning fork flexes backward, it leaves behind an area with fewer than normal air molecules, a condition known as *rarefaction*. When the tines flex forward again, they create another area of compression, and so on (see **Figure 2-1**).

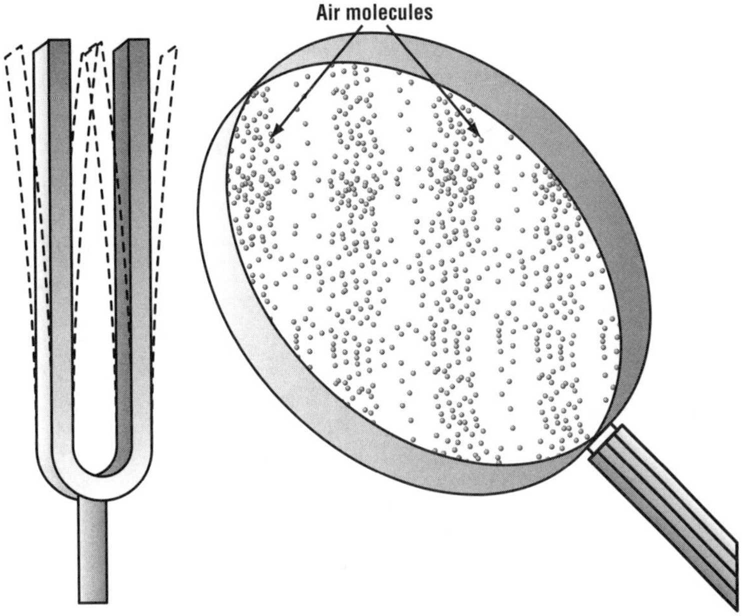

Figure 2-1
The back-and-forth vibrations of a tuning fork create alternating high- and low-pressure disturbances in the air, which propagate outward in all directions.

The alternating regions of compression and rarefaction travel outward from the tuning fork in all directions as the air molecules pass along the alternating states of high and low pressure. It's important to understand that sound waves are not some kind of squiggly beams that fly around the room. Nor are they like ocean waves, which bob up and down. They're rapidly fluctuating patterns of high and low pressure. In other words, a sound wave is actually a type of *pressure wave*.

As an analogy, think of a bucket brigade in which a line of people pass buckets of water from a source to a burning building. Each person in the line moves very little, yet the buckets can travel great distances very quickly by being transferred from person to person. In this case, the people represent the molecules and the buckets represent the areas of high pressure. The individual air molecules don't move much, but the region of pressure moves rapidly as the molecules bump against one another.

When the sound wave reaches your ear, the rapid changes in pressure cause the delicate membrane of the eardrum to vibrate at the same rate. The vibrations of the eardrum are transferred to a fluid-filled canal in the inner ear, where nerve endings are stimulated by the vibrations. Your brain then interprets the messages from the nerve endings as sound.

Waveform Displays

Sound can be perceived and enjoyed on its own, but to employ the type of sophisticated editing and processing that today's audio professionals demand, you can't simply *hear* a sound, you also have to *see* it. That's why all high-end audio-editing programs like Peak Pro devote a significant amount of onscreen real estate to displaying what sound waves look like (see **Figure 2-2**). These *waveform* displays let you freeze a sound in time and view it in great detail, much the way a jeweler uses a loupe to scrutinize a diamond before cutting it.

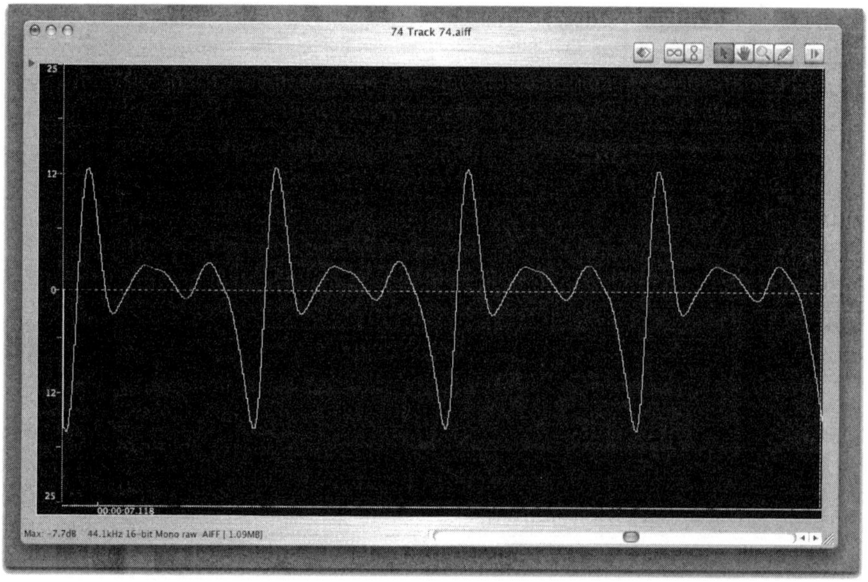

Figure 2-2
Advanced audio-editing programs like Peak Pro always provide a large display where you can zoom in on a waveform to analyze it in detail.

A waveform display, however, is not really a "picture" of a sound. Remember, sound does not consist of squiggly lines that zoom through the air. A waveform display is actually a *graph* of a sound wave; it plots the sound wave's rapidly alternating changes in pressure by using a horizontal axis to show the elapsed time and a vertical axis to show the changes in pressure (see **Figure 2-3**).

Running from left to right across the middle of the graph is a line that represents a zero change in air pressure—that is, the general ambient air pressure or current equilibrium. The bumps and spikes in the waveform that appear above the zero point are called *peaks;* they represent the areas of higher-than-normal pressure.

(The greater the pressure, the higher the peak.) The dips and valleys below the zero point are called *troughs;* they represent the areas of lower-than-normal pressure. (The less air pressure, the lower the trough.) The point at which a peak turns into a trough, or vice-versa, is known as a *zero crossing.* It's the transitional instant when the pressure has momentarily returned to equilibrium.

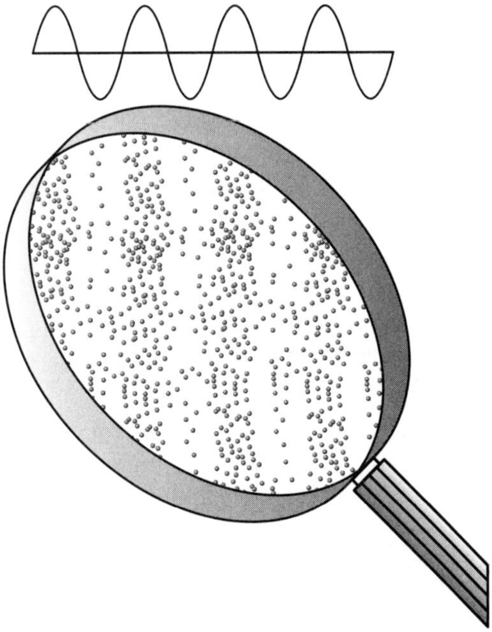

Figure 2-3
Waveform displays are not actually pictures of sound; they're graphs that show the changing pressure levels in a moving sound wave.

Frequency & Amplitude

Sound waves have two important characteristics that determine how we perceive them: *frequency* and *amplitude.* As we've seen, the back-and-forth vibrations (oscillations) of a sound source produce repeating compression/rarefaction patterns. Each of these yin/yang patterns is referred to as a *period* or a *cycle* (see **Figure 2-4**).

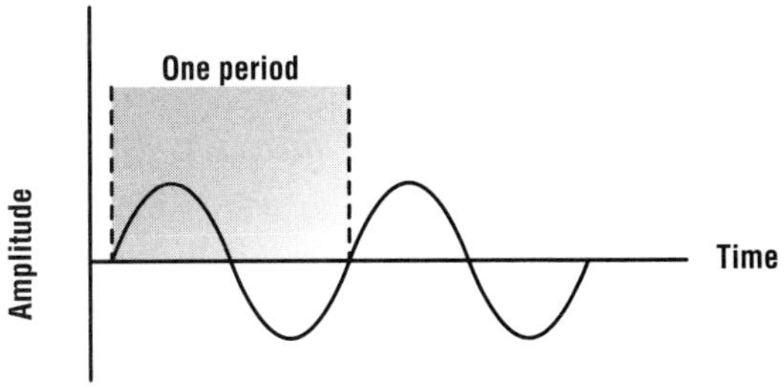

Figure 2-4
One complete high/low pressure pattern is called a period or cycle. Frequency is specified in hertz; one hertz equals one cycle per second.

The term "frequency" refers to the number of cycles that pass a fixed location (such as your ear or a microphone) during a single second. Frequency is expressed in a unit of measurement called *hertz* (abbreviated Hz), which is named after the nineteenth-century German physicist Heinrich Rudolf Hertz. One thousand cycles per second equal one *kilohertz* (kHz). In a waveform display, as frequencies become higher, their peaks appear closer together. As frequencies become lower, their peaks become more spread out.

Young people with good hearing can usually hear frequencies between 20Hz and 20kHz, so that is generally regarded as the range in which sounds are audible. Of course, pressure patterns with frequencies above and below that range exist, but we don't perceive them as sound. (In the case of extremely loud waves in the range between 1Hz and 20Hz, we may feel them even though we can't hear them in the ordinary way.)

The word *pitch* is related to frequency: Sounds that have a high (fast) frequency also have a high pitch, and sounds whose frequency is low (slow) have a low pitch. But pitch is a more general term that mainly characterizes a sound within a musical context. Frequency, on the other hand, is more often associated with scientific units of measurement.

Whereas a measurement of frequency describes how quickly a sound wave's cycles arrive at a given point, a measurement of amplitude describes the amount of difference between the peak (or trough) in a waveform diagram and a zero crossing—or, to look at it another way, the difference between the greatest (or least) amount of air pressure in the sound wave and the ambient air pressure. When the pressure differential between a peak (or trough) and an adjacent zero crossing is larger, we say that the amplitude is higher or greater. In our earlier example, striking the tuning fork gently would produce a faint sound, because little energy would be available to compress the neighboring air molecules. Striking the same tuning fork harder would produce a tone of the same frequency, but the sound would have more volume because the stronger vibrations would create greater pressure in each cycle of the sound wave. In a waveform display, the greater pressure would appear as taller peaks; the distance between peaks (the frequency) would remain the same (See **Figure 2-5**).

The unit of measurement used to indicate a sound's strength is the *decibel* (dB), named after Alexander Graham Bell. The decibel (one-tenth of a *bel*) is based on a logarithmic scale that indicates the ratio between a sound's amplitude (its *sound pressure level*) and a standard reference. The level at which most people can first perceive sounds—the *threshold of hearing*—is assigned a value of 0dB. Other sound levels are then expressed in relation to that reference. Normal listening levels range from 0dB to beyond 120dB—a level commonly referred to as the *threshold of pain.* (In digital audio systems, however, the 0dB reference level is the maximum possible amplitude, and sounds with a lower amplitude are described using negative dB values such as –6dB.)

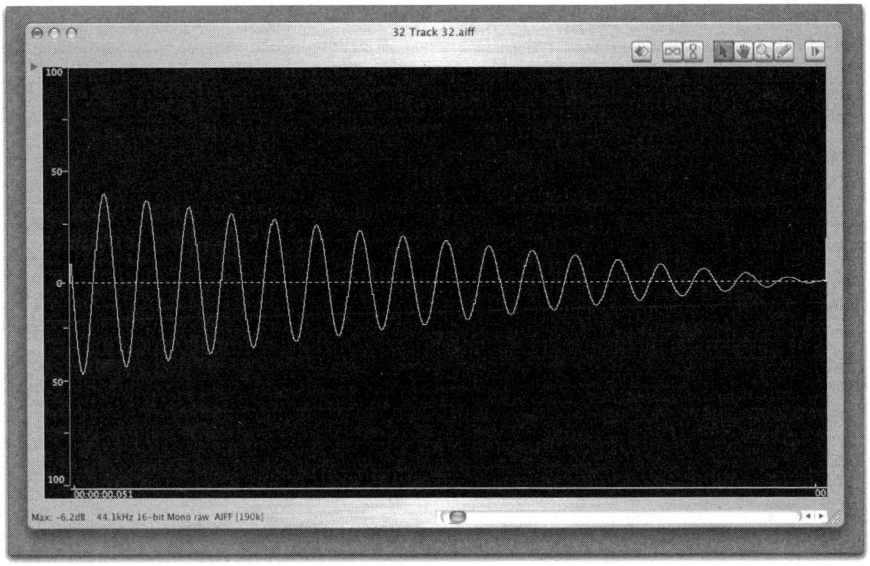

Figure 2-5
You can tell by looking at this waveform that the sound is decreasing in volume. Notice that the frequency stays the same as the amplitude diminishes.

The term *loudness* is related to amplitude, but it's a more subjective term. Our perception of a sound's loudness is influenced by factors other than amplitude. Specifically, our ears tend to be most sensitive to frequencies in the range between 1kHz and 5kHz. As a result, a sound in that range will be perceived as louder than a low-pitched sound that has the same amplitude.

Timbre & Complex Waveforms

As you can see from the above illustrations, our faithful tuning fork generates a relatively "pure" sound that produces a smoothly undulating periodic waveform called a *sine wave.* Sine waves have a discernible pitch, but they're decidedly lacking in character, because they represent an extremely simple type of sound (great for tuning instruments, rather boring as entertainment). Musical instruments and other real-world sounds are substantially more interesting because they consist of various combinations of acoustic building blocks. The best way to visualize these important elements is to examine how a string vibrates.

When a string is set into motion, it vibrates as a whole, producing a frequency called its *fundamental.* Although the string

Did You Know? SOUND LEVELS

When referring to sound intensities, decibel readings can be a bit hard to relate to. To help keep things in context, here are a few common sounds and their *approximate* levels.

Threshold of hearing: 0dB
Whisper (4 feet away) or the rustle of leaves: 10 to 20dB
Recording studio: 20 to 30dB
Quiet residence or a private office: 40 to 50dB
Conversational speech (three or four feet away): 60 to 70dB
Heavy traffic: 80 to 90dB
Pneumatic drill (ten feet away): 90 to 110dB
Threshold of pain: 120dB
Rock concert: 120 to 125dB
Jet engine: 160 to 170dB
Rocket engine: 195dB

vibrates as a unit along its length, it also vibrates in shorter segments that are one-half, one-third, one-fourth, one-fifth, and so on, of the total length (see **Figure 2-6**). These shorter segments produce their own sine waves, which are called *harmonics* or *partials.* Harmonics are higher frequencies that are whole-number multiples of the fundamental frequency. (Harmonics above the fundamental are also referred to as *overtones.*)

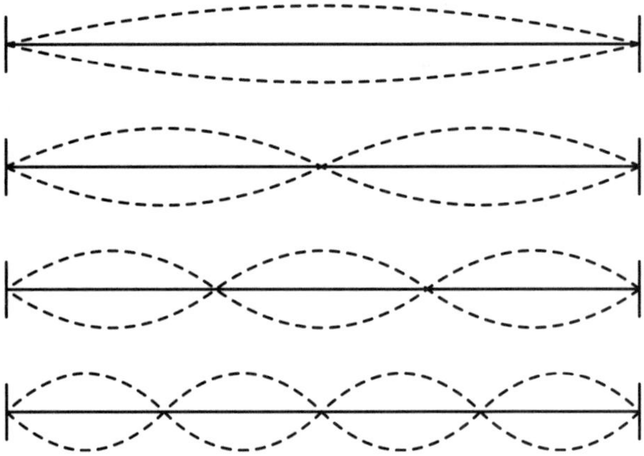

Figure 2-6
When a string is plucked, it vibrates simultaneously in segments of different lengths. These whole-number multiples of the total string length produce higher frequencies called *harmonics.*

The fundamental is considered the first harmonic; the second harmonic (which divides the string in half) has twice the frequency of the fundamental. The third harmonic has three times the fundamental frequency, and so on. A vibrating column of air—as in a woodwind or brass instrument—exhibits much the same characteristics as a vibrating string, producing harmonics at many different frequencies, all of which are approximately whole-number multiples of the frequency of the fundamental. The term "partial" has a more general meaning: It's used to refer to frequency components of a complex sound that *aren't* necessarily whole-number multiples of the fundamental.

The particular combination of harmonics and their relative strengths determines the tone color or *timbre* (pronounced "tam-bur") of a musical instrument or other sound source. In a blind listening test, few people would have a problem distinguishing a clarinet from a trumpet or a viola or a car horn even if all of the sounds were produced at the exact same frequency and amplitude. That's because every sound source has a distinct sonic fingerprint that emphasizes some harmonics over others, and it's this unique harmonic mixture that gives sounds their color and character (see **Figure 2-7**).

Unlike our simple sine wave example, most real-world periodic sounds have much more complex waveforms with myriad extra wrinkles and irregular patterns. That's because the fundamental, which typically starts out as a relatively simple waveform, is altered by the addition of all of the associated harmonics (see **Figure 2-8**). When you pile on those extra harmonics, you end up with a waveform that has many more little peaks and troughs.

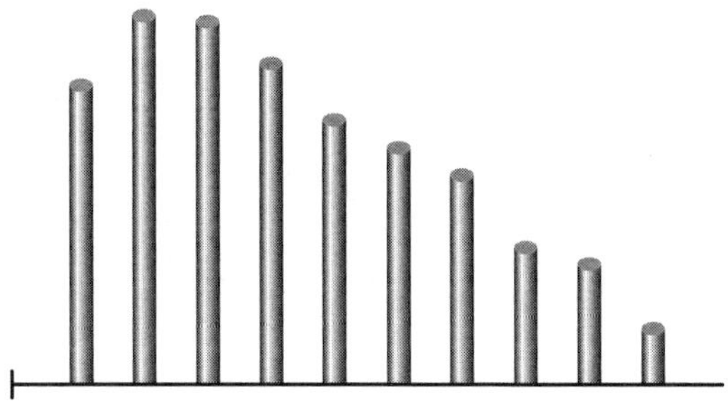

Figure 2-7
The relative strengths of an instrument's different harmonics are responsible for its unique timbre. For example, this bar graph shows the first ten harmonics of a typical French horn tone. Notice how the upper harmonics become progressively weaker—a common characteristic.

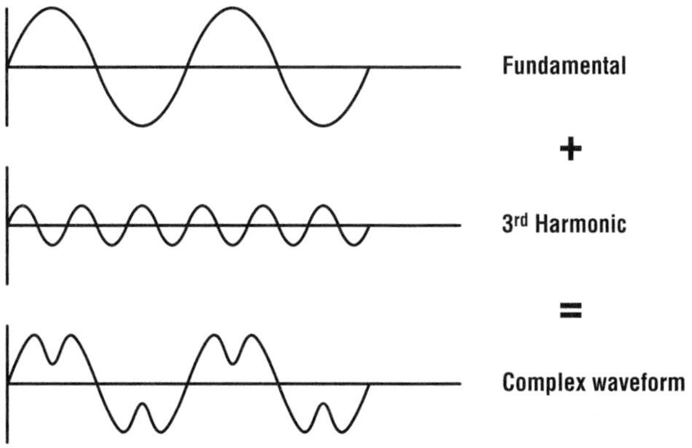

Figure 2-8
When simple waveforms of different frequencies combine, they form complex waveforms.

It's fascinating to realize that essentially any waveform can be deconstructed into a group of sine waves, each with its own amplitude, frequency, and phase characteristics. The mathematics required to perform this trick were explored in the early nineteenth century by French mathematician Baron Jean Baptiste Joseph Fourier (one of Napoleon's engineers). We now refer to his method of examining sounds as *Fourier analysis.* Creating different combinations of harmonics lies at the heart of several electronic music synthesis methods.

It's important to understand that sounds in the real world (or, for that matter, the sound waves displayed in Peak Pro) don't generally look like sine waves. Quite often a sound will not have any visible periodicity at all. A recording of a symphony orchestra, for instance, will quite likely look like random noise, even though your ear is quite capable of picking out the oboe solo.

Sound into Numbers

Regardless of platform or operating system, computers really only speak one language, and it's a language consisting of endless streams of ones and zeros—also known as *bits* (short for *binary digits*). On their own, however, bits have no inherent sound, and nature knows nothing of ones and zeros as it propagates sound waves through the environment. Getting these two worlds together takes some fancy technological footwork, which lies at the root of all of Peak Pro's editing capabilities. To keep the essential terms and concepts clear, let's take a brief look at how sound is translated into digital audio and what pitfalls to watch out for along the way.

The Analog World

Before the advent of computers, sound was strictly an *analog* affair, and even with computers, sound is still mostly an analog phenomenon: A vibrating object produces a sound wave whose pattern of compressions and rarefactions mimics the movement of the object. If the source vibrations become stronger, the waveform as shown on-screen will exhibit peaks and troughs that are higher and lower; that is, the air molecules in the areas of compression are packed more closely together, and the molecules in the areas of rarefaction are more widely separated. If the object's vibrations become more rapid, the regions of compression and rarefaction are closer together. When that happens, more of them will reach your ear within a given period of time, which means their frequency is higher. The peaks and troughs in the graphic representation of the sound wave are, therefore, analogous in shape to the movement of the sound source. Changes in the movement of the source produce the same kinds of changes in the waveform.

Recording onto an analog medium, be it a 33 rpm vinyl record, a cassette, or open-reel tape, follows much the same principles. The original sound source produces a sound wave, which impinges on a small diaphragm inside a microphone. Responding to the sound wave, the vibrating diaphragm produces an electrical signal with continuously varying voltages. The fluctuations in voltage correspond directly to the vibrations of the diaphragm: Higher frequencies cause more rapid fluctuations; lower frequencies cause slower fluctuations. Louder sounds cause the voltage to increase and decrease more; softer sounds produce smaller changes in voltage. In other words, the electrical signal changes in the same way the air pressure changes. We can view a waveform diagram in Peak Pro as showing the voltage fluctuations rather than the changes in air pressure; it makes no difference to the diagram.

An analog recording device then stores the fluctuating voltages as magnetic patterns on tape, as microscopic ripples on vinyl, or in some other form that reflects the changes. On playback, the original signal is re-created and sent to a speaker, which moves in and out in response to the fluctuating voltages, reproducing a more or less faithful copy of the original sound wave. The main point to keep in mind is that throughout the process, each step corresponds to the previous step in that something (air pressure, voltage fluctuations, the shape of the vinyl groove, or the movement of the speaker cone) is changing in a continuously varying physical manner, and that if we graph those changes the graphs will all have the same shape.

Analog aficionados are quick to point out that analog recording has much to offer. Without getting too deeply into that debate, we can say that early digital audio systems distorted the sound in certain ways, as do analog recording systems. But analog distortion usually sounded better to human ears than the forms of digital distortion found in first-generation digital audio gear. Today, improvements in digital recording technology have rendered the analog/digital debate largely irrelevant. The fact remains, analog recording has some serious shortcomings, especially in the area of audio editing. For that and other reasons, the recording, entertainment, and music industries have turned overwhelmingly to digital audio. As you'll discover in the following chapters, breaking the analog connection during the recording process offers unparalleled control in shaping and editing sounds. Before we get to that, however, let's take a look at how sounds enter (and exit) the digital domain.

The Digital Domain

The digital recording process actually starts out the same as the analog recording process. Sound waves impinge on a microphone diaphragm, which generates an analog electrical signal whose pattern of voltage peaks and troughs is (to the extent allowed by the imperfections of the microphone) the same as the pattern of air pressure peaks and troughs in the sound wave. At that point, however, the analog process ends and the digital process begins.

The electrical signal enters an electronic circuit called a *sample-and-hold circuit*. The sample-and-hold circuit grabs the incoming signal and takes a kind of analyzing "snapshot" (called a *sample*) of the voltage level at that instant. The resulting value is then passed to another circuit called the *analog-to-digital converter* (*A/D converter* or *ADC* for short). The ADC converts the momentary voltage into a digital number, which represents the voltage level (amplitude) at that specific instant. The sample-and-hold circuit then takes another snapshot, and the same process repeats again and again—thousands of times per second—generating a series of numbers that represent the fluctuating voltages of the original signal (see **Figure 2-9**).

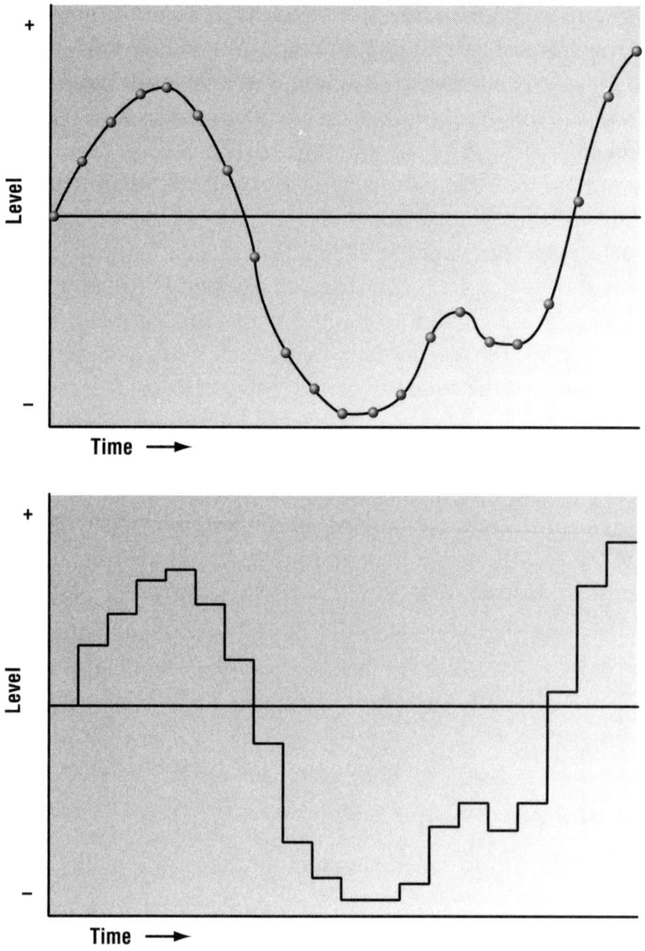

Figure 2-9
With digital audio, the continuous analog signal is represented by a series of discrete values that approximate the overall shape of the original waveform.

Sampling & Aliasing

The process of capturing and reading the incoming analog signal at intervals is referred to as *sampling,* and the number of times per second that the process occurs is therefore referred to as the *sampling rate.* The higher the sampling rate, the more accurately the series of numbers can represent the signal, because the more closely spaced samples can better pick up the fine details and minuscule irregularities in the signal. In short, the higher the sampling rate, the greater the fidelity.

But how high is high enough? Well, for starters, you must have at least two samples for each cycle of the sound wave to capture its shape with even minimal fidelity: one sample to represent the positive part (the peak) and another sample to represent the negative part (the trough) in each cycle (see **Figure 2-10**). If your digital recording device can't capture at least two samples per cycle, it will introduce a troublesome form of distortion called *aliasing*. Without enough samples to properly represent the basic shape of the waveform, the numbers coming from the ADC will appear to represent a frequency that is much lower than the actual sound wave that is being recorded (see **Figure 2-11**). This unwanted artifact is known as an *alias frequency*.

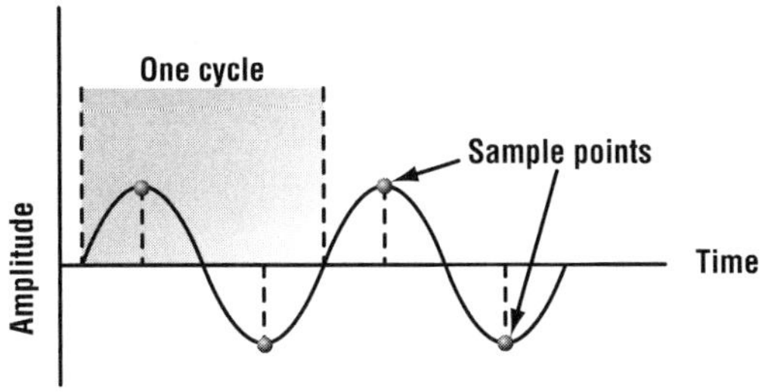

Figure 2-10
To digitally capture an audio signal, you must have at least two samples per cycle so that the levels of the peaks and troughs can be represented.

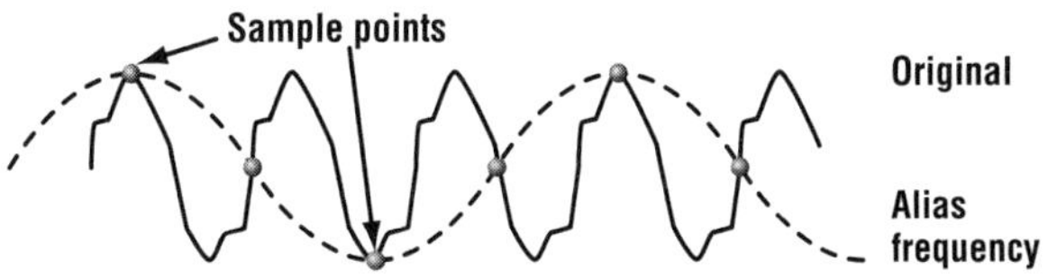

Figure 2-11
Unwanted alias frequencies appear when too few samples are taken to properly represent the signal.

Audio Lingo: SAMPLE

The term *sample* often causes confusion because it's used so loosely and in so many different contexts. As used in discussions of digital audio technology, the term refers to one of the individual "snapshots" of an audio signal as it is converted from an analog signal into a digital stream. For example, the digital audio that is used for compact discs includes 44,100 different samples for each second of audio.

However, the term *sample* is also used to describe an entire digital audio recording of any length. Samples in this sense are usually relatively short (sometimes only a fraction of a second) because they're used to play individual musical notes, sound effects, or short musical phrases. Samples of this type are often combined into larger *multisamples* (with the individual samples assigned to different MIDI notes) to be played from hardware or software instruments called *samplers* or *sample playback modules.* You may even hear multisamples incorrectly referred to as "samples," which only adds to the confusion.

To help you better understand the concept of aliasing, let's look at a common example of visible aliasing—at the movies. In essence, movie cameras work a lot like digital recorders. They "sample" the visual world at the rate of 24 frames per second. That's a lot slower than the thousands of samples per second needed for recording audio. But it's easier to fool your eyes into seeing fluid motion from a series of still snapshots than it is to fool your ears with the audio equivalent.

Although filming at 24 frames per second is fine for most onscreen action, once in a while the illusion breaks down. If you watch a lot of Westerns, in particular, you've probably already noticed the well-known "wagon-wheel effect" when a stagecoach or buckboard is shown racing across the plains. Many times the spokes on the wheels seem to be standing still or even going backwards. (Helicopter blades and airplane propellers often do the same thing.) This is an example of aliasing.

If the spokes on the wheel happen to arrive at the same position every time the movie camera's shutter opens, the camera will be tricked into seeing the spokes as stationary. If the spokes arrive slightly behind the same position each time the shutter opens, they'll appear to rotate backwards. In both cases, the camera's "sampling rate" is simply too slow to accurately capture the rapid movement of the spokes. So, along with the obviously spinning wheels and the scenery whizzing by, we're also confronted with the incongruous image of the stationary wagon spokes.

The same kind of thing occurs when alias frequencies appear in an audio recording. Along with the usual musical sounds, you also get one or more anomalous frequencies that clearly don't belong. And that's why it's important to keep the sampling rate high enough to properly capture all of the audio "action."

Nyquist Limit

As I mentioned earlier, you need at least two samples per cycle to reasonably capture a waveform's shape. This precept is clearly summarized in the *Nyquist Theorem* (named after American engineer Harry Nyquist), which states that the sampling rate must be twice as high as the highest frequency to be recorded. In other words, the highest frequency that you can record without aliasing is one-half of the sampling rate. That frequency is often referred to as the *Nyquist Limit.*

Because the audible range extends up to about 20kHz, an acceptable sampling rate would have to be at least 40kHz. To prevent inaudible high frequencies beyond the Nyquist Limit from generating audible alias frequencies, digital audio recorders employ a type of lowpass filter, called an *anti-aliasing filter,* between the microphone and the sample-and-hold circuit (see **Figure 2-12**).

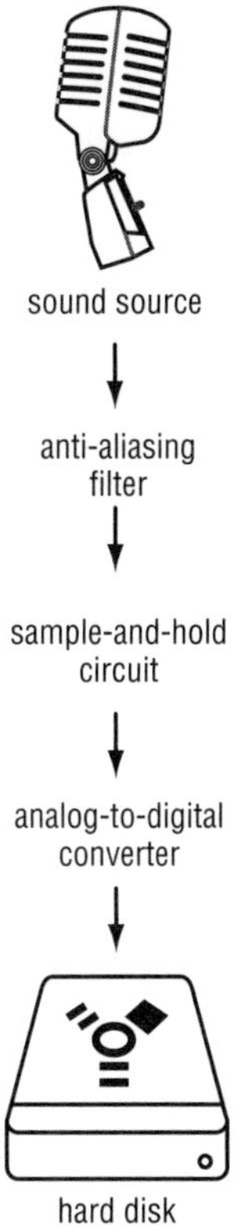

Figure 2-12
Transforming an analog sound into digital data involves several steps.

The compact disc rate of 44.1kHz and the DAT recorder rate of 48kHz provide plenty of leeway for most recording needs without allowing the anti-aliasing filter to color the sound too much. However, thanks to DVDs and fast computers, sampling rates of 88.2, 96, and 192kHz have become increasingly common. They offer an improvement in clarity and "transparency" that is discernible on good playback systems. This clarity is due in large part to the fact that aliasing is more easily avoided in systems that operate at higher sampling rates.

Resolution

The sampling rate is certainly an important parameter in determining the quality of digital audio, but it's not the only consideration. The *resolution* is just as important.

As we've seen, the digital audio process takes a continuously varying sound wave and breaks it down into a series of discrete events. The more samples that are taken per second, the more accurate the representation. The same principle also applies to the ADC each time it assigns a number to represent an amplitude value. This process called *quantization* or *digitization* relies on having enough numerical levels available to accurately describe each sample's amplitude.

The more levels that are available, the more precisely the ADC can match each reading. When a reading falls between levels, the ADC must round off to the nearest binary number, which means that its description of the sample will be less than perfect. The term *resolution* refers to how many gradations are available to the ADC circuit. The discrepancy between the original analog signal and its digital counterpart is known as *quantization error,* and the uniquely digital type of distortion that results is often referred to as *quantization noise.*

The more bits that the ADC has to work with, the lower the level of quantization error. Every bit that is added produces a substantial improvement in resolution. For example, 8-bit digital audio offers only 256 possible levels (2 to the 8th power), but compact discs with their 16-bit audio offer a much more precise 65,536 levels of resolution (2 to the 16th power). With 24-bit audio, you get a whopping 16,777,216 quantization levels! At that resolution, even if a voltage value doesn't land exactly on an available number, it won't be very far off.

In addition to reducing quantization noise, a higher resolution offers a higher *dynamic range.* That's the difference between the loudest sound that a device can handle without distorting and the inherent noise level of the device itself.

To obtain the highest quality digital recordings, you must be adept at steering a path between those two extremes. If you record at too low a level, you'll end up with an intrusive amount of quantization noise. On the other hand, if you set your input levels too high (above zero on the digital input meters), you'll produce an obnoxious form of distortion called *clipping.* It's called clipping because when viewed onscreen, the waveform's tops and bottoms appear to be chopped off (See **Figure 2-13**).

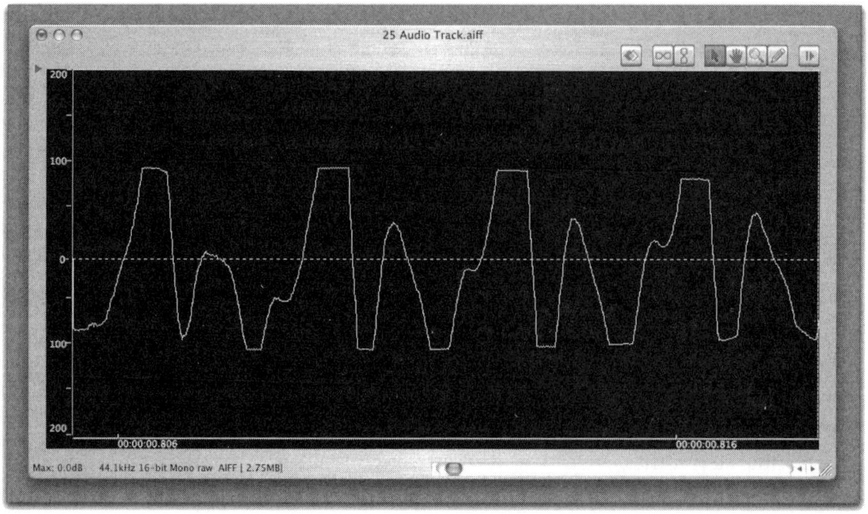

Figure 2-13
When a signal's amplitude exceeds the digital circuit's range, some of the waveform's peaks may get flattened at the upper limit, producing a form of distortion called *clipping.* Notice how some of the peaks and troughs in this example appear to be cut off.

Numbers into Sound

At this point, our original sound wave has been converted from a pressure wave into an electrical signal and then into a stream of binary numbers. Now that it's in the form of data, the "sound" can be stored on a variety of digital media such as DAT, CD, DVD, MiniDisc, or hard drive.

To play back the sound, you simply turn the whole parade around (see **Figure 2-14**). The data on the storage medium is streamed into a circuit called a *digital-to-analog converter* (*D/A converter* or *DAC* for short). The DAC transforms the numbers into a series of voltages.

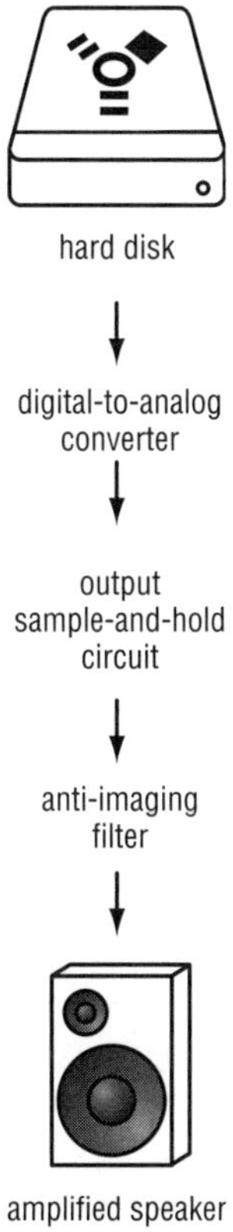

Figure 2-14
The return trip from digital to analog audio is like the analog-to-digital process in reverse.

The reconstructed signal is then sent to an *output sample-and-hold circuit* that helps to stabilize it. At this point the signal is still a bit coarse and typically has unwanted remnants of the conversion process, so it's next sent to an *output lowpass filter*, also known as an *anti-imaging filter*. After that, the fluctuating electrical signal should closely resemble the original analog signal that started the process.

The final step comes when you send the signal to an audio monitoring system where the speaker cone, vibrating in and out, recreates a sound wave that we can listen to.

Chapter 3

The User Interface: Getting Around in Style

Because Peak Pro is designed to perform a variety of tasks, BIAS has created a user interface that is simple yet versatile. The brushed-aluminum look of the toolbars and windows is complemented by an even higher level of customization than in earlier versions, which makes it easy to configure and reconfigure the interface to meet your changing needs.

Exploring Peak Pro's various nooks and crannies and learning how to use the program's many customization options is the best way to optimize your workflow and improve your editing efficiency. With that in mind, let's start by taking a close look at what you see on-screen when you open a typical document (audio file). From there we can investigate some of the more esoteric options that are also available to you.

Buttons & Views

At its simplest, Peak Pro's graphical user interface consists of only three independent but interrelated windows (see **Figure 3-1**). The Audio Document window provides a resizable display area for viewing waveforms, and it also provides a few editing tools along with some useful information fields. The button-filled Toolbar window provides direct access to most of Peak Pro's commands. And the resizable Transport window boasts high-resolution VU meters as well as tapedeck-style controls and a digital readout.

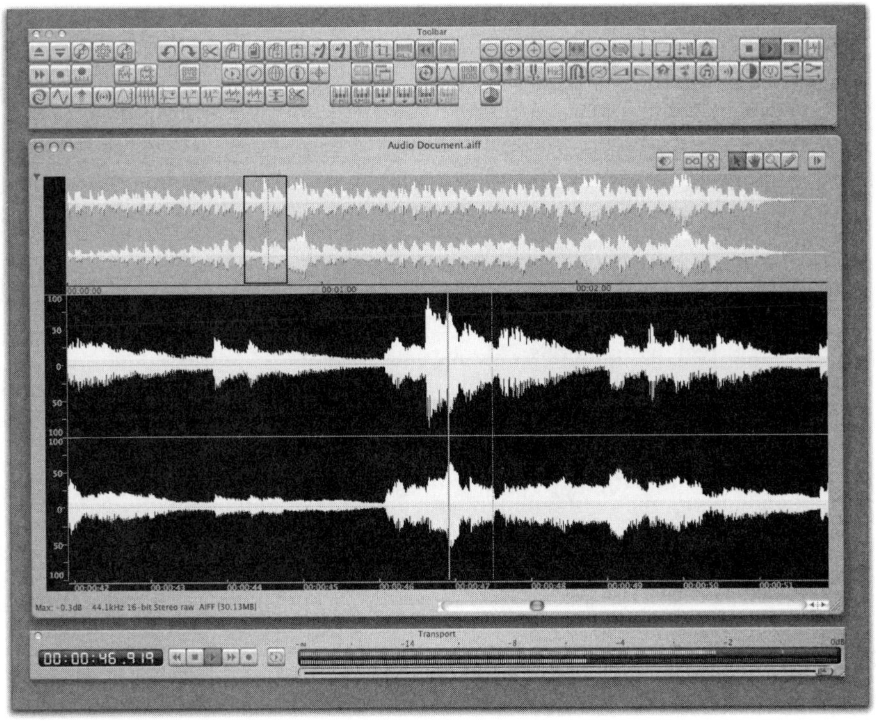

Figure 3-1
Peak Pro's main user interface consists of three independent but interrelated windows (top to bottom): the Toolbar, Audio Document, and Transport windows.

Audio Document Window

The heart of this trio is clearly the Audio Document window. In fact, you can close the other two windows completely and still get a lot of work done in Peak Pro, especially if you memorize a few keyboard commands. In the upper part of the window, an Overview display shows the entire recording, zoomed out far enough to show the complete waveform without scrolling. The larger lower section is the editing area, where you can zoom in on a section of the waveform to view it in as much detail as necessary.

When you click inside the main waveform display, a vertical dotted-line *insertion cursor* appears. As we'll see shortly, it's used in a wide number of editing and playback functions. During playback, a solid, colored line, called the *playback cursor,* sweeps through the waveform, showing where you are in the recording. When the playback cursor reaches the right edge of the display, the waveform updates to reveal the next section of the recording. You can turn this feature on and off at Options > Scroll

During Play. You can also scroll manually to the left or right by holding the Control key and hitting the Left or Right Arrow key.

If you aren't zoomed all the way out, Peak Pro also offers the option of having the playback cursor appear stationary in the center of the display with the waveform moving behind it. Just choose Options > Move Waveform During Play. If you zoom in close using the zoom controls (explained below)—just to the point where the waveform appears as a single line—this option produces a very cool oscilloscope-style display.

In addition, the waveform display is where you can add any of several types of markers for indicating important places in the recording or for delineating the boundaries of regions and loops. (Markers are discussed in Chapter 10.)

Each of the different types of markers, along with the waveform itself and its background, can be assigned any of a wide assortment of colors. Just go to Peak > Preferences > Colors to open the Document Colors dialog box (see **Figure 3-2**). Peak Pro comes with several preconfigured "themes" ranging from simple black and white to garishly bright. Fortunately, you can also put together your own color scheme by choosing your own colors for each of the display elements that you'd like to change. You can also add a 3-D shadow effect to the waveform and specify how dark the shading should be for selections.

Overview Display

The Overview is primarily a navigation and reference tool to help you avoid getting lost in longer audio files. By providing the "big picture" at the top of the window, Peak Pro helps you stay oriented when you're working on details in the lower display. A colored frame (with its own playback cursor) appears around the section of the waveform that appears in the lower area. During playback, the frame and cursor move through the Overview to show you where you are in the recording.

But the Overview is more than a simple visual aid. You can click anywhere in the Overview display (the Arrow cursor turns into a miniature speaker icon when it's in the Overview), and playback will jump to that point. Even better, if you click and hold the mouse button, you can drag the frame and playback cursor forward and backward through the Overview to produce a kind of coarse scrubbing effect. You can also Option-drag in the Overview to scan quickly through the waveform without playing the audio. In either case, the lower display updates continually to stay in sync.

The Overview is therefore an excellent tool for quickly dissecting and auditioning different parts of a recording and for locating areas that you'd like to edit.

Tool Tips:

SCOUTING LOCATIONS

If you're having trouble finding a specific location in a recording, click and drag the Overview frame for quick-and-easy audio/visual scrubbing through the waveform. Option-drag to scan without sound. Scroll the main waveform display to the left or right by holding Control and hitting the Left or Right Arrow key.

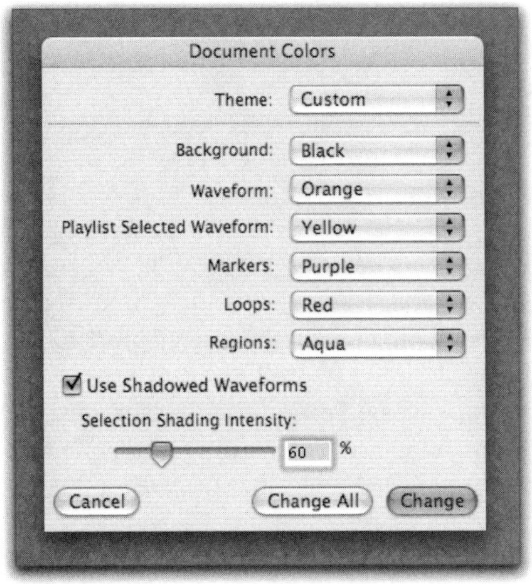

Figure 3-2
Use Preferences > Colors to create your own color scheme for displaying waveforms and markers.

Waveform Display

Most of the Audio Document window is devoted to the main waveform display. As in the Overview, stereo files appear in a split screen with the left channel on top and the right channel on the bottom. If you forget which is which, just move the mouse cursor into the upper half of the top waveform or the lower half of the bottom waveform; a small R or L appears to the right of the cursor indicating the channel.

On the left side of each waveform, a vertical scale indicates the amplitude level from zero to 100 percent of maximum. At the bottom of the window, elapsed time is shown in one of several formats: minutes/seconds/milliseconds, bars/beats, samples, CD frames, or one of six SMPTE timecode rates. You can change the format under Options > Time Units.

If you're working on a relatively small screen or you just want to maximize your view of the main display, click the tiny triangle near the upper-left corner of the Audio Document window. It toggles the Overview display on and off, which allows the main display to expand into the full window. (You can do the same thing from Options > Show Overview or by holding the Command key and hitting the comma key.)

> **Tool Tips:**
> **OVERVIEW TOGGLE**
> You can turn the Overview on and off by hitting the **Command** key and the **comma** key together.

To resize or reshape the entire Audio Document window, just grab the lower-right corner and drag. Regardless of the final size or shape, the visible part of the waveform remains the same. If you check the Live Resize box in the

Peak > Preferences > Window Preferences dialog box, the waveform will grow and shrink in real time as you drag.

Audio File Info Bar

Several pieces of important information are provided in the lower-left corner of every Audio Document window (see **Figure 3-3**). The first number indicates the highest amplitude point in the waveform. (Note that the highest amplitude may be either a positive-going or negative-going peak. "Highest" doesn't mean "the uppermost point in the waveform.") That reading, in dB, offers some insight into how fully the current audio file has used the available dynamic range. It might be useful, for example, in deciding if you'll need to use the Normalize command (see Chapter 6) during editing. For a more detailed look at this high (or low) point in the waveform and to find its precise location, Option-click on the word Max (in the lower-left corner) to open an information sheet with additional data (see **Figure 3-4**).

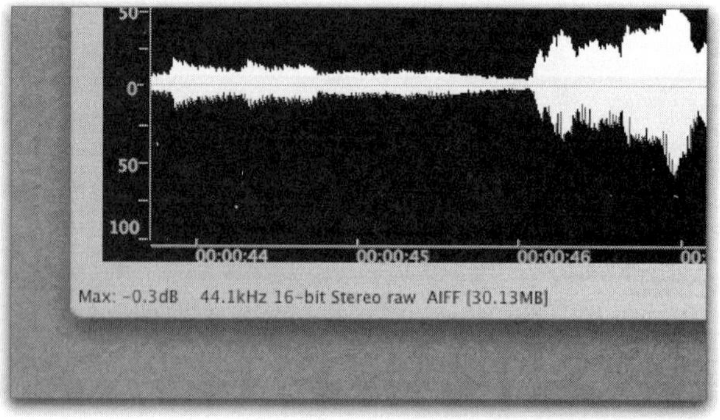

Figure 3-3
The Audio File Info Bar (in the lower corner of the Audio Document window) provides helpful data about the current file.

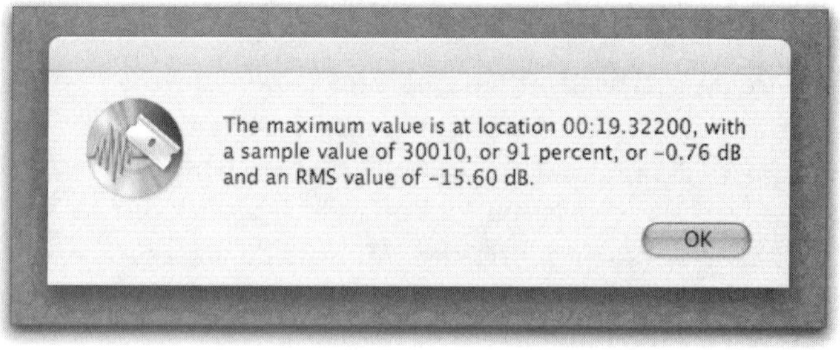

Figure 3-4
Peak Pro provides a handy information sheet that identifies and locates the greatest positive or negative point in the waveform.

The next numbers in the lower-left corner show the recording's sampling rate and resolution, and those are followed by an indication of whether this is a stereo or monaural file (which should be obvious from the waveform display). The last bits of information show the file format and the size of the document—two things to keep in mind when saving and exporting files (see Chapter 4). If you want a more detailed look at the current file's parameters, click on either of these data displays (or hit Command-I) to open the Audio Info dialog box (see **Figure 3-5**).

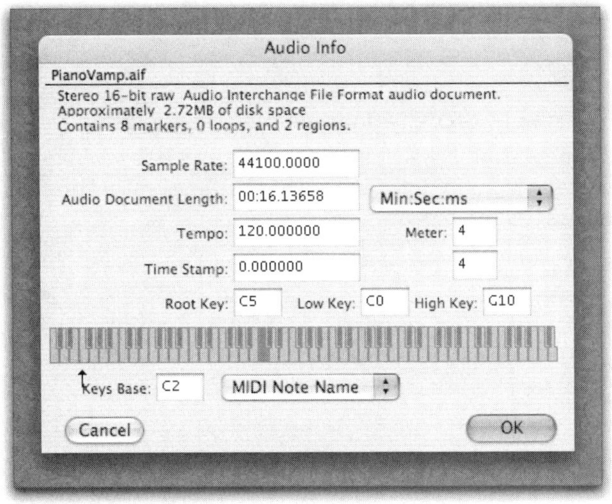

Figure 3-5
You can get a detailed look at the current file's parameters in the Audio Info dialog box.

Blending Tool

Several buttons in the upper-right corner of the Audio Document window provide direct access to important tools (see **Figure 3-6**). The first button on the left toggles the adjustable Blending feature on and off. Blending adds a very short crossfade at the edit point whenever you cut, copy, paste, or insert audio. It's designed to minimize clicking or popping when the waveform is cut at a point other than a zero crossing (see Chapter 5) or when you're attempting to splice two sections with slightly different amplitudes.

Figure 3-6
The Audio Document window has its own set of tool buttons in the upper-right corner.

Lock Mode

The next button is the Horizontal Lock button. It lets you couple the beginning and ending markers of a loop or region so you can move them as a unit to a different location without changing the duration of the region. (More on loops, regions, and markers in Chapter 10.) To the right of the Horizontal Lock button, the Vertical Lock button lets you grab two or more markers of various kinds at the same location and move them all at once.

Arrow Cursor

The next section of tools begins with the Arrow Cursor button. This button selects the standard cursor, which is actually only an arrow when it's outside of the waveform area. Inside the main waveform display, the cursor turns into an I-beam, and in the Overview it becomes a tiny speaker.

In the main waveform display, the Arrow (I-beam) cursor lets you click and drag through a section of the waveform for editing or creating loops or regions. Drag through the upper or lower half of a stereo display to select only one channel; drag through the center to select both channels.

Hand Cursor

The Hand Cursor button lets you grab the waveform and drag it smoothly left and right. This is a far better and less frustrating way to position the waveform than using the scroll bar at the bottom of the window. It's great for when you need to carefully locate a specific point in the audio file as long as you don't have to cover too much territory.

If you have to move rapidly over a lot of terrain, use the scroll bar, or try moving the Hand cursor into the Overview display; it will turn into an arrow. While holding down the mouse button, drag left or right. You'll see the Overview frame move rapidly through the waveform. When you get to the general area that you want, release the mouse button and return to the main waveform display. The cursor will become a hand again and you can carefully reposition the waveform.

Zoom Tool

The next button activates the Zoom tool. The Zoom tool cursor is a small magnifying glass with a plus sign in the center of the lens. Position the lens over the part of the waveform that you want to examine more closely, and click the mouse button. Each time you click, Peak Pro zooms in closer, while keeping the same point in the waveform centered under the magnifier. This context-sensitive zooming is an important feature because it lets you zoom in on pops and single-cycle clicks without losing them offscreen as the waveform expands. To zoom out, just hold down the Option key (the plus turns to a minus) when you click. You can also zoom in and out within the Overview display, but here the Zoom tool works differently. Click and drag across the region you want to zoom in on, and the main waveform display will be resized to show the region you selected.

Peak Pro's Action menu contains commands that let you independently zoom vertically (to better view low-level sounds) or horizontally (to move in toward the sample level as with the Zoom tool). You can also access these as well as several other zoom commands using keyboard shortcuts, as explained in the "Zooming Ahead" sidebar, or by clicking the appropriate buttons in the Toolbar window.

Tool Tips:
ZOOMING AHEAD
Here are several shortcuts for zooming:

Command-]: zoom in
Command-[: zoom out
Control-Up Arrow: increase vertical zoom
Control-Down Arrow: decrease vertical zoom
Shift-Command-]: fit selection
Shift-Command-[: zoom out all the way
Shift-Left Arrow: zoom to single-sample level or zoom to sample level at the start of a selection
Shift-Right Arrow: zoom to single-sample level at the end of a selection

Pencil Tool
Once you've zoomed in far enough to see individual cycles in the waveform, you can use the Pencil Tool button (to the right of the Zoom Tool button) to activate the Pencil Tool cursor. It lets you redraw the waveform directly into the display to repair problems of various kinds. If you hold down the Option key while using the Pencil tool, you'll activate the Magic Pencil Tool feature, which is especially handy for removing pops and clicks (see Chapter 6 for more on the Pencil tool). Option-clicking on the Pencil Tool button opens the Draw Tool dialog box (see **Figure 3-7**). It lets you specify how much Peak Pro smoothes out the lines that you draw. The smoothing feature could be a big help if you're working with a balky mouse or you don't have a steady drawing hand. You can try it out by setting the slider to 100 percent. Zoom in to the sample level and redraw a section of the waveform, giving it a sharp vertical edge. Then zoom out one or two levels and back in, and notice how the drawn-in section has been smoothed.

Figure 3-7
Peak Pro's Pencil Tool includes a built-in smoothing function to help improve the results when you redraw a section of a waveform. You can turn on the smoothing feature and adjust its strength with the Draw Tool dialog box.

Contents Drawer

The final button in the upper-right corner of the Audio Document window opens the handy Contents Drawer—an OS X-style feature that was introduced in Version 4. The Contents Drawer slides out from the right side of the window and provides several kinds of helpful information (see **Figure 3-8**).

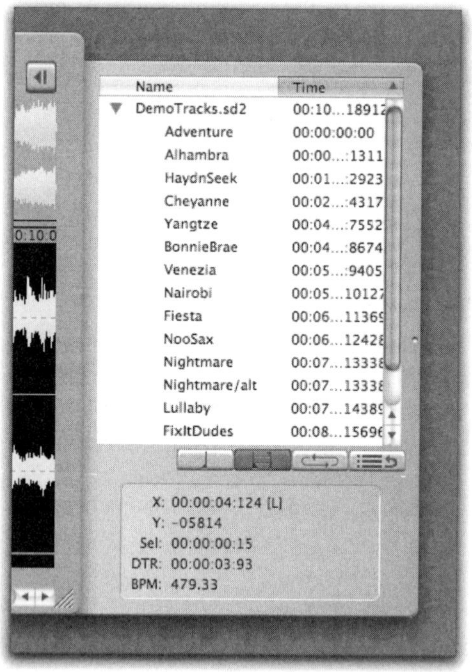

Figure 3-8
With the click of a button, Peak Pro's Contents Drawer slides out from the right side of the Audio Documents window. Its upper area shows region, marker, and loop information. The lower part shows the current cursor position and related data.

At the bottom of the drawer, the Cursor Info area lets you "read" the waveform by moving the cursor through it. The X parameter shows the elapsed-time position of the cursor along the horizontal axis. The Y parameter shows the positive or negative amplitude levels of the waveform as you move the cursor horizontally across the waveform display.

The Cursor Info area also shows which channel (L or R) the cursor is in, the duration of any selected part of the waveform (Sel), the distance from the cursor to the next Reference marker (DTR), and the tempo in beats per minute (BPM) when appropriate.

If you'd rather have all of this information follow the cursor around as you work, toggle on the Cursor Overlay field. (You

> **Tool Tips:**
> **CURSORY CHANGES**
> Use the **Esc** key to quickly cycle through the cursor modes in the Audio Document window.

can get to it in the Options menu or by hitting Shift-Command-T.) The Cursor Overlay provides the same data as the Contents Drawer but in a floating transparent panel that stays next to the cursor as it moves about (see **Figure 3-9**).

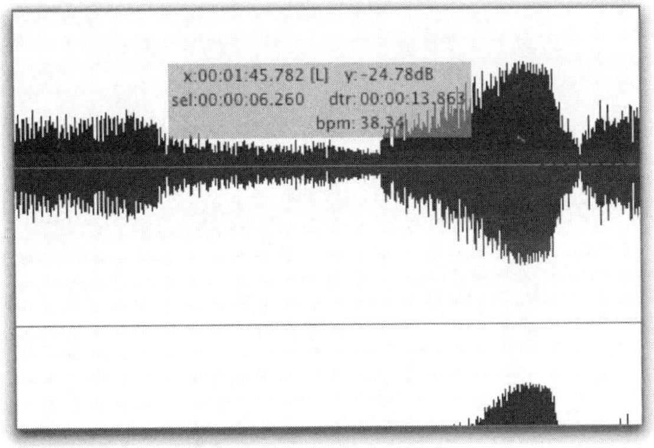

Figure 3-9
The Cursor Overlay includes the same information as the bottom part of the Contents Drawer, but it provides it in a floating transparent field that follows the cursor around.

> **Tool Tips: OPTIONAL OVERLAY**
> Use **Shift-Command-T** to turn the Cursor Overlay on and off.

The upper part of the Contents Drawer shows the current file name and lists all of the waveform's regions, markers, and loops along with their timings. Below the list, four buttons let you specify which items appear in the list: markers, regions, loops, or the edit history. You can sort by name or time by clicking the corresponding column's title bar and then clicking the small triangle that appears. Double-click any entry and the waveform display jumps to that location. Option-double-click any of the region entries to open the Edit Region dialog box; do the same for a marker to open the Edit Marker dialog box. Option-double-click a loop entry to open Peak Pro's handy Loop Tuner feature. (More on loops in Chapter 10.)

Contents Window

Peak Pro lets you have several Audio Documents open at one time, each with its own dedicated Contents Drawer.

Try this: Open any four audio files, one after another. Peak Pro initially stacks the Audio Documents on top of each other, but you can quickly improve the view. Choose Tile Windows from the Window menu or hit Command-T to make all of the waveforms visible at once.

Although each of the windows has a separate Contents Drawer, it soon becomes apparent that having all of the drawers open at the same time can cause problems in seeing the waveforms themselves. Scrunched-down displays and overlapping drawers in multiple documents can make it difficult to find the data that you need. For that reason, Peak Pro provides a resizable floating Contents window (Window > Contents) that provides the same information and features that are found in the upper part of the Contents Drawer (see **Figure 3-10**).

Unlike the document-specific Contents Drawer, however, the Contents window includes marker, region, and loop data from all of the open documents simultaneously. That makes it easy to keep track of loops and edits in a group of documents without having to open each Contents Drawer separately. Moreover, because it's fully resizable (from tiny to full-screen) and floating, you might find the Contents window useful to keep open even for a single document.

> **Tool Tips:**
> **WINDOW SHOPPING**
> If you have multiple Audio Documents open, hit **Command-T** to tile the windows, so you can see them all at once. If your windows are stacked or overlapping instead of tiled, you can bring any of the first nine windows to the front by hitting **Command** and one of the **number keys** (1 through 9) on your QWERTY keyboard. The windows are numbered in the order in which they were opened; the corresponding window will jump to the front of the pile.

Figure 3-10
Unlike the Contents Drawer, which is dedicated to its attached Audio Document window, the Contents window (Window > Contents) can simultaneously show marker, region, and loop information from several open audio files.

The Toolbar & Shortcuts

Beginning with Version 4, Peak Pro's Toolbar has become a much more flexible part of the user interface (see **Figure 3-11**). The Toolbar buttons now reside in a separate window that you can customize and resize/reshape to suit your needs. You can even have the tools disappear completely if you don't need them, but since you can have as few or as many buttons as you like, it's easy to put together a user-friendly combination that provides access to your favorite commands and functions, many of which are available for button assignment.

Figure 3-11
You can stuff Peak Pro's Toolbar window with dozens of buttons (as shown here) or just include a few of your favorites to keep things simple.

To add or remove buttons to the Toolbar window, go to Peak > Preferences > Shortcuts/Toolbar Preferences. That opens the Shortcuts & Toolbar dialog box, in which you can assign keyboard shortcuts and/or buttons to dozens of commands (see **Figure 3-12**). To add a button, simply select a command from the list on the left. If an icon appears in the Toolbar area, you can add that button by clicking the Place in Toolbar checkbox. The new button immediately appears in the Toolbar window. You can also add a pop-up label to the button. (The identifying label appears if you pause over the button without clicking on it.)

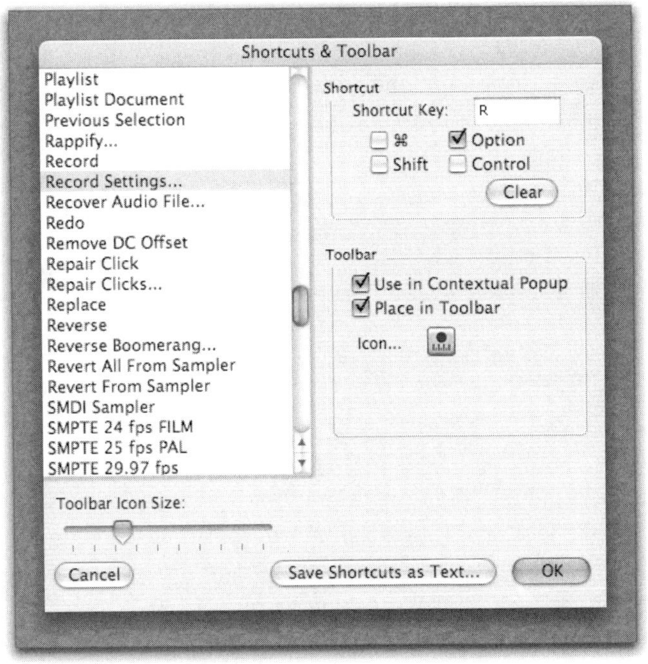

Figure 3-12
The Shortcuts & Toolbar dialog box lets you create or change key commands and add, remove, and resize the Toolbar buttons.

If the command has a default keyboard shortcut, it will appear in the upper Shortcut area. You can get rid of the shortcut with the Clear button or change it to something else by hitting the key combination that you'd like to use. If that combination is already taken, an alert warning will appear. To remove an existing button, just select the command on the left and uncheck the Place in Toolbar checkbox.

Once you've assembled your preferred bunch of buttons, you can adjust the button size to accommodate your workspace. The slider at the bottom of the Shortcuts & Toolbar dialog box lets you set the button dimensions from a Lilliputian 16 × 16 pixels to an elephantine 64 × 64 pixels. If your eyesight ain't what it used to be, or you're just tired of trying to nail the microscopic icons in other programs, having giant buttons to click can be a big relief. On the other hand, if you're the type who likes to have a mountainous collection of buttons to play with, keeping the button size small lets you have a full Toolbar without it taking over the whole screen.

I prefer to only keep buttons for commands that I use on a regular basis. The commands that I need only once or twice a year, I can access from the various menus. For example, I do a lot of zooming when I'm editing, so I keep a complete set of zooming commands in my Toolbar. And I keep a Marker button handy to quickly drop in a marker as I listen to an audio file.

I also have a complete set of transport buttons in the Toolbar. Because my Toolbar is relatively sparse, I can enlarge the buttons quite a bit, and that lets me have an oversized set of transport buttons at the top of the screen in addition to the controls in the Transport window, which I keep at the bottom of the screen. Everyone's approach to editing is different, however, so it's best to experiment with different Toolbar collections until you find the one that works best for you.

In addition to letting you choose the size and number of Toolbar buttons, Peak Pro also lets you change the position and shape of the Toolbar window. Drag the title bar at the top to move the window around; drag the lower-right corner to reshape and resize the window. By dragging, you can configure the Toolbar as one or more horizontal rows, as one or more vertical columns, or as a rectangular cluster of almost any size or shape.

Transport Window

Peak Pro's floating, resizable Transport window has three component parts (see **Figure 3-13**). On the left, a nine-digit, faux-LED counter shows elapsed time as well as several other types of information. In the center, six buttons provide tape-deck-style transport controls. They are, from left to right, Return to Zero, Stop, Play, Go to End, Record (see Chapter 4), and Loop During Playback (see Chapter 10). On the right, a stereo set of multicolor peak-hold VU meters is paired with a single master output fader.

Figure 3-13
Peak Pro's Transport window consists of three parts (from left to right): an LED-style counter display, a set of transport controls, and an expandable set of high-resolution VU meters.

Counter Display

The counter is extremely useful for locating and defining specific areas for editing. For example, click anywhere in the main waveform display and the counter jumps to that timing point. Want to know how long a recording is? Just hit the Go To End transport button, and the end timing appears in the counter.

The counter is especially helpful when working with loops and regions. Let's say you need exactly five minutes of audio beginning with a strong beat in the middle of a file. First locate your downbeat and click on it. Then drag to the right (while holding down the mouse button) until the counter shows five minutes of elapsed time. When you release the button, you'll have a selection of exactly five minutes beginning on your downbeat. When you first click on a waveform location, the counter shows the timing for that point, but as soon as you begin to drag the cursor, the counter jumps to the elapsed time beginning from where you began your selection.

If you need to locate to a specific point in the waveform, simply click on the counter to open the Go To Time dialog box (see **Figure 3-14**). Type in a location and click OK. The playback cursor jumps to the appropriate place in the waveform and appears on the far left side of the main display, ready for playback.

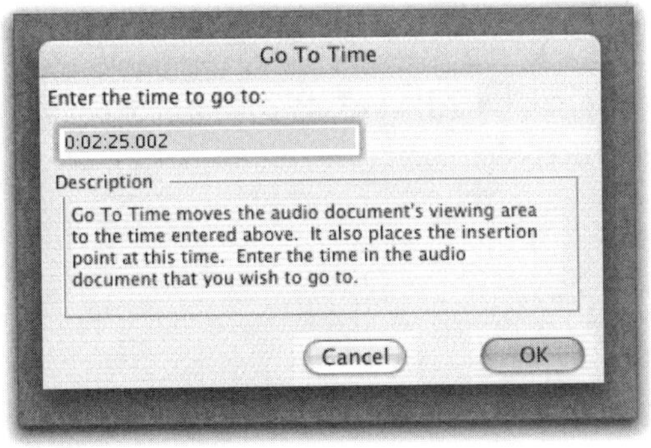

Figure 3-14
To jump to a specific place in a recording, just click the counter and enter the timing in the Go To Time dialog box.

Logically enough, the counter displays its timing information in the same format as is used by the waveform display. If you want to change the counter's format (as well as the waveform display's), go to Options > Time Units to choose something else.

Playback Options

Peak Pro offers a versatile assortment of playback options in addition to the usual Play button. For example, with playback stopped, click anywhere in the waveform and hit the Spacebar; playback begins at that point. Hit the Spacebar again to stop playback. Better yet, double-click anywhere in the waveform and playback jumps to that place. This works whether or not the audio is playing. Hit the Return (Enter) key or click the Stop button twice to return to the beginning of the audio file (or to the insertion point).

You may have noticed that there is no Pause button in the Transport controls. That's because Peak Pro's Play button serves double duty in that capacity. Hit the Spacebar (or click the Play button) to begin playback. When you hit the Spacebar (or click the Play button) again, the program moves the insertion cursor to that point. When you hit the Spacebar (or Play button) a third time, playback picks up where it left off (at the Insertion cursor), just as it would with a Pause button.

If you have an area selected for editing, hitting the Spacebar (or Play button) begins playback at the beginning of the selection. Hitting the Spacebar (or Play button) again stops playback and jumps the cursor back to the start of the selected area. That's very helpful when auditioning different parts of a recording.

Try this: Select an area in the waveform, and hit the Spacebar to start playback. As the audio plays, select a new region and hit the Spacebar twice. The cursor jumps to the new region and playback starts almost immediately from there. You can do this over and over again while searching for a particular section in a recording.

Here's another handy feature: Hold down the Command key when you hit the Spacebar and Peak Pro adds a user-definable pre-roll and post-roll time to the playback. In other words, playback begins just before and ends just after the actual selection. (You can also select the command from a menu at Audio > Play With Auditioning.) To set the pre-roll and post-roll times go to Peak > Preferences > Auditioning (see **Figure 3-15**).

Figure 3-15
For playing selections, Peak Pro lets you set a pre-roll and/or a post-roll time in the Auditioning dialog box.

Peak Pro's Stop & Extend Selection command is a little-known but cool feature. Here's how it works. Make a selection and hit the Spacebar as usual, but this time, hold down the Shift key before you hit the Spacebar. Continue to hold the Shift key as the audio plays; playback will proceed through the selected area and beyond. After playback continues for awhile, hit the Spacebar again (or the Return key) without releasing the Shift key. The audio stops playing, and the selection expands or contracts to include everything from the beginning of the selection to the place where playback stopped. If you hit the Spacebar before reaching the end of the selection, the right selection border jumps back to the stopping place, leaving you with a smaller selection. You can hit the Spacebar again (without the Shift key) to audition your new longer (or shorter) selection.

Triggering Multiple Files

Peak Pro also includes a powerful feature for realtime playback from multiple audio files. As I mentioned earlier, Peak Pro lets you have several audio documents open at the same time. Each time you open another document, the program assigns it a number based on the order in which it was opened. For example, if you open five audio files, Peak Pro will assign them numbers 1 through 5. If you forget which is which, just go to the Window menu. There you'll find the list of open documents along with their assigned numbers. To play any of the files, just hit the number key that corresponds to that document.

You don't even have to wait for each document to finish playing before you trigger the next one. You can hit several number keys in rapid succession, and Peak Pro will cue them up, playing each in turn all the way through. If you want to interrupt a file that is playing and skip to the next one in the sequence, just hit the Return (Enter) key.

> **Tool Tips:**
> **TRANSPORT TRIGGERS**
> Here are some important transport-control shortcuts:
>
> **Spacebar:** play and/or pause
> **Spacebar:** play selected region from beginning
> **Return (Enter):** stop and rewind to Insertion cursor or beginning of selection
> **Shift-Return:** stop and extend (or reduce) selection to stopping point
> **Command-R:** record

This is a great way to try out sound effects on the fly or to trigger narration, dialog, or music clips in real time to see how they work. It also has some potential for live performance; I love the way it lets you improvise with audio clips on the spur of the moment.

You can have up to nine open documents (numbered 1 through 9). To start playback, you have to use the number keys on the QWERTY keyboard, not the ones on the numeric keypad. (You can actually have more than nine documents open at once, but only the first nine are assigned numbers.)

VU Meters

On the right side of the Transport window, Peak Pro provides two high-resolution bar-graph meters that show playback levels in decibels. With the peak-hold function enabled, a floating meter segment (representing the highest level) in each channel stays lit to improve readability. At the far right of the meters, red indicators light up to alert you to the presence of clipping and possible distortion.

As with the peak-level indicators, the clipping indicators have options for setting the hold times. Choosing Audio > Meters opens a small dialog box (see **Figure 3-16**) that lets you turn off the hold function, have the hold segments stay lit until playback is stopped, or have the segments hold for three seconds (or until that level is exceeded).

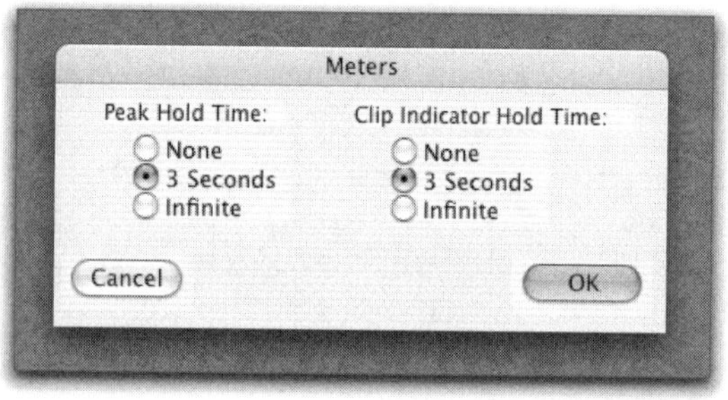

Figure 3-16
The peak-hold VU meters and the clipping indicators have options in the Meters dialog box for setting their hold times.

Directly beneath the VU meters, a single fader lets you set the master playback level. If you drag its lower-right corner, you can stretch the Transport window to accommodate any size monitor. However, only the meters and master fader expand; the longer the window, the longer the meters. It's kind of like a zoom control for your VU meters. With a dual-monitor setup, you could easily have your meters extend over a two-foot range. That makes it easy to read even from a distance and makes small adjustments of the output fader a breeze.

When they're not being used for their primary tasks, the counter and the VU meters provide other useful information. For example, the counter reads out the remaining time during DSP processing operations, and the meters become a progress bar when opening and saving documents.

Other Windows

In addition to the main windows described in this chapter, Peak Pro includes three other windows that add to the power and flexibility of the program. These are the Movie window for displaying QuickTime movies in sync with audio; the VBox window, in which you can combine and route multiple effects plug-ins; and the Playlist window, which is used for organizing and preparing regions for CD burning and other tasks. We'll explore each of these windows in greater detail later in the book: the Movie window in Chapter 12, the VBox window in Chapter 9, and the Playlist window in Chapter 11.

In the next chapter, we'll look at how to get audio—in one form or another—into and out of Peak Pro.

Chapter 4
Ins and Outs: Recording, Playing, Importing, and Exporting

Before you can get down to serious editing (or any kind of editing, for that matter), you first must get a digital audio file into the computer. Peak Pro provides a number of ways to accomplish that task. For starters, the program supports a prodigious panoply of popular (and not-so-popular) audio formats, and Peak Pro makes it a breeze to import tracks directly from an audio CD or from a QuickTime movie. The program supports the standard interleaved-stereo formats (such as AIFF and WAV) as well as the ubiquitous dual-mono Sound Designer II format that is native to such popular programs as Digidesign Pro Tools, MOTU Digital Performer, and BIAS Deck.

Although many people view Peak Pro simply as an editing environment for importing, processing, and exporting audio files, Peak Pro also boasts some sophisticated recording capabilities. That makes it an excellent front end for stereo field recordings as well as for studio use.

Later in this chapter, we'll explore the issues of importing and exporting pre-existing audio files. First, let's take a close look at Peak Pro's recording features. We'll start with a review of some important considerations for setting up and optimizing your audio recording and playback system.

Core Audio Hardware

Although Peak Pro supports the Mac's built-in audio capabilities, you'll typically get much better performance and more versatility if you use a high-quality Core Audio-compatible audio interface. BIAS recommends using a FireWire, USB, or PCMCIA

(CardBus) external interface or an internal PCI card. In any case, you must be sure to install the dedicated Core Audio driver that comes with the device.

Core Audio offers several advantages over earlier audio engines, including low latency, multichannel support, high resolution and adjustable sampling-rate support, and the ability to easily share your audio interface among several other audio programs.

After installing the necessary hardware and software, you can verify that OS X has recognized the new device (and enable or disable the device in the future) by opening the Mac's System Preferences window (Apple menu > System Preferences) and choosing the Sound control panel (see **Figure 4-1**). If everything is okay, you should see your audio interface listed as an audio input and output option.

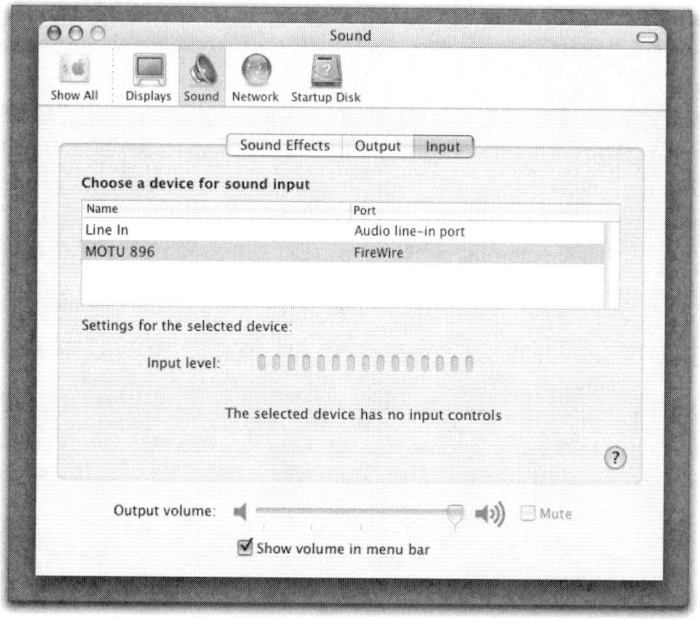

Figure 4-1
Check the Mac's Sound control panel to verify that your audio interface is recognized and selected as the input and output device.

For a more detailed look at your audio interface's available parameters, open the Audio MIDI Setup utility (see **Figure 4-2**). You'll find it in the Utilities folder inside the Applications folder. The Audio MIDI Setup panel lets you set such things as the sampling rate, the input and output channels, and the audio signal's clock source.

In addition to the audio utilities built-in to OS X and the dialog boxes in Peak Pro (more on those in a moment), most audio interfaces provide their own control panel, which often provides access to more settings than are found elsewhere (see **Figure 4-3**). If your audio interface has such a control panel, open it first to set up the hardware the way you want it. Then verify your settings in OS X.

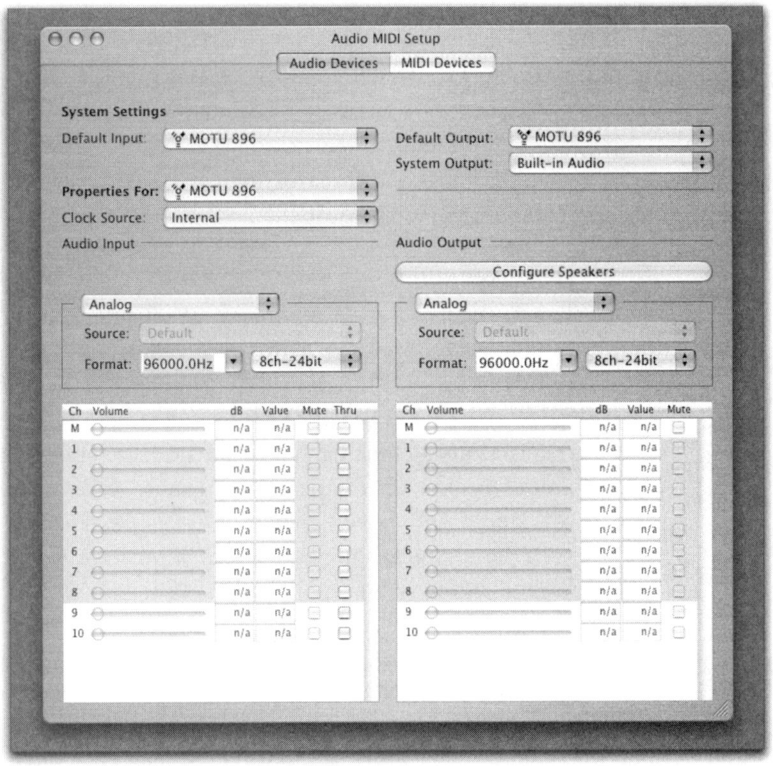

Figure 4-2
The Audio MIDI Setup utility provides a detailed look at your audio interface and its parameters.

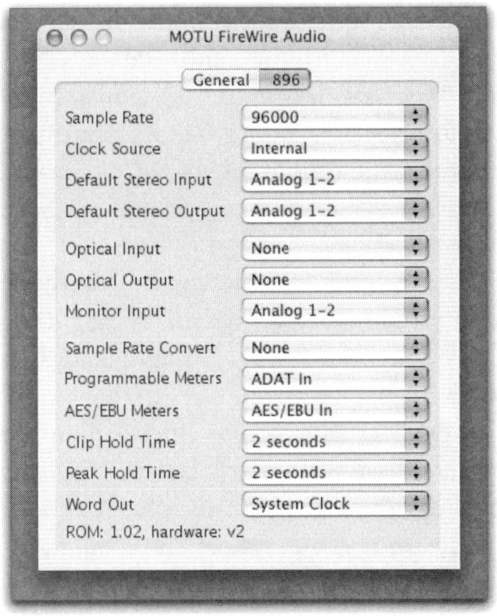

Figure 4-3
Most high-quality audio interfaces include a dedicated control panel providing direct access to a range of settings.

OS X Audio HAL

Although Peak Pro defaults to Core Audio (it will be checked in the Audio > Sound Out submenu), it also supports the Mac's built-in OS X Audio HAL engine, the successor to Apple's old Sound Manager. A few audio devices don't work with Core Audio but do support Audio HAL, which is a simpler I/O protocol. If you use HAL, however, you won't be able to use Core Audio plug-ins, so use Core Audio if possible.

> **Tool Tips: ON THE LINE**
> Before plugging a line-level source into your Mac, be sure to check its output level. Professional audio devices (such as mixing boards, synths, and tape decks) typically have a +4dBu output level. The Mac, on the other hand, requires an input of –10dBV. You may have to turn down the output of the audio source to keep from overloading the Mac's input. Better yet, use a +4dBu to –10dBV line-matching transformer to minimize distortion.

FireWire DV

The FireWire DV option at the top of the Sound Out menu lets you connect a FireWire digital video camera or similar device and use its inputs for recording or its outputs for monitoring the playback from Peak Pro. Most of the time you'll get the best results from a third-party audio interface, but there may be times when a digital video camera must serve as the hub for your audio system. For those situations, Peak Pro lets you integrate the audio capabilities of your DV device with your recording and editing setup.

Hard Drive Issues

Before you can start recording, there's one other consideration to take into account. You must decide where your recorded audio will be stored. Peak Pro defaults to using the largest drive available as the Record Disk, but you can select a different drive in the Peak > Preferences > Scratch Disks box. New recordings will always be made to whatever disk you've specified. (You can always move the file somewhere else later.) If you're running a single-drive system, you can certainly record with Peak Pro, but recording onto the same drive as your operating system and applications could cause problems because you may be overextending the capabilities of the drive's read/write head. Most pros record their audio onto a separate, dedicated audio drive with an access time of better than 12ms and a rotation speed of at least 7,200 rpm.

Fragmentation

The problem with using a single-drive system is that it forces the hard drive read/write head to jump all over the place as it attempts to run the computer, access the program, and record or play back audio files. That can push the limits of its capabilities and may, in extreme cases, cause glitches to appear in the recordings. Moreover, the main system drive will quickly become *fragmented* as different programs add and modify files.

As the hard disk fills up and becomes more cluttered, new files get divided into parts that are spread around the surface of the disk. That may not be a big deal for a text document, but it spells trouble for audio files, which need large blocks of contiguous space to maintain smooth and efficient data streaming. Recording onto a fragmented disk can split your audio file into disparate pieces, slowing access time and making it harder for the drive to maintain a steady flow of data during recording and playback. Since Peak only records or plays back one stereo file at a time, fragmentation is unlikely to cause difficulties as long as you're using CD-standard 16-bit, 44.1kHz audio, but can become troublesome with high-resolution/high-sampling rate files.

A little fragmentation is tolerable, but too much fragmentation leads to errors during recording and/or playback. If you're starting to get unexplained clicks or dropouts during recording, check the condition of your drive. For an audio drive, when the fragmentation rises above about 10 percent, it's time to use a hard-drive maintenance program such as MicroMat's TechTool Pro (www.micromat.com) to defragment or optimize the disk (see **Figure 4-4**).

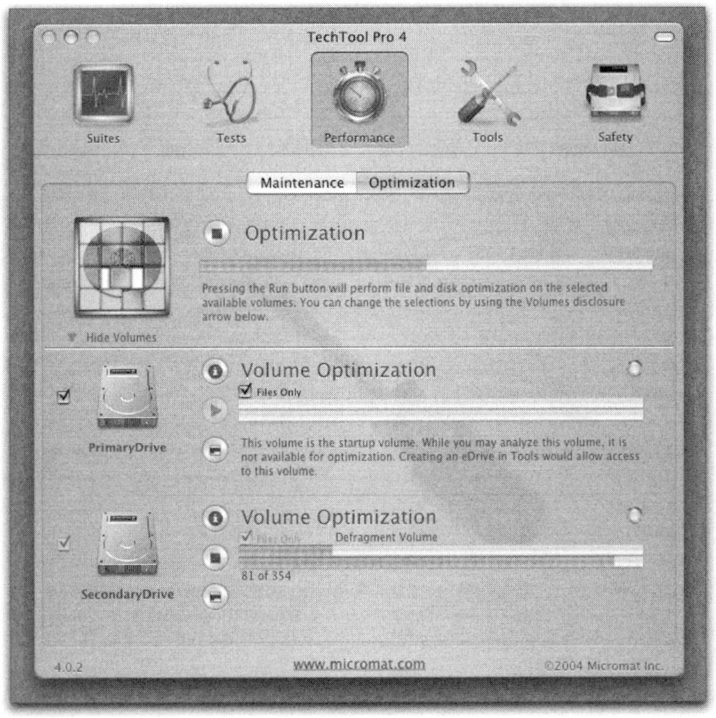

Figure 4-4
A good hard-disk maintenance program, such as TechTool Pro, is an essential complement to your other studio software.

With a separate drive devoted specifically to audio recording, the drive will usually contain only a few dozen large files rather than hundreds or thousands of smaller files. As a result, it's easier to keep track of the drive's condition. In addition,

> **Tool Tips: IN STORAGE**
> Don't forget to provide plenty of storage space for your recordings. 16-bit/44.1kHz stereo recording consumes roughly 10MB per min.; 24-bit/44.1kHz stereo requires 15MB per min.

it's a good idea to archive your recordings on a reliable storage medium and routinely reformat the audio drive (rather than just deleting files) to ensure that it's totally clean and ready for optimum performance. Your computer will also function more efficiently with a second drive simply because it can simultaneously employ two drive-head mechanisms to seek data instead of placing the entire burden on one. Again, this type of optimization is more important with multitrack audio programs than with Peak.

If you decide to use an external drive, choose a FireWire drive or better yet a FireWire 800 drive (if your computer supports one). FireWire drives typically handle streaming data more efficiently than USB drives.

Recording Setup

Recording in Peak Pro is relatively straightforward. However, before you begin, you must make several decisions about how you want your audio system and Peak Pro to interact. A good place to start is with the Core Audio Settings dialog box. You'll find it in the Audio menu under Hardware Settings (see **Figure 4-5**).

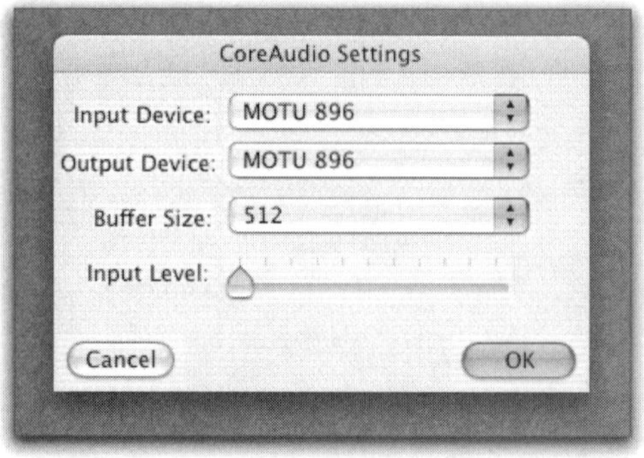

Figure 4-5
Before recording with a Core Audio interface, make sure that it appears as the input and output device in the Core Audio Settings dialog box. The Input Level slider may be grayed out, as it is here.

Be sure that your audio interface is selected as the input and output device and that the Input Level slider is not all the way to the left. (The slider may be grayed out if the Core Audio driver overrides it.) The drop-down Buffer Size menu lets you adjust your hardware's buffer. If you're having problems with funny noises or odd distortion when you begin recording, try increasing the buffer size.

The next step is to open the Record Settings dialog box (Audio > Record Settings). It provides several important options for creating and handling your audio file (see **Figure 4-6**). At the top, you can use the drop-down menu on the left to assign one of your drives as the Record Disk. On the right, another drop-down menu lets you specify the file format for the recording. The right side of the dialog box also has six checkboxes for setting other parameters.

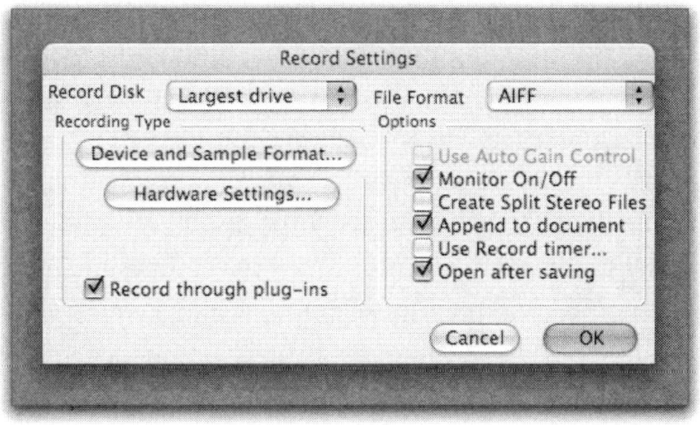

Figure 4-6
The Record Settings dialog box provides several important options that determine how Peak Pro handles the recording process.

Use Auto Gain Control applies to devices that use the Macintosh mic inputs with Mac OS X Audio HAL. If your recording device has an auto-gain-control feature, you can enable or disable it with this box. If you're using a Core Audio interface, this item will likely be grayed out.

Create Split Stereo Files lets you record your stereo input as dual mono files (as used by Pro Tools, Digital Performer, and Deck) rather than as a single interleaved stereo file.

Append to Document lets you add your recording to an existing file. Open the Audio Document that you would like to add to and place the insertion cursor at the point where you want to insert the new material. You can insert your recording at the beginning or end of the Audio Document or at any point in between without overwriting any of the original. Or you can select an area, in which case whatever is in that area will be replaced with new audio. (The new material will continue to replace the original past the selection area until you stop recording.)

Use Record Timer opens a separate dialog box where you can specify a duration for the recording (see **Figure 4-7**). Once you start recording, Peak Pro automatically stops when the appropriate elapsed time (in seconds) has been reached. (For longer times, you'll have to do a bit of math to calculate the time in minutes and seconds.)

Figure 4-7
The Recording Time dialog box lets you specify ahead of time how long a recording will be.

Open After Saving is handy if you want to view your recorded waveform right after hitting Stop. If you're doing multiple takes, you might want to leave this box unchecked. That way you can look only at the takes that are of particular interest.

Don't overlook the lone checkbox in the lower-left corner.

Record Through Plug-Ins is a powerful and very cool feature. It lets you record through any of your installed plug-ins, so you can add reverb to your recording or process the audio with noise reduction, EQ, or other effects in real time. This option is a great time-saver, and it offers a terrific way to experiment with recording techniques. However, for serious recording, it's usually best to record "dry" and do your processing after you have a clean, edited audio file to work with. We'll take a close look at plug-ins and Vbox in Chapter 9, but here's a quick summary of how to use this feature. Open an Audio Document and then open Vbox by choosing Vbox from the Plug-Ins menu. Add the effects plug-ins to Vbox that you'd like to record through, and then begin recording as explained below.

The two large buttons on the left of the dialog box provide ready access to several hardware-related settings. The Device and Sample Format button opens the Core Audio Record Settings dialog box (see **Figure 4-8**). It lets you choose which channels to record through (for multichannel interfaces), the sample rate and resolution, the clock source, and the number of channels to record (mono or stereo).

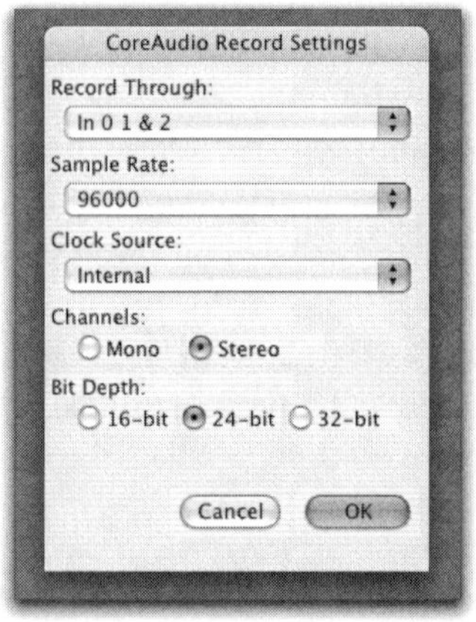

Figure 4-8
Peak Pro's Core Audio Record Settings dialog box lets you change the resolution, sample rate, and other parameters.

The second button in the main Record Settings dialog box is labeled Hardware Settings. It opens the same Core Audio Settings dialog box that we opened earlier (see **Figure 4-5**).

Other Settings

As I mentioned earlier, Peak Pro defaults to Core Audio as the preferred protocol for recording and playback. However, it also supports the Mac's internal inputs and outputs as well as third-party external devices that are natively supported by the Mac OS. If you're using such a setup, you'll encounter some differences in the dialog boxes that appear when you click the Hardware Settings button and especially the Device and Sample Format button in the Record Settings dialog box.

When using the OS X Audio HAL audio engine, the Hardware Settings button may not produce a dialog box at all if there aren't any special settings to be made, or it might produce a dialog box with options that are specific to the hardware.

The Device and Sample Format button opens a three-tab dialog box where you can set the usual parameters such as resolution, sampling rate, input source, number of channels, and so on (see **Figure 4-9**). The tab on the left labeled Compression offers options for different QuickTime-supported compression schemes. However, compression isn't supported in Peak Pro during recording, so you should just leave the setting on "None."

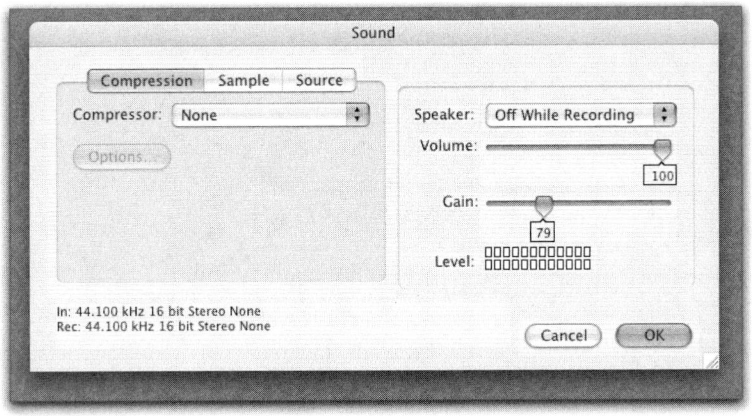

Figure 4-9
If you aren't using a Core Audio interface, the Sound dialog box changes appearance. Peak Pro doesn't support data compression during recording, so the Compressor drop-down menu should have None selected.

Recording

Once all of your hardware settings are configured, it's time to get down to recording. Plug a mic, a line-level output from a mixer, or an electronic instrument into your audio interface. Click the Record button in the Transport window or in the Toolbar window if this button appears there. You can also select Record in the Audio menu or just hit Command-R. Whichever method you use, the result is the same. The Record window appears (see **Figure 4-10**), and the meters in the Transport window come alive, showing input activity. (If they don't, recheck your hardware settings as described earlier and make sure that the input gain on your audio interface is set high enough.)

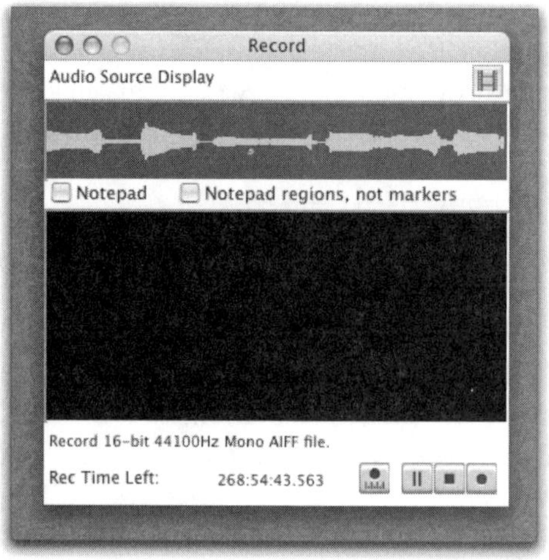

Figure 4-10
During recording, the Record window provides a real-time waveform display of the incoming audio. The handy Notepad area lets you mark and label important places in the file as the recording is being made.

Set the input levels by keeping a sharp eye on the meters. Adjust your audio interface's signal level to keep Peak Pro's meters registering as high as possible without tripping the red Clipping indicators. As a rule of thumb, it's a good idea to allow about 5 or 6dB of headroom on the meters to ensure that you stay safely below the clipping threshold (0dB on the meters).

> **Tool Tips: ON THE LEVEL**
> When setting your input levels, it's best to keep the signal as hot as possible but with about 5dB of headroom below the clipping level (0dB). That should give you a healthy looking waveform yet protect you from accidentally clipping, which could ruin an otherwise fine recording.

Staying below clipping is definitely a good thing, but don't make the mistake of playing it too safe and setting your levels too low. That produces a puny waveform that doesn't take full advantage of the available bit depth (resolution) and therefore the available dynamic range. The result will be a recording with unnecessary noise in it. If you increase the waveform's amplitude through processing at a later date, you'll just increase the noise level as well.

The Record window has three main sections. At the top, the Audio Source Display area provides a real-time waveform display of the incoming audio. In the center area, the Notepad lets you annotate—on the fly—important places in the recording. And at the bottom, an information display shows the current record settings (from the Core Audio Record Settings dialog box or its equivalent if you're using one of the other protocols) along with a real-time counter showing the available recording time (hours:minutes:seconds) based on the remaining hard disk space.

The buttons in the lower right include a Record Settings button (the first on the left), which opens the main Record Settings dialog box (see **Figure 4-6**). That can come in handy if you want to change some of the recording or hardware options at the last minute. The remaining buttons let you pause, stop, and begin recording.

This Record button is the real deal: When you click it, recording begins, and a miniature waveform starts to scroll across the top of the dialog box. You can interrupt recording momentarily by clicking the Pause button, or you can put an end to the recording by clicking the Stop button. When you do that, a Save dialog box appears, prompting you to name the audio file. The recording is then saved in the format that you specified earlier in the Record Settings dialog box, but you can change it at a later date with the Save As command.

Notepad

The Notepad is definitely one of the coolest features in the Record window. It lets you add Notepad Cues (markers) to the main waveform display during the recording process. Here's how it works: Select the Notepad option in the Record window and then begin recording. When an important point in the recording occurs, hit the Return key and type in a short label. Actually, your labels don't have to be short; if you're a fast typist, you can create labels that are several sentences long. However, only the first couple dozen characters appear in the display (followed by an ellipsis). You can view the entire text in the Contents Drawer by pausing the cursor over any truncated entry to produce a contextual pop-up label.

When the next event that you want to label occurs, hit Return again and type in another label. You can repeat this process as often as necessary until you stop recording. After saving the Audio Document, take a look at the waveform display. There you'll find all of your Notepad Cues with their corresponding labels. If you open the Contents Drawer (or the Contents Palette), you can view the markers in list form. Double-click any item in the list to jump to that place in the waveform.

The Notepad feature has a very handy variation called "Notepad regions, not markers." If you select *both* checkboxes above the Notepad text field, you can create regions on the fly as you record. The procedure is essentially the same as described above. The first time you hit Return it creates the beginning of a region with a Region marker, which you can then label. When you hit Return again it marks the end of that region and the beginning of a new region (which you can then label). Hitting Return again ends that region and starts a new one, and so forth.

When you view the waveform display, you'll see a series of region markers with labels. In the Contents Drawer you'll see the regions in list form. Double-click on an item to jump to that place in the waveform and to also highlight the region for playback and editing. Hitting the Spacebar or clicking the Play button in the Transport window plays the selected region. That makes it easy to jump around and audition the different regions.

If you don't like the idea of having a series of contiguous regions, simply avoid labeling the areas between the regions that are important to you. In the waveform display, only the important regions will be labeled. In the Contents Drawer, you can click the

Name column title bar to group the labeled regions together (see **Figure 4-11**). That's a quick way to organize the regions so you can locate the ones that are important. (The unlabeled regions also appear together in their own group, and you can still jump to them in the waveform by double-clicking the corresponding times.)

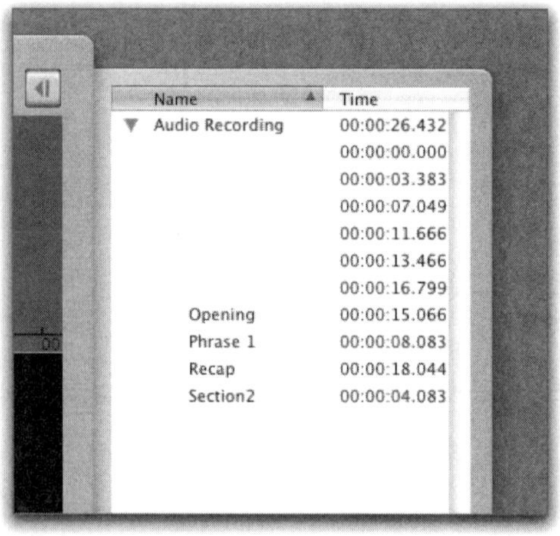

Figure 4-11
Clicking the Name title bar in the Contents Drawer lets you separately group the labeled and unlabeled Notepad markers. Click a name or time to jump to that place in the waveform display.

To use the Notepad effectively for live recording, you'll need a studio setup where the clatter of the computer keyboard can't enter the microphones. And someone else will have to do the performing, so you can attend to dropping in markers and typing in labels. Of course, if you're recording a line-level source from an existing recording, you don't have to worry about any of that.

In either case, the Notepad can be a powerful way to improve your workflow when it comes time to edit. For example, if you're recording a band, you can use Notepad to tag the sections in a piece as it's recorded, such as Intro, Verse 1, Verse 2, Chorus, Bridge, and so forth. Or if you're planning to record several short takes in a single recording, you can keep them straight with a few well-placed labels. For recording narration and dialog, you can use Notepad to help you later locate specific phrases by typing in the first few words in each marked phrase.

Moreover, once the markers are in the waveform, you can move them around, relabel them, and do all kinds of other things. The subject of markers and how to work with them is covered in Chapter 10.

Recording into QuickTime

If you have a QuickTime movie that needs a soundtrack, you can record the soundtrack directly into the movie with Peak Pro. First, open a new (blank) Audio Document (File > New) and then open the QuickTime movie using Peak Pro's Open command (File > Open).

Click the Record button in the Transport window to open the Record window. Before recording, however, click the Record Settings button, and choose Append to Document in the Options section on the right (see **Figure 4-6**). Click the OK button, and then click the Movie button in the upper-right corner of the Record window, if you want the movie to play along. When you've completed your recording, choose Save As in the File menu, and select QuickTime as the file format. (You'll find more about working with QuickTime movies in Chapter 12.)

Importing Audio

Instead of recording new audio, you can import existing files into Peak Pro. The program can open, edit, and resave a variety of file types. Peak Pro's default file type is the interleaved-stereo format AIFF, but you can also import the dual-mono Sound Designer II (SDII) format, as well as WAV, QuickTime, Jam Image, Raw, Mac System 7, MP3, and several other formats (including several compressed formats; see Appendix II).

To open an audio file, choose Open from the File menu or hit Command-O on your keyboard. Peak Pro presents you with a dialog box in which you can browse through your system and locate the necessary file. When you select an audio file whose type Peak Pro supports, a display in the lower left shows the file's sampling rate, resolution, file format, and duration (see **Figure 4-12**). A handy Play button lets you audition the file before you actually open it in Peak Pro.

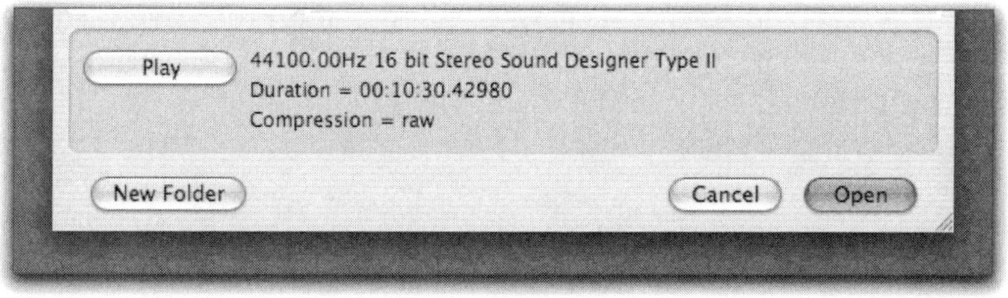

Figure 4-12
The Play button in the lower-left corner of Peak Pro's Open dialog box lets you audition an audio file before importing it. The file's specs appear next to the button.

That approach works well if you're not sure which file you need. However, if you know what you want, you can bypass the Open dialog box entirely by simply dragging the appropriate audio file and dropping it onto the Peak Pro application icon. Peak Pro then instantly opens the file in a new Audio Document window, and you're ready to go.

If you want to work on several recordings, you can drag-and-drop multiple files at once. Peak Pro rapidly opens all of the files in a stack of Audio Document windows. You can even drag a folder full of various types of files and drop it on Peak

Pro's icon. Peak Pro then searches through the folder for supported files and automatically opens them in separate windows.

One easy way to use the drag-and-drop method is to first open Peak Pro so that its icon appears in the Dock. You can then simply drag files to the icon in the Dock. I also keep an alias of the Peak Pro application in the Finder's Sidebar area. That way, I don't even have to open Peak Pro first; I just drag an audio file to the icon in the Sidebar, and it automatically launches Peak Pro and opens the file. If you don't use the Sidebar, you can simply plant a Peak Pro alias icon anywhere in the Finder and use it the same way.

Dual Mono

As mentioned earlier, Peak Pro's native file format is interleaved stereo, but importing dual-mono files is a snap. First, go to the Options menu and make sure that Auto-Import Dual Mono is checked. Then select Import Dual Mono from the File menu to bring up the Open dialog box.

When you find the recording that you want, choose either the left or right audio file and click Open. Peak Pro creates a new interleaved stereo Audio Document, which appears in a stereo display. The two mono files must have the same sampling rate and the exact same name except for the L or R suffix that identifies the channel. Also, keep in mind that because Peak Pro creates a new stereo file during the conversion process (in addition to the source files), you'll need as much free disk space as the original two mono files take up together.

> **Tool Tips: MONO A MONO**
> If you only want to import one side of a dual-mono recording, just uncheck the Auto-Import Dual Mono feature in the Options menu. Then, import the individual file as usual to open a monaural Audio Document window.

After you've finished editing and processing a stereo file, Peak Pro lets you export it in Dual Mono format. Just choose Save As from the File menu and select Sound Designer II from the File Type drop-down menu in the Save Audio Document dialog box.

CD Tracks

Peak Pro makes it easy to import and edit audio tracks from compact discs as long as you have a CD-ROM drive that supports Apple-standard audio extraction (as most Mac-compatible drives now do). The quickest way to grab a track is to literally grab a track. Put a CD in your CD-ROM drive, and when the CD icon appears, click on it and select the track that you'd like to import. Drag the track icon over to the Dock and drop it on the Peak Pro icon. If you haven't added Peak Pro to the Dock beforehand, just open the program to make the icon appear. (You can also drag-and-drop using the main Peak Pro application icon or an alias of it.) After a few seconds, the entire track appears in an Audio Document window.

If your audio-extraction needs are a bit more complicated, skip the drag-and-drop approach, and instead choose Import CD Track from the File menu. (You can also click the CD button in the Toolbar.) When the Import CD Audio dialog box appears, select a track to import and click the Mark button (see **Figure 4-13**). You can select and mark several tracks for importing or just click Mark All if you want the whole shebang.

Figure 4-13
Peak Pro's Import CD Audio dialog box lets you select one or more tracks to import. If you have an Internet connection and iTunes, the CDDB track names (from commercially released CDs) automatically appear in the list.

If you have iTunes installed on your computer and you're connected to the Internet, Peak Pro will recognize and display the track names from commercial CDs by reading each track's International Standard Recording Code (ISRC) as it is registered with the online CD Database (CDDB). You can use the existing names for the imported tracks, or you can save any track to disk with a new name by clicking the Track Name button to open the Name Track dialog box (see **Figure 4-14**).

If you don't need an entire track, you can save yourself some editing time by only importing part of a track. Select a track for importing as described above (you don't have to mark it), but before clicking the Import button, click the Set Import Times button (or simply double-click the track name) to open the Import CD Track Range dialog box (see **Figure 4-15**).

At the top of the box, you'll see a timeline bar that represents the entire length of the track. The left and right edges of the bar are actually sliders that you can move toward the center to isolate a section of the track. (You can also click along the timeline to jump a slider to that position.) As you drag the sliders, a time readout shows where you are in the track. To see if you've chosen the right area,

Audio Lingo: ISRC

The International Standard Recording Code (ISRC) originated in 1986 and is part of the data that appears on commercial compact discs and other media. It's included as part of the subcode data of each track or recording, and its main purpose is to ensure proper royalty payments. The ISRC provides information such as the country of origin, the producer, the serial number, and a reference date.

click the Play button to audition the selected portion. When you're satisfied with your selection, click OK, and then click the Import button in the Import CD Audio dialog box.

If you just want to import one or more tracks directly to disk (as AIFF files) without having them appear in Peak Pro, uncheck the box labeled "Open tracks after import."

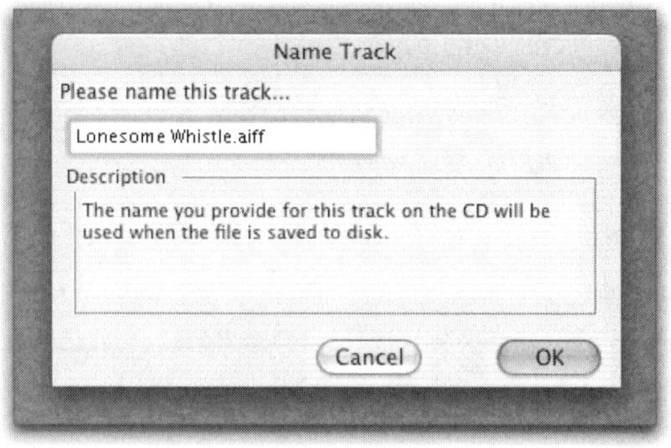

Figure 4-14
The Name Track dialog box lets you name or rename any imported track.

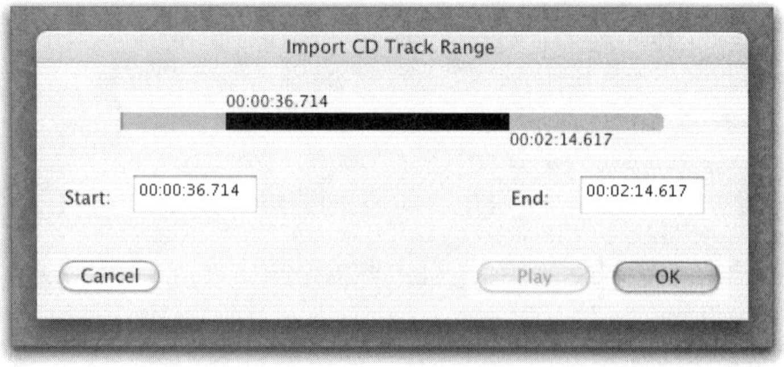

Figure 4-15
If you don't need to import an entire track, use the Import CD Track Range dialog box to specify the portion that you want. The Play button lets you audition your selection before importing.

Saving Files

In addition to the standard Save command, Peak Pro offers two kinds of Save As commands to accommodate different editing approaches. The regular Save As command lets you save a copy of the current file with a different name. When you choose Save As, the original file is closed and the renamed file appears onscreen in the Audio Document window. You can then continue working on the new file, and choose Save As again—each time you reach a crucial point in your edits—to preserve that file and continue on with another newly named document.

The great thing about Save As is that you can use it to save successive stages in a project and quickly return to an earlier state whenever you want. I always add numbers to my labels (for example, LoveSong1, LoveSong2, LoveSong3, etc.), so I can easily keep the versions in chronological order long after the editing session.

The Save A Copy As command works a little differently. As its name suggests, it saves a copy of the current file, but instead of replacing the original file with the renamed file in the Audio Document window, it lets you stash away the copy for safekeeping while you continue to work on the original. With the Save A Copy As command, you can generate a string of previous versions to keep in case you need to revert to them at a later date. But you can also continue working on the original file, which is important because it lets you preserve the original Undo history, so you can undo edits that go back before you chose the Save A Copy As command.

Both of the Save As commands are nondestructive, because they leave the original file intact, but their differences make them suitable to different working styles.

Compressed Formats

Peak Pro supports the same compression formats that QuickTime supports, which means that you can open and save compressed recordings in those formats as well as in AIFC, the compressed version of AIFF. (For a list of supported file formats, see Appendix II.) To save a Peak Pro document in a compressed format choose Save As (or Save A Copy As) in the File menu to open the Save As dialog box. Use the drop-down Compression menu to choose one of the available compression options (see **Figure 4-16**).

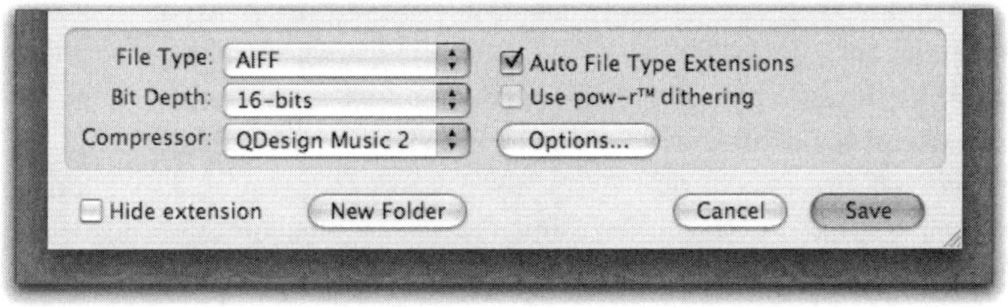

Figure 4-16
At the bottom of Peak Pro's Save As dialog box, you can change the resolution of an audio file and apply one of several compression algorithms before saving.

Dithering

The Save As dialog box also offers you the option of reducing the resolution before saving. For example, if you've been working on a 24-bit file, but you want to prepare the recording for a compact disc, use the Bit Depth drop-down menu to select 16-bits. For Web site sound effects, try 8-bits.

Of course, reducing the resolution inevitably degrades the audio somewhat, so to counteract the effect of using fewer bits, Peak Pro includes Pow-r Consortium's POW-r (Psychoacoustically Optimized Wordlength Reduction) dithering algorithm. You can activate it by checking the POW-r Dithering box next to the Bit Depth menu. Peak Pro actually offers three variants of the POW-r algorithm, which you can select by clicking the POW-r Dither Preferences button in the Peak Pro Preferences dialog box (see **Figure 4-17**).

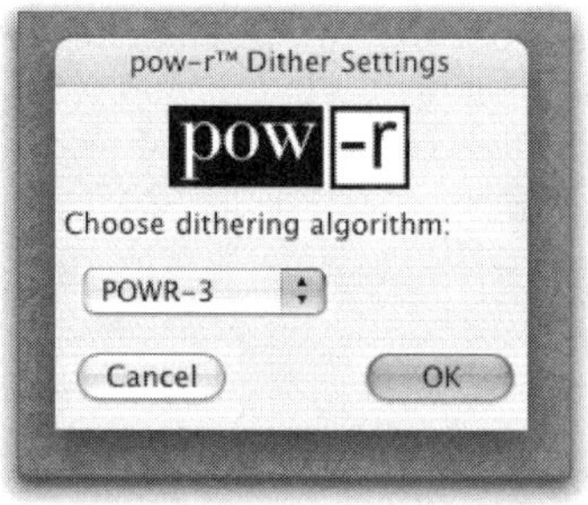

Figure 4-17
For achieving better results when reducing an audio file's resolution, Peak Pro offers three forms of the high-quality POW-r dithering algorithm.

The POWR-1 option is best suited to monaural recordings or stereo recordings with a narrow stereo field, such as you might encounter with a solo performance. For a typical stereo recording with a standard stereo spread, use POWR-2. For recordings with a full audio spectrum and a wide stereo spread, you'll likely get the best results with POWR-3.

Audio Lingo: DITHERING

Dithering is a highly complex and technical topic that involves a number of theories and approaches. To put it in its simplest terms, dithering is a process wherein a small amount of low-level broadband noise is added to a digital recording to improve the audio quality. It may seem counterintuitive, but the added noise, in essence, helps the digital audio system make better use of the available resolution (bit depth). It's therefore particularly useful in counteracting the distortion that appears in a recording when its resolution is reduced, leaving fewer bits to represent the waveform.

In theory, the mostly inaudible noise introduced by dithering is more than made up for by the reduction in distortion. There are many types of dithering algorithms that incorporate different approaches to processing, and as expected, dithering algorithms vary in effectiveness. However, high-quality dithering algorithms, such as those in Peak Pro, can certainly go a long way toward maintaining the audio quality of high-resolution digital recordings that must be compromised for CDs, the Internet, and other media.

It's important that dithering be applied to a given file only once. For this reason, dithering is usually performed during the final stage of audio processing (such as reducing 24-bit audio to 16-bit in order to create a CD master).

MP3

Peak Pro can save and export files in MP3 format, but first you have to install a free encoder utility called Lame. You can get it by going to Apple's Lame for OS X Web page at http://homepage.mac.com/awk/lame. Look for the file named LameLib_Bundle.sit, and click its Download button (see **Figure 4-18**). Unstuffing the file reveals the LameLib.bundle file.

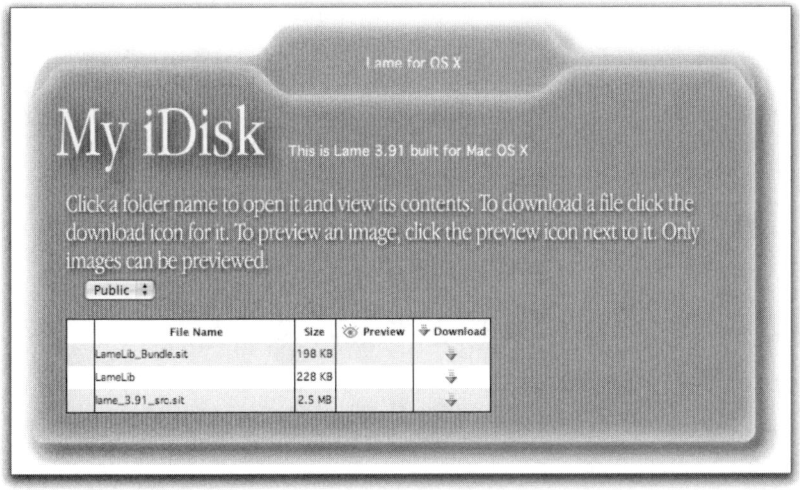

Figure 4-18
You can download the free Lame encoder utility from the Lame for OS X Web site.

With Peak Pro closed, locate the application icon and highlight it by clicking on it once. In the Finder, choose Get Info from the File menu (Command-I). In the Peak Pro Info dialog box that appears, click the triangle next to Plug-ins to open the Plug-Ins viewer section (see **Figure 4-19**). Click the Add button, navigate to LameLib.bundle, and click the Choose button. (Be sure to choose only the entire LameLib.bundle folder, not the individual items inside.)

Close the Plug-Ins viewer section and reopen it. LameLib.bundle should appear in the list. Close the dialog box and re-launch Peak Pro.

In Peak Pro's Save As dialog box, the MP3 option should now be available. To save an audio file in MP3 format, it must have a 16-bit (or lower) resolution and a sampling rate of not more than 48kHz. If you are starting with a 24-bit file, use the POW-r dithering option when lowering the resolution.

Peak Pro defaults to a high MP3 bit rate, but you can choose a lower-quality rate (from 8 to 320 kbps) by clicking the Options button in the Save As dialog box (see **Figure 4-16**). That opens the MP3 Encoder dialog box (see **Figure 4-20**), which also provides spaces for adding tag information, such as the artist's name and the musical genre.

Figure 4-19
In Peak Pro's Info dialog box, add the Lame encoder to the Plug-Ins section.

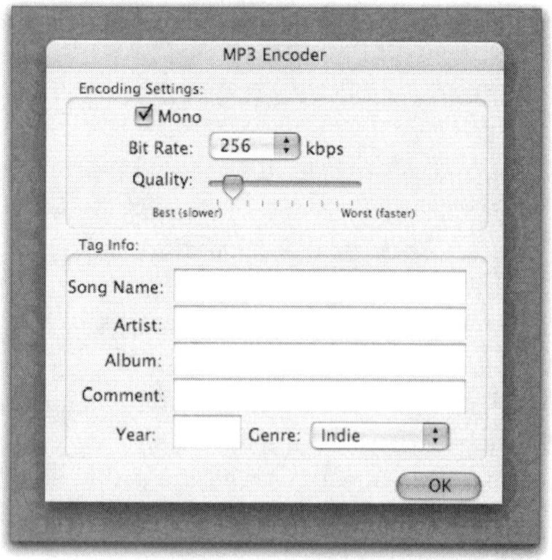

Figure 4-20
The MP3 Encoder dialog box provides a Quality slider and a drop-down Bit Rate menu along with several fields for adding tag information.

Samplers

Although they're under attack from a growing number of increasingly powerful software samplers, hardware samplers are still in widespread use. And many desktop musicians are quite attached (figuratively, in most cases) to their modules and keyboards. Unfortunately, hardware samplers with their diminutive displays often make it difficult to properly edit samples.

If you have a sampler that supports the SMDI protocol, however, you can use Peak Pro as your editing front-end. You'll have to have your sampler connected to your computer with a SCSI cable for SMDI to work. Peak Pro supports several SCSI-compatible samplers, including the E-mu E-IV, E-64, E-5000, ESI-32, and ESI-4000; the Kurzweil K2000, K2500, and K2600; the Peavey SP/SX; and the Yamaha A3000, A4000, and A5000. With any of these (and possibly other SMDI samplers), Peak Pro lets you import samples, edit and process them, and return the samples to the sampler.

The procedure is relatively straightforward. Choose SMDI Sampler or one of the specific sampler names from the Sampler menu to open the SMDI Sampler Transfer dialog box (see **Figure 4-21**). Peak Pro displays a list of samples that it has detected in the device. Click any item in the list to view detailed information—such as the sampling rate, resolution, and other data—in the Info area. Select a sample and click the Receive button to transfer the file to Peak Pro where it appears in an Audio Document window. You can Shift-click to choose more than one sample.

Audio Lingo: SMDI

SMDI stands for SCSI Musical Data Interchange. It's a transfer protocol that enables SCSI-compatible instruments to exchange data at a much higher rate than the standard MIDI protocol allows. Of course, to use SMDI you must be able to connect your Mac to your sampler with a SCSI cable. If you're using one of the newer Macs, that means adding a SCSI card or converter.

Figure 4-21
Peak Pro's SMDI Sampler Transfer dialog box supports several specific models of hardware samplers.

After editing, you can send the sample back to your sampler by clicking the Send button. If several documents are onscreen, Peak Pro sends the front-most document to the sampler. Before sending the sample, you must first select a sample in the SMDI Sampler Transfer dialog box's list. The sample in Peak Pro is then sent to that memory location in the sampler and replaces the existing sample (if there is one) with the edited one.

What's Next?

Now that we've looked at how to get audio into and out of Peak Pro, let's dive into the editing process and explore the program's basic editing tools.

Chapter 5

Basic Editing: Getting the Most from Everyday Tools

Peak Pro's vast editing capabilities range from the mundane to the amazing, and most users quickly gravitate toward their favorite surgical techniques for fixing problems or toward their favorite audio processors for shaping and mangling sounds. We'll get to both of those categories and many more in the next several chapters, but before diving into the program's more exotic capabilities, it's important to have a solid grounding in the basics.

In this chapter, we'll look at the essential tools, techniques, and features that most people use (and often under-use) every time they begin an editing project. These bread-and-butter capabilities may not be especially flashy, but you'll find yourself using them over and over again as you clean up, reconstruct, and enhance your audio files. In fact, you may be surprised at just how much you can really accomplish with Peak Pro's basic set of editing tools.

Nondestructive Editing

It's important to understand that Peak Pro takes a nondestructive approach to editing. In other words, none of the editing operations that you perform on a waveform are permanent until you save the audio file. If you do something and realize it was a mistake, you can easily Undo it (Command-Z). In fact, with Peak Pro's unlimited Undo capability, you can retrace your steps all the way back to the last time you saved the document (or to its original state if it hasn't been saved yet). Conversely, you can Redo (Command-Y) any edit that has just been undone.

These two commands are not only good for retreating from bad editing decisions, they also offer a great way to quickly compare before-and-after edit states. Try out an edit, and if the effect is too subtle to readily perceive, or if you're just not sure if you like the result, do several A/B comparisons with the Undo and Redo commands. Just remember that the Redo command only works in tandem with an Undo command; as soon as you perform another edit, you lose the ability to Redo until you Undo something later.

The Edit List

Peak Pro enables you to step backwards through a series of edits by maintaining an internal edit list. In that way, the program keeps track of the sequence of events that have led to the waveform's current state. Stepping back sequentially through your edits works fine in many cases, but Peak Pro also lets you jump directly to any previous state (since the last save) by accessing the edit list directly. This is a fantastic time-saving feature when you're working on complex projects with lengthy strings of alterations.

After making a number of edits to a file (I'll describe several good candidates in a moment), just choose Edits from the Edit menu to open the Edits dialog box (see **Figure 5-1**). It displays a chronological event list (with times and dates) showing all of your editing operations since the last time the file was saved.

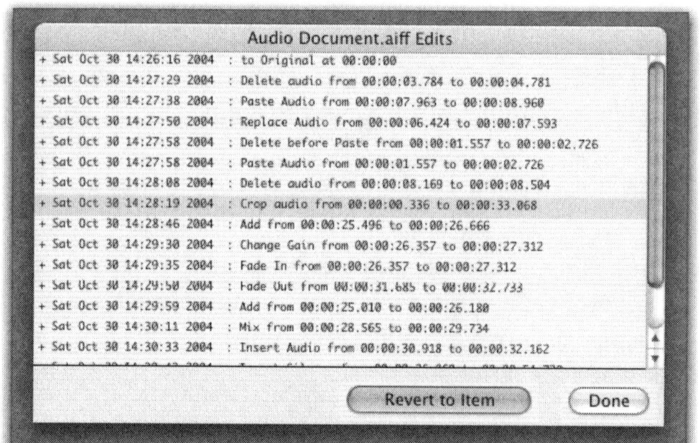

Figure 5-1
The Edits dialog box shows your editing operations in a chronological event-list format.

To return to a previous edit state, select an edit description from one of the events and click the Revert To Item button. (You can also just double-click the description.) The waveform immediately returns to that prior state. Click Done to leave the Edits dialog box.

Remember, if you jump to an earlier edit state, you can Redo your way back out of it or just jump to a different place as long as you don't perform any new edits first. Once you perform a new edit, you lose the edit history after that point (the preceding history is still there), and when you save the file, the entire edit history disappears completely.

Show Edits

In addition to the edit list, Peak Pro can also display a graphic indicator of where in the waveform your edits have occurred (since the last save). It may not be as detailed as the edit list, but it can be a helpful visual aid, showing which parts of the waveform are the same as the original file and which parts have been changed (see **Figure 5-2**). To activate this display mode, choose Show Edits in the Options menu. Altered waveform areas appear within cross-hatch-bordered frames, which disappear when you save the edits.

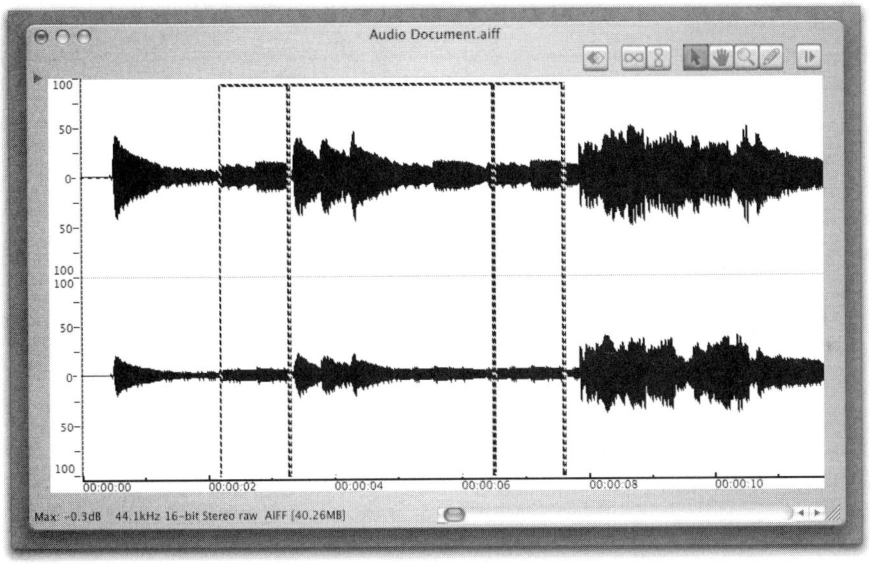

Figure 5-2
Peak Pro's Show Edits feature (Options > Show Edits) indicates which parts of the waveform have been altered. Edited areas are highlighted with cross-hatched borders.

Selecting & Inserting

At its simplest level, Peak Pro is much like a word processor for audio documents, and as such, it offers the same kinds of Cut, Copy, and Paste commands commonly found in most programs. Before you can perform an edit, however, you must decide where it should occur. Using Peak Pro's Arrow (I-beam) cursor you can click at a location to deposit an insertion point (a vertical dotted line) or click-and-drag through an area to create a selection. The insertion point identifies a specific place along the timeline where an edit will occur. A selection highlights a segment of audio for copying, editing, or processing.

> **Tool Tips: REAL-TIME EDITS**
> Peak Pro's editing capabilities aren't just nondestructive, they're "interactive" as well. For example, you can cut out a chunk of audio, paste it at the end of the waveform, change its pitch, and fade it out, all while the audio is playing back. When playback reaches the edited material, it will sound as if it had been that way from the start. In other words, you don't have to stop the whole show just to make a few simple edits. If you're the multitasking type, you can listen and edit at the same time.

That pretty much sums up the basics for specifying an editing location, but because Peak Pro is more complex than your typical word processor, there are several other important considerations to take into account. For example, when working with a stereo file, click on the line dividing the two channels (or a little above or below the line) to create an insertion point that affects both channels. Click-and-drag to create a stereo selection. You can also insert a cursor or create a selection in the right or left channel alone by clicking above the left-channel or below the right-channel zero-crossing line. (When you're in the right zone, a tiny L or R appears next to the I-beam cursor.)

There are some limitations when working with a single channel of a stereo document. For instance, you can select an area and process it in a number of ways, but you can't cut, paste, delete, or do other kinds of edits that would alter the waveform's timing in relation to the other channel. Since this is an interleaved stereo file, the two channels are tightly linked.

Zero Crossings

When adding or removing audio, you'll usually get the best results when the insertion point or the borders of the selection occur at zero-crossing points (see Chapter 2). Cutting into a waveform at one of the peaks or troughs typically causes clicks or pops when you paste in new material (or remove existing material), because it creates a transition at a high-energy point in the waveform, where even a slight mismatch in the waveform shape is most apparent.

At a zero crossing, on the other hand, the waveform is at a no-amplitude transition in an audio cycle, and your editing transitions are more likely (although by no means certain) to be successful at that point. We'll look at how to fix pops and clicks in the next chapter, but it's always best to avoid trouble in the first place if you can.

Snap To

The problem with locating zero crossings is that you must first zoom in to a level where you can see individual cycles. Once you're at that level, it's impossible to see enough of the waveform to make any but the smallest of selections. Fortunately, Peak Pro offers an easy solution. Go to the Action menu and under the Snap To command, select Zero Crossings (Action > Snap To > Zero Crossings). Then go to the Options menu and choose Auto Snap. (These two items work as a team.)

With Auto Snap switched on and Snap To set to Zero Crossings, Peak Pro slightly expands or contracts your selections until the borders land on the next available zero-crossing points (see **Figure 5-3**). The same feature also works with the insertion point, jumping it to the nearest zero crossing. (You can also set Peak Pro to snap to any of several other increments, such as CD frames or units for specific game platforms.)

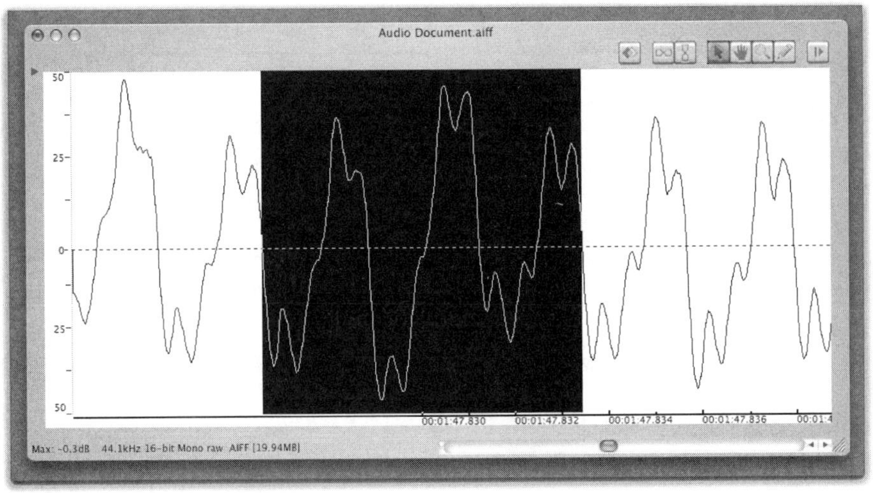

Figure 5-3
With the Snap To command set to Zero Crossings and Auto Snap active, Peak Pro automatically expands or contracts your selection to position the borders at the nearest zero-crossing points.

Try this: With Auto Snap set to Zero Crossings (as described above), open any audio file and zoom in until you can clearly see individual cycles. Click the I-beam in the middle of one of the peaks and watch as the insertion point automatically jumps to the closest zero crossing. Once you know that Peak Pro is finding the zero crossings, you can confidently create your selections at a more practical zoom level.

Keep in mind, however, that in a stereo file, the zero crossings seldom line up perfectly between channels, so a compromise is almost always necessary. Rather than let Peak choose zero crossings for you, you may prefer to zoom in and manually find a spot where there's a zero crossing in one channel and a low-level waveform in the other channel.

Adjusting Selections

When making selections, it's not uncommon to discover that one of the borders is in the perfect position but the other one isn't. Or perhaps you realize that the selection is slightly too large or too small. Rather than starting over again by creating a new selection, you can adjust the borders by holding the Shift key and dragging the left or right edge of the selection. Instead of dragging, you can also just click where you want the border to be, and it will jump to that position. Remember, if Auto Snap is active, when you let go of the mouse button, the selection edges will pop into place at the nearest zero crossing (or other specified time unit or increment).

Tool Tips: BORDER LINES

You can use either of a selection's borders to create an insertion point. Choose the Insertion Point at Selection Start command from the Edit menu (or hit the Up Arrow key). The selection disappears leaving an insertion point at the previous start point. You can do the same thing using the selection's end border by choosing Insertion Point at Selection End (or by hitting the Down Arrow key).

> **Tool Tips: SELECT SOUND**
> Remember: you can always audition a selection by clicking the Play button in the Transport window, choosing the Play Selection command in the Audio menu, or by simply hitting the Spacebar on your keyboard.

Set Selection

If you must establish a selection at a precise location or for a precise duration, you can use Peak Pro's Set Selection dialog box (Edit > Set Selection). It lets you specify exact timings (in one of several time formats) for the start, end, or duration of the selection (see **Figure 5-4**). If you have already made a selection before opening the dialog box, the current selection's parameters appear, so you can make changes as needed. The Set Selection command can be used on either or both of the channels in a stereo file.

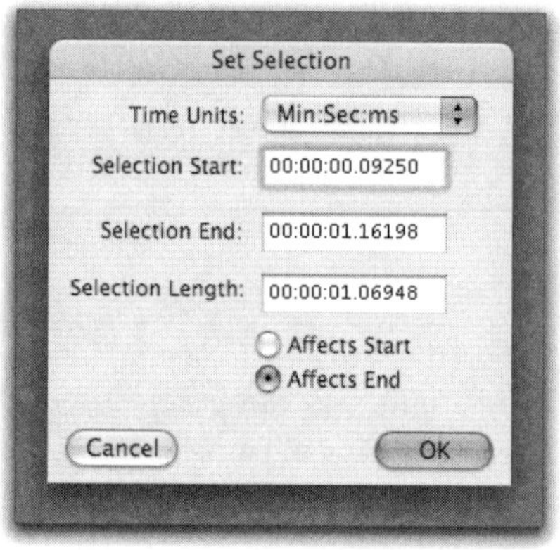

Figure 5-4
To specify exact parameters for a selection, use the Set Selection dialog box.

Next Selection

Peak Pro has leveraged its powerful Undo/Redo capabilities to provide a specialized feature for working with selections. It lets you recapture a previous selection for making quick comparisons or for retracing your steps if you change your mind.

Try this: Open any Audio Document and click-and-drag to make a short selection. Then create another selection and another one. Now choose Previous Selection from the Edit menu (or hit Shift-Command-Left Arrow). Peak Pro jumps back to the previous selection. Use the command again to jump back to the selection before that one. You can move in the other direction by choosing Next Selection (or by hitting Shift-Command-Right Arrow).

This is a terrific tool for auditioning different parts of a recording without having to add markers or extract regions. Just hit Shift-Command-Left Arrow and then hit the Spacebar to hear the previous selection. Then do the same thing again to hear the selection before that one. You can quickly cycle through several selections in either direction and listen to whichever ones you want.

Moreover, the same commands work with the insertion point in essentially the same way. Click in several places along the waveform, and then jump from one point to another with the Previous Selection or Next Selection commands. In fact, you can even mix selections and cursor positions and jump from one to the next in the sequence. This can be a very handy tool for comparing multiple takes of the same sound effect or section of dialog.

Document From Selection

It's not uncommon to find yourself working on an Audio Document with multiple music cues, sound effects, or dialog parts in it. In those cases, it's often best to break out the different elements so you can edit and process them in separate windows. Peak Pro makes that task easy to do. Make a selection in an Audio Document and choose Document From Selection (File > New > Document From Selection) or hit Control-N. Peak Pro instantly creates a new untitled Audio Document containing a copy of the selection. You can name the file later, and you can even save it in a different format than the original.

Tool Tips: SELECT ALL

To quickly select all of the audio in an Audio Document, choose Select All in the Edit menu or hit Command-A. To select everything in only one channel, place the insertion point in the appropriate channel only, and then choose Select All (or Command-A). In either case, you can deselect the audio by clicking anywhere in the waveform display.

Removing Audio

At the most basic level, cutting and copying in Peak Pro is much the same as in a word processor. Drag to make a selection and then choose Copy (Command-C) to copy the selection to the Clipboard. The original waveform remains unchanged, and the copied material is available for pasting or for other edits, which we'll get to shortly. The Cut command (Command-X) also sends a copy of the selection to the Clipboard, but it removes the selection from the waveform at the same time. The audio to the right of the selection then snaps to the left to fill in the gap. To remove a selection without copying anything to the Clipboard, hit the Delete key (or choose Delete from the Edit menu).

One of the most common reasons for deleting part of a waveform is to trim away dead air before and after a music cue, sound effect, or sample. The quickest and easiest way to accomplish that task is with the Crop command. Simply select the part of the waveform that you want to keep, and choose Crop from the Edit menu or hit the Command and apostrophe keys (Command-'). Peak Pro preserves the good stuff and removes everything else.

Another common editing problem occurs when you need to remove a section of audio without disturbing the timing of the surrounding waveform. Let's say you're editing a section of synchronized dialog and you need to remove a cough during a pause. If you choose Cut or Delete, all of the dialog after that point will be out of sync, because the waveform after the cut will jump to the left to fill the gap. The solution is to use Peak Pro's Silence command. Select the area that you want to remove and choose Silence from the Edit menu (or hit Command-E). Peak Pro replaces the selected audio with a silent section of the same length; the offending audio is gone and the timing remains unchanged.

Adding Audio

Peak Pro offers a range of options for adding audio in various (and often subtly different) ways to an existing waveform. For starters, there's the ubiquitous Paste command in the Edit menu (Command-V), which adds the Clipboard contents to a waveform. Click anywhere in a waveform to add an insertion point and then choose the Paste command. The new material from the Clipboard is added at the insertion point. The waveform to the right of the insertion point moves farther to the right to accommodate the new audio.

You can also use Paste to replace a selection. In that case, the Clipboard material completely replaces the selected area, which is deleted just before the new material is added. If the selection is shorter than the Clipboard material, the waveform to the right of the selection moves farther to the right to accommodate the new audio. If the selection is larger than the Clipboard material, the file shrinks in length as the material on the right moves to the left to fill in the waveform.

Two other commands—Insert and Replace—offer variations on the Paste command. When adding audio at an insertion point, Insert functions exactly the same as Paste. New material is added, and the waveform expands. Replace, however, substitutes the Clipboard material for the same amount of audio starting at the insertion point. In other words, if you copy ten seconds of audio and choose Replace, the Clipboard contents replace the ten seconds of waveform following the insertion point. The overall length of the waveform stays the same.

> **Tool Tips:**
> **CLIPBOARD CLEANING**
> Because of its nondestructive approach to editing, Peak Pro must store any cut or copied audio on your hard drive so it can retrieve the data and restore it if it needs to. With extra-large edits, that can amount to a sizable chunk of disk space. If you're running low on storage and you're absolutely sure you won't need the material, you can flush out the Clipboard and regain the space with the Clear Clipboard command in the Edit menu.

Unlike the Paste command, Insert and Replace don't behave differently when working with selections. They simply treat the left border of the selection as if it were an insertion point. Insert is therefore handy if you like to add audio—for instance, a short snippet of background noise, which dialog editors call *room tone*, at the start of a selection. Replace is useful for overwriting sections of a waveform without having to make a selection first.

If you work with rhythm tracks, hip-hop loops, or long ambient pads, you'll appreciate Peak Pro's Duplicate command (see **Figure 5-5**). It lets you paste (insert) any number of copies of the Clipboard contents into your Audio Document at the insertion point. When you choose Duplicate from the Edit menu, a small dialog box provides a slider (with a range of 0 to 100) and a number box (where you can type in any number) to specify how many repetitions of Paste to employ. The waveform expands to accommodate the new material.

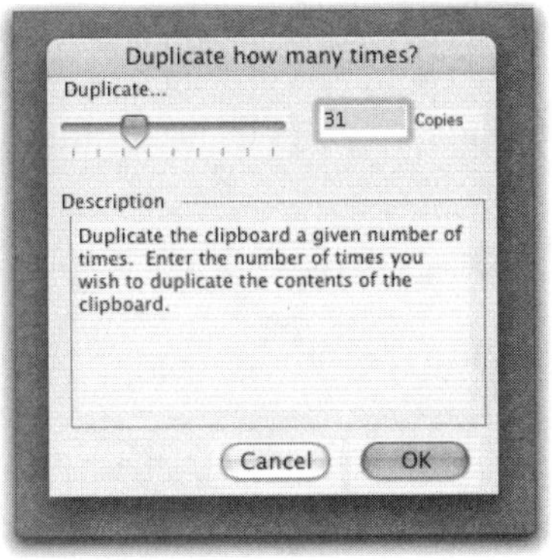

Figure 5-5
Peak Pro's time-saving Duplicate command opens a small dialog box where you can specify the number of Clipboard copies to paste into the waveform.

Mixing Audio

So far, the editing commands that we've looked at have either inserted or replaced audio from the Clipboard. But Peak Pro also has commands that let you *combine* the Clipboard contents with the existing (target) waveform. The Add and Mix commands have nearly identical dialog boxes and they work in much the same way.

To use the Add command, copy some audio to the Clipboard and click in the waveform display where you want to have the added audio begin. Choose Add from the DSP menu to open the Add dialog box (see **Figure 5-6**). Use the slider at the top of the box, or type in a percentage to adjust the level of the Clipboard material before mixing it in. This is an important step because adding together the target waveform samples with the Clipboard samples can easily cause clipping, especially when working with loud passages.

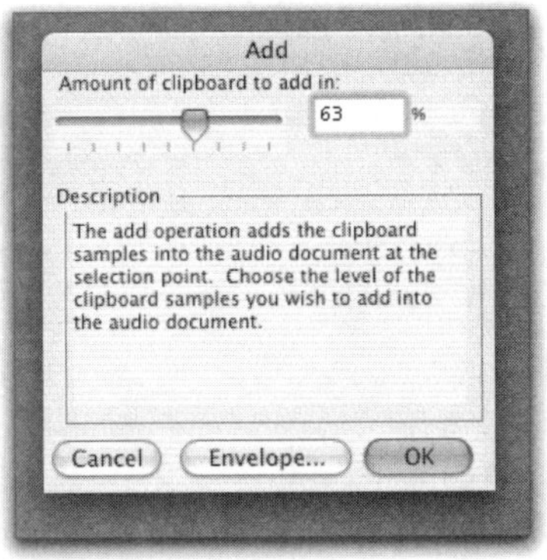

Figure 5-6
Peak Pro's Add command lets you blend the Clipboard contents at any level with the existing waveform.

If you want the Clipboard audio to fade in or fade out, click the Envelope button. That opens a separate Edit Envelope dialog box (see **Figure 5-7**) where you can choose from a list of preset fade in/out shapes. You can also modify the envelopes by dragging control points on a graph. Click the Save button to preserve your custom shapes. Click the Change button to apply the envelope, then click the OK button in the Add dialog box. The Add command provides an excellent way to lay in music behind narration, to add sound effects to dialog, or to create audio-montage-style soundtracks.

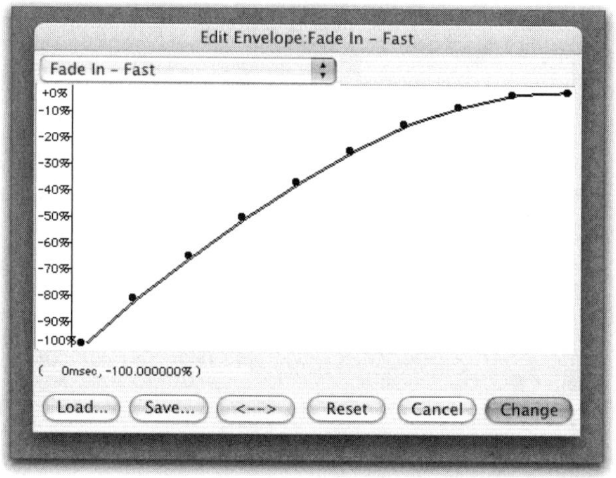

Figure 5-7
By using the Add command's Edit Envelope dialog box, you can fade the Clipboard audio in or out when blending it with the target audio.

The Mix command is also in the DSP menu, and it uses the same kind of dialog box as the Add command does (see **Figure 5-8**). The Envelope button opens the same Edit Envelope dialog box. The difference between the two commands is that Mix attenuates both the Clipboard audio and the target audio and thereby prevents the resulting waveform from clipping.

Figure 5-8
The Mix command uses the same kind of dialog box as the Add command, but the slider at the top of the Mix dialog establishes an inverse relationship between the levels of the target audio and the levels of the Clipboard audio.

Here's how it works. If you set the slider to 100 percent, you'll end up with 100 percent Clipboard and 0 percent target audio. At 50 percent, you'll get 50 percent Clipboard and 50 percent target audio. At 40 percent, you'll get 40 percent Clipboard and 60 percent target audio, and so forth. It's as if the Clipboard and the target audio are on separate mixing board faders that are linked inversely: as one goes up, the other goes down. That yields a distinctly different result than the Add command, which leaves the target audio as-is and simply adds in the Clipboard at the specified level.

Deciding which command to use depends on the type of mix that you want. For example, if the target audio is the primary material and must not be altered, use the Add command to judiciously blend in some of the Clipboard. To quickly establish the relationship of the two sources as you combine them, use the Mix command. Remember, in both cases, you can use the Envelope feature to vary the levels over time.

Fading In & Out

Peak Pro's Edit Envelope dialog box for the Add and Mix commands is actually only one of several types of envelope controls that the program offers. The ones that I use most often are the Fade In and Fade Out commands. They're quick and easy to use and they can solve a wide range of common problems.

To create a fade-in, select the area in the waveform where you want to apply the fade. Then click the Fade In Envelope button in the Peak Preferences dialog box (Peak > Preferences > Fade In Envelope). That opens the Fade In Envelope Editor, where you'll see your waveform selection with an amplitude-envelope graph superimposed on it (see **Figure 5-9**). The waveform's appearance reflects the changes that the current envelope will produce. The vertical scale on the left shows the amount of attenuation: 0% (at the top) indicates full (original) volume; –100% (at the bottom) indicates zero amplitude.

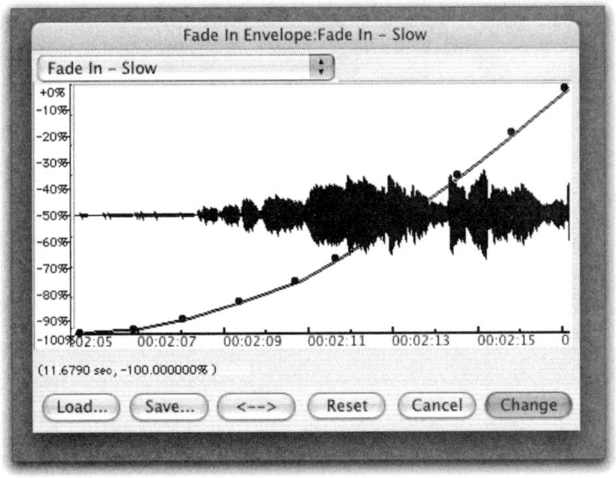

Figure 5-9
The Fade In Envelope Editor lets you choose from several preset envelope shapes, or you can create and save your own envelopes.

You can use the drop-down menu at the top of the Editor to choose one of the preset envelope shapes. Each time you choose a new preset, the waveform in the Editor changes to show the effect that the current envelope will have.

If you want to create your own envelope, start with one of the presets and drag the graph's breakpoints into whatever positions you want. To add more breakpoints, just click on the line where you need other points. To remove a breakpoint, click on a point to select it and hit the Delete key. You can create a mirror image of the curve (reverse it) by clicking the <—> button. Click the Save button to store your new fade-in curve in the Peak Envelopes folder. You can then select your custom preset from the drop-down menu in the Editor.

Once you've settled on a fade-in envelope, click the Change button to make it the current setting and to close the Editor. To apply the fade-in to the audio document, choose Fade In from the DSP menu. Most people end up using the same fade envelope over and over again, so once you've saved your envelope choice with the Preferences, you can quickly apply that fade-in anytime you want with only two clicks: Click-and-drag to select an area for the fade-in, and then choose the Fade In command (or click the Fade In button in the Toolbar).

The Fade Out command works exactly the same as the Fade In command (see **Figure 5-10**). In fact, you may have noticed that the Fade In Envelope drop-down menu includes fade-out as well as fade-in options. The same is true of the Fade Out Envelope drop-down menu. (That's because the different envelope menus draw from the same Peak Envelopes folder.)

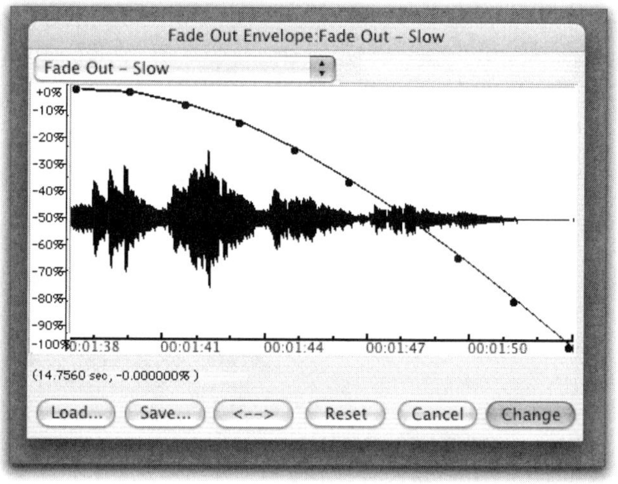

Figure 5-10
The Fade Out command offers the same options as the Fade In command.

If you really wanted to, you could actually set the Fade In command to produce a fade-out, while the Fade Out command produced another kind of fade-out. Or Fade In could produce one of the standard types of fade-in, while Fade Out produced one of your custom fade-in envelopes. You could even reverse the commands, so that In was Out and Out was In. The <—> button makes that especially easy to accomplish. This is all far too confusing for my tastes, so I like to keep my In and Out commands as nature intended. The point is, though, that Peak Pro offers a lot of flexibility in how you apply your fade envelopes.

Here's another thing to keep in mind. All of the preset fade-ins begin at zero (–100%) and build from there, but there's no reason why you can't start your fade-in from, say, 50 percent, thus preserving an attack transient or keeping a music bed at a low level for a while before it starts to swell. Just drag the first breakpoint up to the –50% mark (or wherever you'd like to start). The same is true for the Fade Out command; you can have it end wherever you want. Moreover, you can also create a custom envelope that fades in for awhile and then fades out, or vice versa (see **Figure 5-11**).

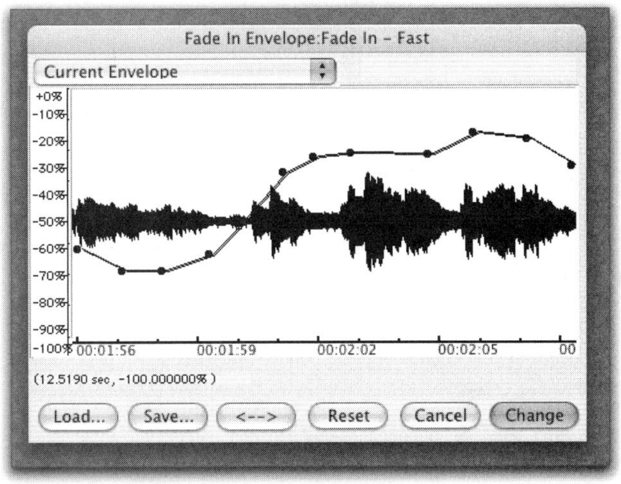

Figure 5-11
Fade In and Fade Out envelopes can begin and end at any level, and they can even change directions.

Remember, the length of the selection affects the speed of the fade-in or fade-out. A linear fade-in applied to a three-minute selection will creep in at a snail's pace because the change in amplitude will be spread out over such a long time (and it will take awhile for the audio to reach listening level). Long fade-ins are a great way to sneak an ambient pad in behind dialog or to add subtle changes to a music cue.

On the other hand, a fade-in applied to a short selection, such as a half second, happens so fast that it barely registers with the listener. In fact, applying an extra-short fade-in or fade-out can be a valuable technique for smoothing out edit points or other abrupt transitions. We'll explore that technique more in the next chapter. For now, just be aware that you can adjust the speed of your fade-ins and fade-outs by changing the size of your selection.

Blending

As mentioned previously, fading in and out can be an effective way to smooth out edits, and Peak Pro can actually do it automatically with its Blending function. Activate Blending by clicking the Blending button at the top of the Audio Document window (see **Figure 5-12**) or by hitting the Caps Lock key on your keyboard. (The button turns blue when Blending is active.) With Blending enabled, Peak Pro applies a very brief crossfade whenever you edit a waveform with Cut, Delete, Paste, Insert, or similar commands that typically leave abrupt transitions.

Figure 5-12
You can activate Peak Pro's Blending feature by clicking the Blending button at the top of each Audio Document window.

You can specify the duration of the crossfade by clicking the Blending button in the Peak Preferences dialog box (Peak > Preferences > Blending) and entering a number in milliseconds in the Blending dialog box (see **Figure 5-13**). Although you can type in four-digit numbers for the duration, Blending is designed to apply extremely short, unnoticeable crossfades at edit points, so you'll usually get the best results if you keep the setting to around 100 to 500ms.

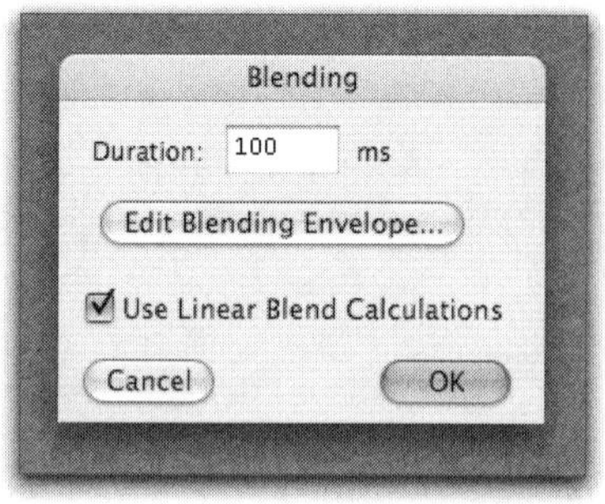

Figure 5-13
The Blending dialog box lets you specify a crossfade duration for the automatic Blending feature.

Peak Pro also offers two options for calculating the crossfade effect: logarithmic or linear. In most cases the differences are probably imperceptible, but if you encounter a stubborn edit transition, try switching options. I prefer using logarithmic calculations as a default, but if you get better results with linear calculations, click the Use Linear Blend Calculations checkbox.

For even more control over the crossfade, Peak Pro lets you edit the crossfade envelope shapes. Click the Edit Blending Envelope button to open the Blend Envelope

Editor (see **Figure 5-14**). There you'll find the familiar fade-in and fade-out envelope graphs together in the same display with the same drop-down envelope preset menu at the top. One of the fade graphs has breakpoints that you can move; the other graph moves automatically to form a mirror image. You can click anywhere along the primary line to add more breakpoints for greater control over the final shape. You can also save your custom crossfade shape in the Peak Envelopes folder.

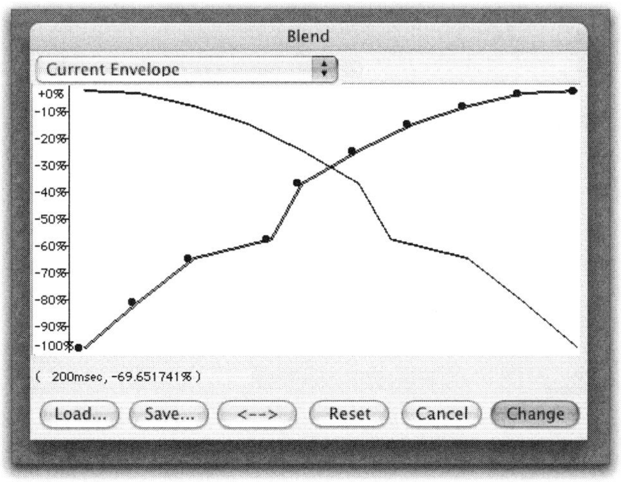

Figure 5-14
In the Blend Envelope Editor, you can choose a preset crossfade type or create your own.

The Current Envelope menu in the Blend Envelope Editor box provides easy access to the contents of the Peak Envelope folder (which is found in your user directory on the hard drive, in the Library folder, in the Preferences subfolder). By default it includes three crossfade types: Linear Blend, Equal Power Blend, and Block. Linear creates a simple X-shaped crossfade which can work well if the transition occurs at a pause, a low energy point in the audio, or with certain types of intermittent content. If you're trying to splice together sections with more continuous music or sound effects, however, the linear shape may produce a dip at the transition point. In those situations (and in many others), the Equal Power option often yields better results. If you've chosen the Use Linear Blend Calculations function in the Blending dialog box, BIAS especially recommends using the Equal Power Blend X-Fade envelope to avoid the slight drop at the crossover point.

The Block preset is a bit more unusual. With its default shape it doesn't actually produce a crossfade at all. Instead, it appears to create the digital equivalent of a butt splice. However, by dragging the breakpoint at the top of the "transition" to the left and

> **Tool Tips: BLENDING OFF**
> It's a good idea to leave Blending off until you specifically need to use it for improving cutting and pasting results. In some cases, the Blending function can cause problems with processing commands in the DSP menu, such as Fade In, Fade Out, and Normalize. Peak Pro includes the Blending On/Off button at the top of every Audio Document window, so it's readily accessible; the button turns blue when the Blending feature is active.

dragging the bottom breakpoint to the right, you can create a mini-crossfade. For a more exotic shape, try dragging the upper-left-corner breakpoint down a little and doing the opposite with the lower-right-corner breakpoint (see **Figure 5-15**). The possibilities for creating complex linear combinations are endless, especially when you start adding more breakpoints. The Block preset may not be the most predictable or the most practical for routine editing, but it lends itself well to experimentation.

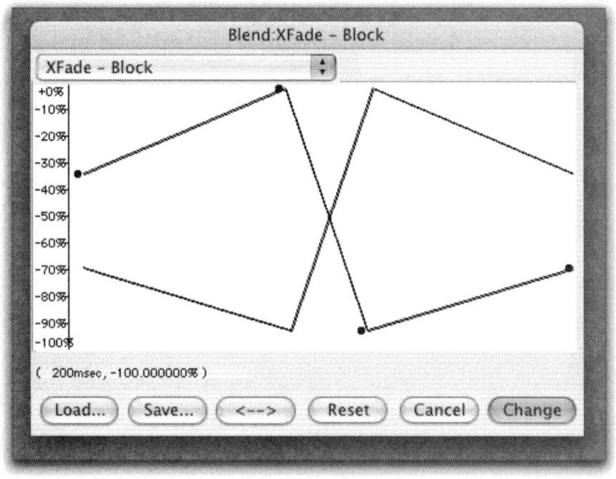

Figure 5-15
The Block preset in the Blend Envelope Editor offers the potential for some unusual cross-fade shapes.

Scratch Disk

Peak Pro's nondestructive approach to editing means that it must continually save large chunks of audio to be ready for an Undo command. Cutting, copying, and other editing operations produce temporary "scratch" files that must be stored somewhere until the file is saved. If you have more than one hard drive in your system, Peak Pro lets you specify which drive to use for holding your temporary files. Click the Scratch Disks button in the Peak Preferences dialog box (Peak > Preferences > Scratch Disks) to open the Scratch Disks dialog box (see **Figure 5-16**).

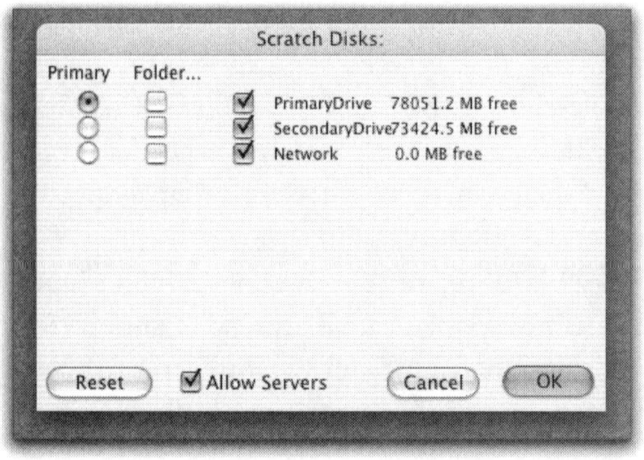

Figure 5-16
The Scratch Disks dialog box lets you specify which of your hard drives (or file servers) should be used for holding temporary editing files.

You can select one drive as the Primary drive (be sure to choose a drive with plenty of free space), and you can even specify a particular folder to use for scratch files. If you're connected to a fast file server (high-speed Ethernet or Media Net, for example) you can use it by clicking the Allow Servers checkbox.

What's Next?

In the next chapter, we'll expand on the basic editing commands and explore Peak Pro's tools for preparing audio files and fixing common problems.

Chapter 6

The Fix-It Shop: Repairing Common Audio Problems

One of the reasons why so many Mac-based studios add Peak Pro to their arsenal of music and audio software is because Peak Pro excels at solving the kinds of problems that typically occur in recordings. Whether it's getting rid of digitally induced clicks and pops, trimming away unwanted sounds, or smoothing out the crackles and scratches from an old 78, Peak Pro has the tools to get the job done. And Peak Pro's versatile zooming and scrubbing capabilities enable you to effectively zero in on the problem areas, which is at least half the battle.

In this chapter, I'll focus on cleaning up and preparing audio files for a variety of uses, such as CD mastering, sound effects production, and dialog editing. These areas are all explored more fully in the next chapters, but before you delve into any of the fancy stuff, you have to be sure that the original file is properly prepped and ready to go. Let's begin at the beginning.

Preparing the Attack

One of the first things that I do when I record or import an audio file is to trim away the unwanted material at the beginning of the recording. That moves the desirable part of the recording to the left so that the beginning is right up against the left side of the Audio Document window.

Trimming the file makes it smaller, so saving is faster. It's not unusual for a music recording to have several seconds of dead air at the beginning as the musicians get organized and wait for the downbeat after the Record button has been clicked. Keep in mind that 20 seconds of background noise or even silence takes up just as much disk space as 20 seconds of a Beethoven symphony.

Trimming is therefore important, but trimming *thoughtfully* is even more important. For example, let's say you're editing samples for use in a sampler. Leave too much space before the attack, and your sound effect or sampled instrument will always have a noticeable lag when it's played from a MIDI keyboard. Trim too close, and you might clip off some of the attack transients. Attack transients are important both for sampled instruments, where a missing attack will adversely change the character of an instrument's sound, and for dialog, where the transients are important in distinguishing between consonants and thus making the words understandable.

I use a two-step approach: First I trim away most of the dead air while staying well away from the actual attack (see **Figure 6-1**). Then I zoom in on the area around the attack and trim further after analyzing the situation in detail. In most cases, if you zoom in far enough to view the waveform as a single undulating line, you can see the point where the waveform suddenly rises out of the primordial ooze of the background noise (see **Figure 6-2**). In those cases, I back off several milliseconds and make the cut.

For safety's sake, I always leave at least a smidgen of space before the actual start. How much space depends on how the file is to be used. Sampled instrument sounds need to be cut pretty close to avoid a lag when played. The same is true of sound effects that must be tightly synchronized and locked to picture; they're much easier to work with if they don't have a built-in pause before sounding. Nevertheless, a few milliseconds at the start are usually not perceptible, and you can always trim a little more later. If you've snipped off too much, you may have trouble restoring it.

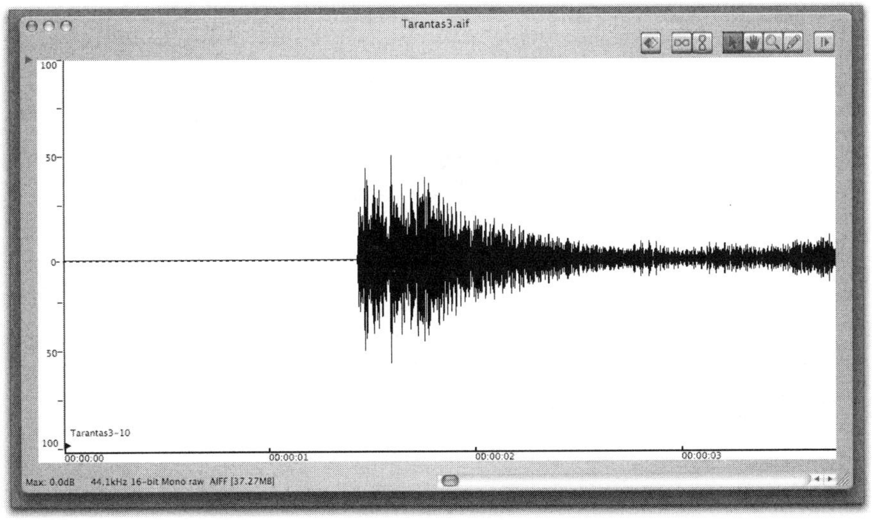

Figure 6-1
When a waveform is zoomed out too far, you can't see the actual beginning of the attack. What appears to be the start of the attack could prove to be deceptive, so it's best not to trim too closely until you zoom in further.

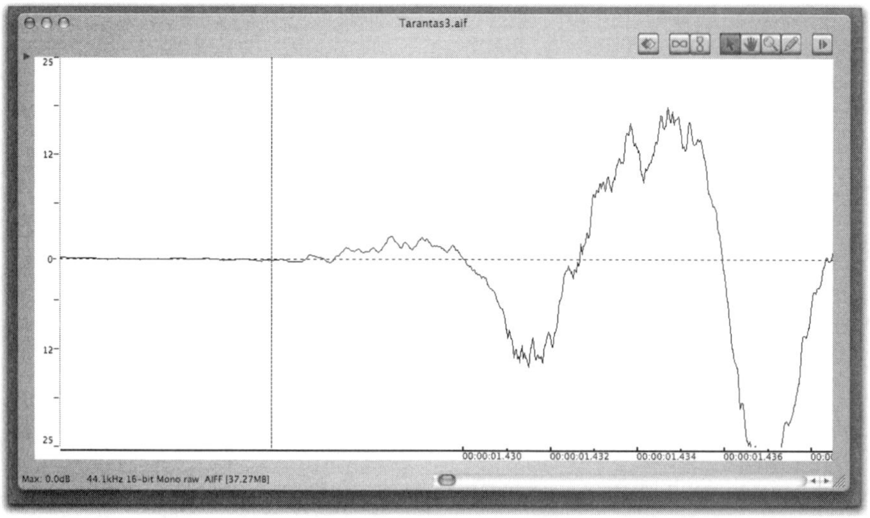

Figure 6-2
If you zoom in close enough you can usually see the exact point where the waveform begins to stand out from the background noise.

Regardless of the amount of space that you leave before the attack, it's important to create a smooth entry. This is especially true in recordings with a noticeable amount of background noise or "room tone" (see **Figure 6-3**). I therefore always apply a fade-in to the space leading into the attack. Select the area from the very beginning of the file and include the first cycle of the attack. Choose Fade-In from the DSP menu.

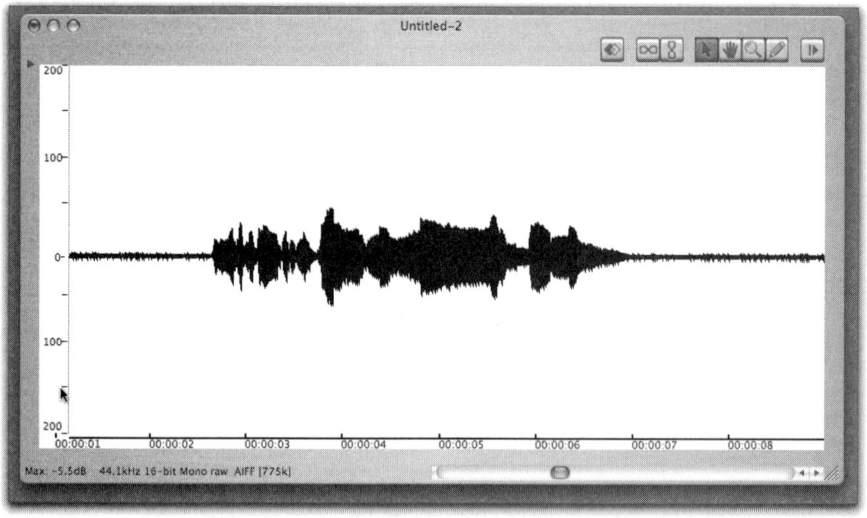

Figure 6-3
This recording has a lot of background hiss, making it difficult to establish the exact attack and end points.

A linear fade-in often works fine, but I usually prefer the Fade-In Slow preset (Peak > Preferences > Fade In Envelope) as a starting point. It depends on the nature of the attack and the length of the fade. Allowing a short section for applying a fade-in before the attack usually yields a smoother entrance. It also guarantees that the audio file begins at zero amplitude, so the sound will start cleanly, without a click.

Attacks don't always have an easily discernable start point. Sometimes recordings begin with a very quiet entrance (see **Figure 6-4**). In those cases you'll have to exaggerate the appearance of the attack by boosting the vertical zoom. After zooming in close enough to see the waveform as a single line, choose Increase Vertical Zoom from the Action menu or hit Control-Up Arrow.

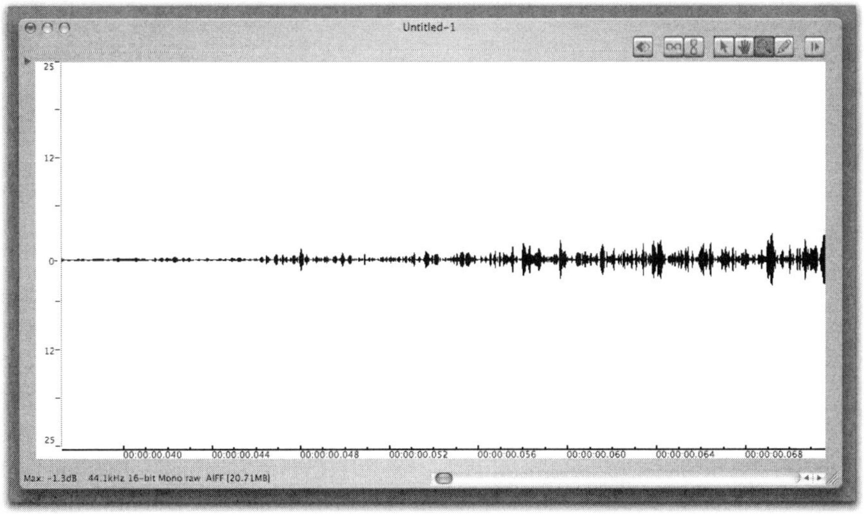

Figure 6-4
When a recording begins very quietly as shown here, it can be tricky to distinguish the performance from the background. Be sure to audition each of your edits to make sure you aren't cutting into the desirable material.

If the recording has a quiet entrance *and* a lot of background noise, finding the actual attack can be tricky. You may have to increase the vertical zoom or decrease it (Control-Down Arrow) in combination with the other zoom tools until you see a likely transition from background to attack (see **Figure 6-5**). After finding the best spot to trim the recording and then fading into the attack, be sure to audition the opening few seconds to verify that the entrance isn't too abrupt or unnatural-sounding.

Depending on the type of work that you're doing, it might be a good idea to save some of the background noise before you throw it away. For dialog editing, soundtracks, and sound designing it could come in handy to have a clip of the room tone to use instead of pure silence when replacing unwanted sounds or extending pauses. The room tone produces a more natural filler than absolute silence. You could even assemble a library of different background and room-tone clips.

In addition, many noise-reduction programs need a few seconds of clear background sound (such as air conditioner hum or wind noise) to analyze in order to eliminate those sounds from the main recording. If you think you might have a use for the background sounds at a later time, select a representative area before the attack and choose Document From Selection (File > New > Document From Selection) or hit Control-N. You can then save the background sound as a separate file.

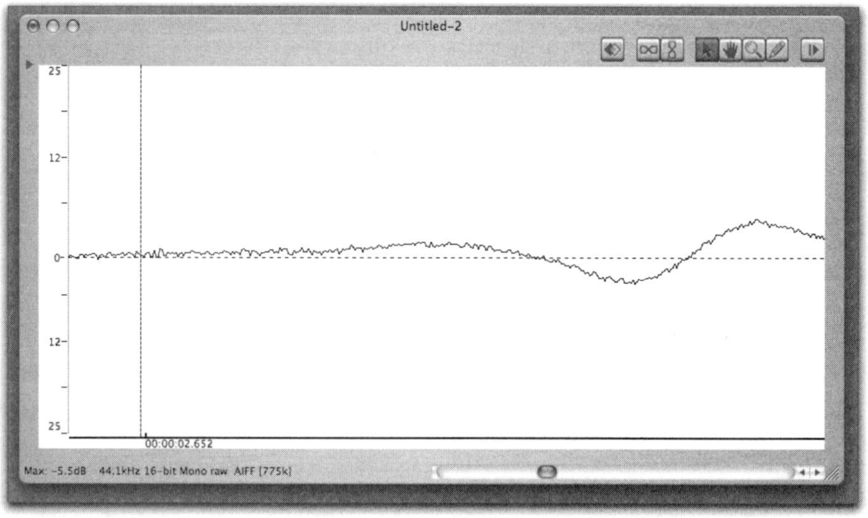

Figure 6-5
With background noise leading into the attack, you'll have to zoom in vertically and horizontally until you find a likely transition. Fading into the attack makes the background noise less apparent.

Trimming the Tail

Removing excess material from the end of the file is much the same as removing it from the beginning. At the end, however, the recording disappears back into the background noise. In most cases, when you zoom in close, you'll find yourself looking at the reverb tail (whether natural or electronic) as it fades away (see **Figure 6-6**).

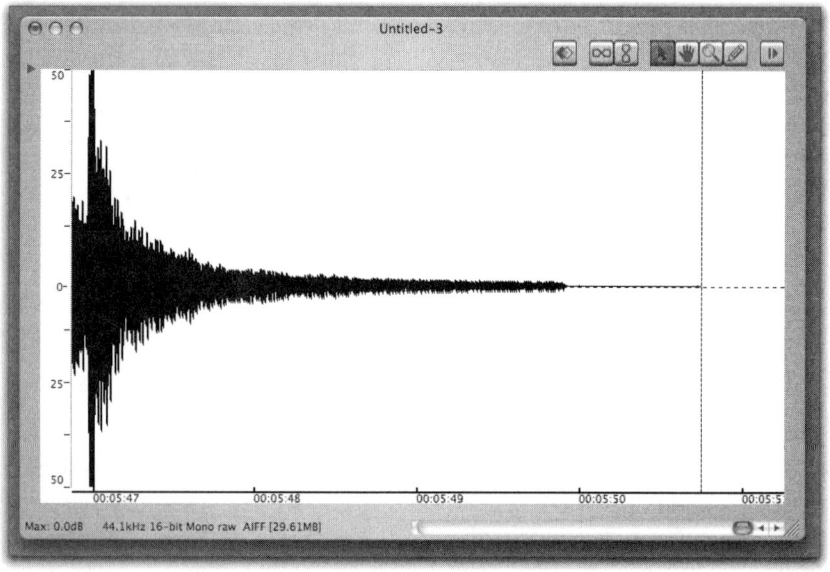

Figure 6-6
When trimming the tail, be careful not to cut off the last bit of reverb. That could make the recording sound more "dry" than it did originally.

Cut somewhere past the end of the tail and then fade out from the last bit of reverb to the end of the file. It's important that you not cut into the reverb tail and thereby leave an abrupt and unnatural ending. Try using the Fade-Out Fast envelope (Peak > Preferences > Fade Out Envelope) or as an alternative try a Linear fade-out.

Sometimes the reverb tail is so long that a large part of it is practically inaudible. This could be a problem for CD tracks, because it creates the perception of an unusually long pause between the current track and the next one. If you find yourself in that predicament, you'll have to locate a workable place to cut the tail and fade it out. (This also comes up with sound effects.) Experiment with the type and length of the fade-out until you find something that sounds natural and doesn't seem truncated. If you go too far, you'll notice that the recording sounds "dryer" than the original, which could be a good thing if that's the desired effect.

As with the attack area, the end of a recording is also a good place to look for room tone to save as filler or as a reference for noise reduction.

Normalize

One of Peak Pro's most commonly used tools is its Normalize command. Normalize exists in some form in virtually all audio-editing programs. It quickly increases the overall amplitude of an audio file that has been recorded at too low a level. In its simplest implementation, the Normalize command searches through the waveform, locates the highest peak, and scales the waveform (multiplies the value of every sample word) so that the highest peak is at the 100 percent amplitude level. In other words, Normalize raises the amplitude of the waveform as much as possible without clipping. (The zero crossings stay where they are, but the rest of the waveform expands outward.)

To use the Normalize command, choose Normalize from the DSP menu, which opens the Normalize dialog box (see **Figure 6-7**). If nothing is selected, Peak Pro automatically selects the whole audio file, but you can also select any area to normalize separately.

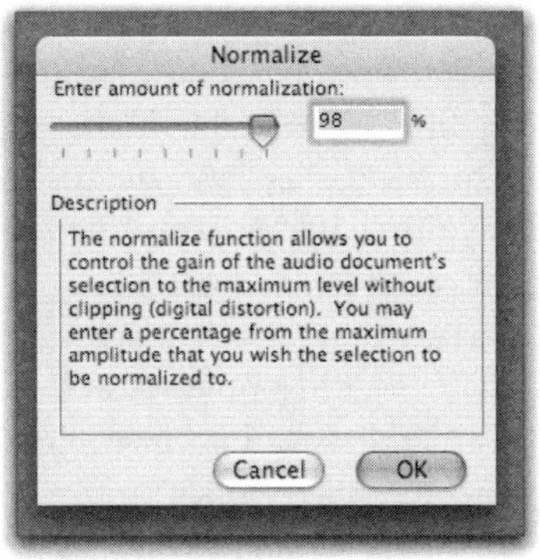

Figure 6-7
Peak Pro's Normalize command raises the overall level of the recording without clipping.

It's important to understand that Normalize is never a substitute for properly setting the recording levels in the first place. That's because when Normalize is applied, everything gets increased: the background noise as well as the recording itself. The proportion of background noise to recorded material stays the same. The great value in having a Normalize command is that it offers an easy way to bring all of your different audio files up to a more-or-less uniform level, which makes them easier to audition, mix, and edit. The normalized waveform also fills the display area more fully and makes it easier to see and hear what you're working on (see **Figure 6-8**).

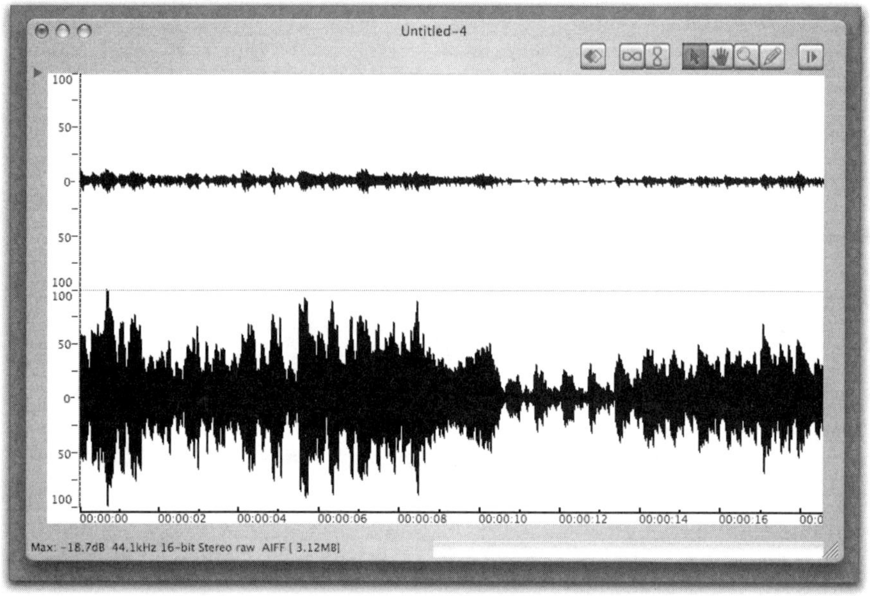

Figure 6-8
This stereo file was recorded at too low a level. I've normalized only the right channel (to 100 percent) so you can see the difference. The normalized waveform is much clearer and easier to edit.

A quiet recording with a single loud drum hit (or other spike) may not change much when normalized because that one hit could be at or near 100 percent already. In those cases, you'll need to use other strategies for increasing the level of the recording. For example, you can select areas around the peak and normalize them, or reduce the level of the peak before normalizing the entire file. Furthermore, if you're normalizing a stereo file with different overall levels between the channels, Peak Pro adjusts the amplitude based on the higher-level channel, so the other channel may not be normalized all the way up to 100 percent. There are times, therefore, when normalizing the left and right channels independently is a good idea. However, this will sometimes affect the left/right panning of sounds within a mix by moving them further toward the side that was lower in amplitude before normalizing.

Unlike some programs, Peak Pro lets you normalize to levels other than 100 percent, and that's an important advantage. You'll notice that the Normalize dialog includes a slider and value field where you can set an amount from zero to 100 percent.

Where you set the slider depends in part on where you are in the editing process. If you're at the end of your editing workflow and getting ready to move on to the next audio file, it makes sense to normalize the current waveform to 100 percent so that it takes advantage of the full amplitude range and matches your other files.

However, if you're just starting to edit the waveform and you plan to do some processing in the future (I'll talk more about processing in Chapter 9), it would be a mistake to max out the waveform's peaks. That's because many plug-ins, such as EQ and reverb, can increase the overall gain during processing, and if your waveform already peaks at 100 percent, the processing can cause clipping.

If you're about to start editing a file that has been recorded at too low a level and may need later processing, the smartest approach is to take advantage of the Normalize slider. Adjust the amount to around 90 percent (you can also type the amount directly into the value field). This boosts the overall amplitude, but leaves a little headroom for processing. Remember, you can always normalize again later if you have to.

In truth, I seldom set the slider to 100 percent, even at the end of the editing process. To allow for some variation in different audio systems, I like to leave a little safety zone. So I usually set the Normalize slider to around 98 or 99 percent. It's hard to hear a 1 or 2 percent difference, and I sleep a little sounder at night knowing that the peaks are just below the clipping threshold.

Find Peak

If you're curious about where the highest peak in the waveform is, you can use the Find Peak command in the DSP menu; it works on selections as well as entire files. When you choose Find Peak, a small dialog box pops up describing in detail where and how high (positive or negative) the highest point in the waveform or selected area is (see **Figure 6-9**).

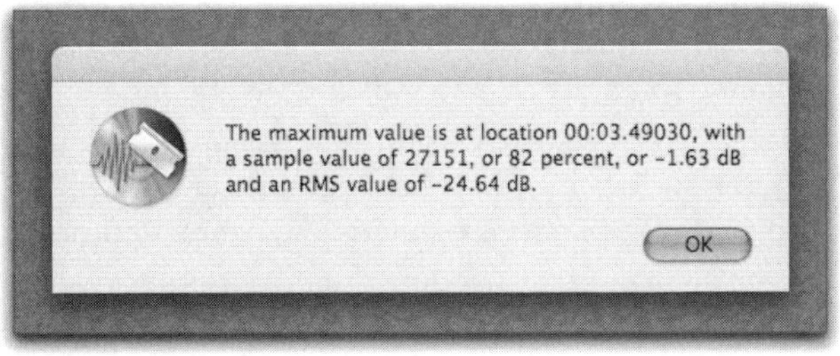

Figure 6-9
The Find Peak dialog box tells you the amplitude level and the exact location of the highest point in the waveform.

It also places an insertion point at that location. If the insertion point is not in view, hit the Left Arrow key to bring it to the center of the Audio Document display. Hit Shift-Left Arrow to move the insertion point into view and also zoom in to the single-cycle level. This is a great tool for locating clicks and pops, as discussed later in this chapter, but it's also useful for determining how much normalizing is possible in a file or selection without further editing.

Normalize RMS

Peak Pro's new Normalize RMS command enables you to adjust the overall level of a waveform or selection based on the average RMS value of the signal. RMS stands for "root-mean-square" (the square root of the mean of the squares, for those of you who are mathematically inclined). This variant of the Normalize command uses RMS calculations to adjust the average levels in a waveform to a specified setting. The result is a more uniform perceived level of loudness when applied to multiple audio files, which is especially important when preparing tracks for CD burning or when editing narration, voiceovers, and dialog.

Choose Normalize (RMS) from the DSP menu to open the RMS Normalize dialog box (see **Figure 6-10**). The Digital Ceiling field lets you establish an upper limit to avoid clipping, in case the RMS values would boost the level too much. The RMS Level field is where you set the normalization amount. For best results, choose a setting of –6dB or lower. The default setting is –10dB.

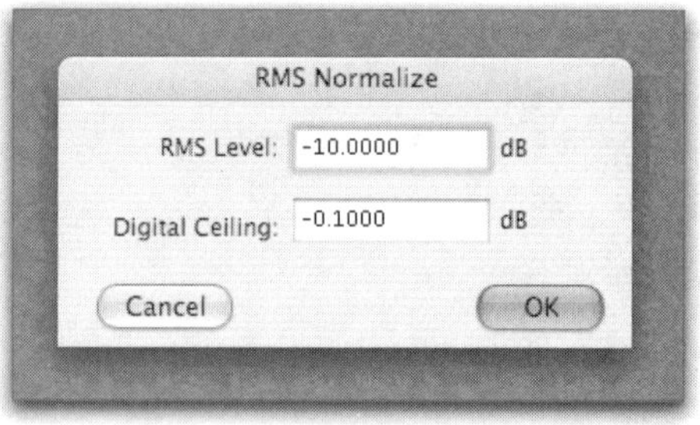

Figure 6-10
Peak Pro's new Normalize RMS command enables you to match the perceived overall levels of multiple audio files.

DC Offset

If you work exclusively with high-quality audio gear, you may never encounter a DC offset. It mainly occurs when a sound card or other audio hardware introduces a bit of extra direct current (DC) into the recorded signal. (A DC offset can also be caused by certain types of waveform modulation in synthesizers, and by poorly designed digital reverbs.) As a result, the waveform appears to be hovering slightly above (or below) the usual zero line. In other words, what ought to be the zero crossing point is shifted out of position (see **Figure 6-11**). You can have a DC offset without it being readily apparent, but if you zoom in far enough, you can usually detect the problem.

A DC offset can be problematic for a number of reasons: It may cause a click or pop at the beginning or end of an audio file, and it can prevent some effects processors from delivering the best results. Moreover, with the zero crossings out of place, cutting, pasting, and splicing files will not likely produce the smoothest edits possible.

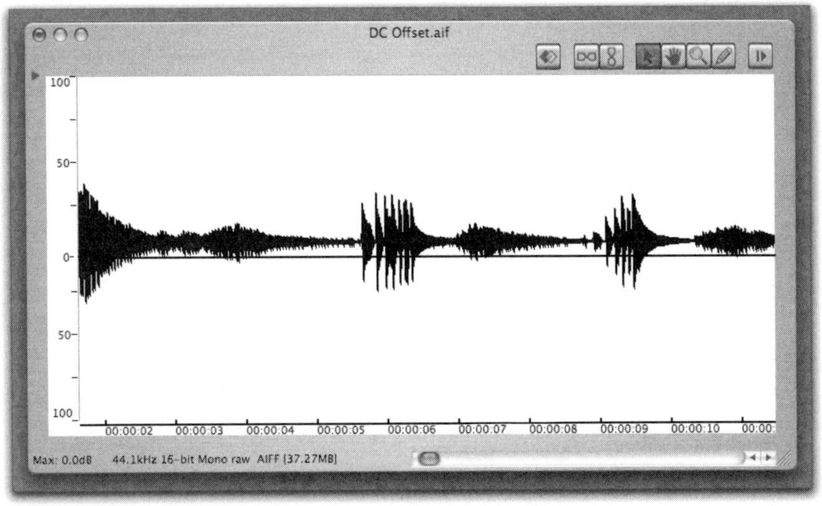

Figure 6-11
When a recording has a DC offset, the waveform does not appear centered on the zero-crossing line.

Fortunately, getting rid of DC offset is a snap. Just choose Select All (Command-A) in the Edit menu and then choose Remove DC Offset from the DSP menu. Peak Pro scans the left and right channels separately to determine the presence of a problem and then corrects the offset.

Invert

You may occasionally encounter a situation where the left and right channels in a stereo recording are out of phase with each other. That can adversely affect the clarity of the stereo image and may lead to undesirable effects, such as a drop in volume in the bass frequencies.

The solution is simple: Select one of the channels and choose the Invert command in the DSP menu. Peak Pro flips the waveform over 180 degrees (reverses the polarity) by replacing the positive values with negative values and vice versa.

If you invert a mono file, you won't hear any difference, but the Invert command might come in handy nevertheless. For example, flipping over the waveform can sometimes make it easier to create a smooth transition when splicing selections or combining loops. Zoom in close to see how the shapes of the two waveforms go together at the edit point. It's a trick to keep in mind when struggling with a difficult transition.

Swap Channels

If you record or import an audio file and later decide that the channels ought to be exchanged, you don't have to do any copying and pasting. Just choose the Swap Channels command in the DSP menu. Peak Pro automatically selects the entire document and switches the channels. You can also make a selection and swap channels in that section only.

Mono To Stereo/Stereo To Mono

Peak Pro makes it easy to create stereo files from mono recordings. With the Audio Document open, choose the Mono To Stereo command in the DSP menu. Peak Pro selects the entire waveform and presents the Mono to Stereo Conversion dialog box (see **Figure 6-12**). It provides a Pan slider for setting the relative levels in the right and left channels. Instead of moving the slider, you can also type a specific percentage value in the field on the right. Positive numbers move the pan position to the right; negative numbers pan to the left.

Tool Tips: 2 INTO 1 AND 1 INTO 2

You can convert from mono to stereo and from stereo to mono while copying and pasting files. For mono to stereo, open a mono document and choose Select All (Command-A) in the Edit menu. Then open a new stereo document (File > New > Stereo Document) and choose Paste (Command-V) in the Edit menu. Peak Pro detects a difference in the number of channels and opens the Mono to Stereo Conversion dialog box.

Going from stereo to mono works essentially the same way. Start with a stereo recording, select it, and paste it into a new mono document. That opens the Stereo to Mono Conversion dialog box. In either case, you don't have to paste into a blank document; you can also paste into an existing file, and of course you don't have to select the whole file, you can also select part of the document to paste.

Figure 6-12
The Mono To Stereo Conversion dialog box lets you create a stereo file from a monaural recording.

Converting a stereo recording into a monaural file works pretty much the same way. Choose Stereo To Mono in the DSP menu to open the Stereo to Mono Conversion dialog box (see **Figure 6-13**). This time the Pan slider determines the relative left/right ratio when blending the channels into the mono document. Bear in mind that if the left and right sides of a stereo signal are out of phase, converting to mono will cause phase cancellation. Certain frequencies will be reduced in volume, or entirely disappear.

Figure 6-13
The slider in the Stereo To Mono Conversion dialog box determines the left/right mixture as it blends the stereo channels into a single mono file.

Bit Usage

When diagnosing problems in audio files, Peak Pro's new Bit Usage display could come in handy. Select an area of the waveform that you would like to analyze and choose Bit Usage in the DSP menu to open the Bit Usage dialog box (see **Figure 6-14**). To get the best results, select at least a quarter of a second; long selections also work fine.

The dialog box consists of a rectangular graph that plots the number of bits in use along the vertical axis and the elapsed time along the horizontal axis. The tiny green tiles that make up the graph appear in different shades representing the varying levels of usage at different points in time: the darker the green, the more usage is present. Because each miniscule tile typically represents a large number of samples, the graph usually appears as a speckled green block sometimes with fuzzy streaks and shadows that correlate to variations in the waveform.

The main thing to look for is whether or not the full resolution is represented. In a 16-bit file, for example, you should see the block extending downward from the 00-bit level through the 15-bit level. If the audio has been degraded in some way (such as from processing), you'll see a disruption of the usual green pattern in the higher-bit levels (see **Figure 6-15**). Black and white stripes in the upper bits may indicate a problem and/or a loss of resolution.

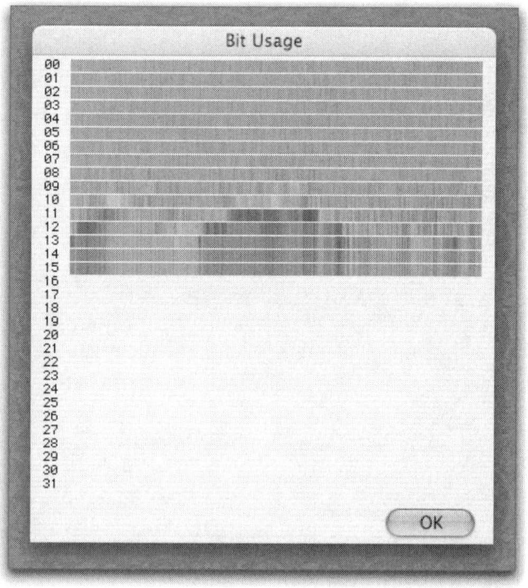

Figure 6-14
The Bit Usage display shows the number of bits that are being used in a selected region. A normal recording should appear as a speckled green block with the proper bit range (vertical axis) and elapsed time (horizontal axis) filled in.

Figure 6-15
Audio that is not using all of the available bits will have black and white streaks in the upper bit area of the Bit Usage display.

You can also use the Bit Usage display to verify that a recording from an outside source really has the resolution that it's supposed to have. A 16-bit recording saved into a 24-bit document will not appear the same as a true 24-bit recording. You can determine the actual bit depth (resolution) by studying the range in the graph.

Snap, Crackle, & Pop Removal

Peak Pro has an excellent arsenal of weapons to use in the war against clicks and pops. Some automate the task for applying to large sections of audio, others are for individual micro-surgery. Let's begin with the broad-based Repair Clicks command.

Repair Clicks

The Repair Clicks command in the DSP menu searches out and eliminates clicks in much the same way that the search-and-replace function does in a word processor. It scans through the selected audio and seeks out any sudden and extreme changes in amplitude values that occur over a very short time, such as a single cycle. It then employs a smoothing algorithm that redraws the waveform based on the neighboring samples.

To use the Repair Clicks command, select all or part of the current waveform and choose Repair Clicks from the DSP menu. That opens the Repair Clicks dialog box, which includes three parameters for controlling how the command works (see **Figure 6-16**). As a starting point for setting the parameters, try the 50-50-50 approach.

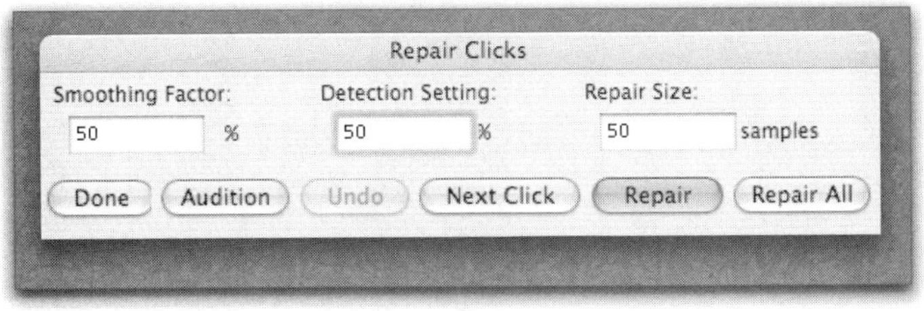

Figure 6-16
The Repair Clicks dialog box has three parameters that control the repair process.

Smoothing Factor lets you specify how smooth to make the repairs when clicks are located and removed. You don't want to set the percentage too high or you may start to remove some desirable high-frequency content. Try starting with 50 percent and see if you like the results. If you're working in an area with a lot of high frequencies, you may have to lower the setting to, say, 40 percent. For more aggressive smoothing, try 60 percent.

The Detection Setting parameter controls how zealously the program searches for clicks. With higher values (around 70 or 80 percent), Peak Pro only goes after the worst offenders. With lower values (around 40 percent), the program can detect less obvious clicks. I suggest starting with 50 percent and seeing how it goes.

You can set the values quite a bit below 40 percent, and in some cases you might get good results. But the lower the setting, the more likely the program is to identify some legitimate sounds as clicks or pops. You don't want to have the program stop at every side-stick or clave tap that the drummer plays. You'll get the best results if you gradually lower the percent value in 5- to 10-percent increments and check the results as you go.

The Repair Size setting lets you specify how many samples on either side of the extracted click Peak Pro will use in reconstructing the waveform. A practical range is from about five to around 100 samples, and 50 is again a good place to start experimenting.

Once you have some preliminary settings, click the Next Click button at the bottom of the dialog box. Peak Pro searches the waveform for clicks based on your parameter values. If it can't locate any clicks, try lowering the Detection Setting value and try again. When Peak Pro finds a click, it highlights it in the waveform display (see **Figure 6-17**). Click the Audition button to hear the click and verify that it isn't something that belongs in the recording. When playing the highlighted click, the Audition button uses the pre-roll and post-roll settings from the Auditioning dialog box (Peak > Preferences > Auditioning; see **Figure 6-18**).

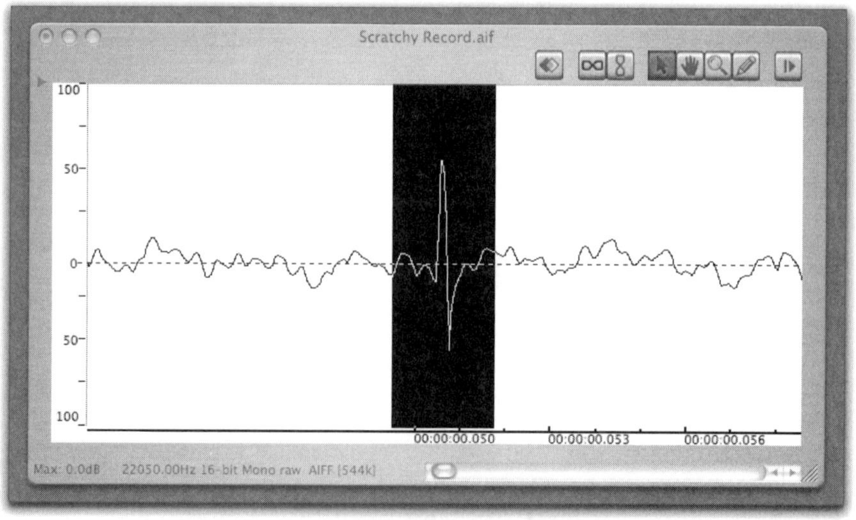

Figure 6-17
When Peak Pro finds a click or suspicious spike, it selects it for repair.

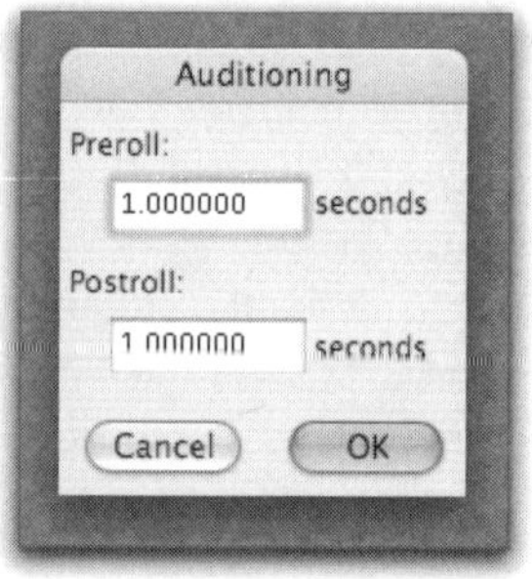

Figure 6-18
When playing clicks for verification, Peak Pro uses the Auditioning dialog box settings for the pre-roll and post-roll times.

To fix the click, use the Repair button and then use the Audition button to listen to the results (see **Figure 6-19**). If the results are not satisfactory, click the Undo button, change the Smoothing Factor and/or Repair Size settings, and try again. As you change the numbers in the Repair Size field, you can see the highlighted waveform area increase or decrease. Depending on the recording, you may find that focusing tightly on the click delivers the best results. At other times, allowing a broader range of samples may yield a smoother repair. It may take some trial and error.

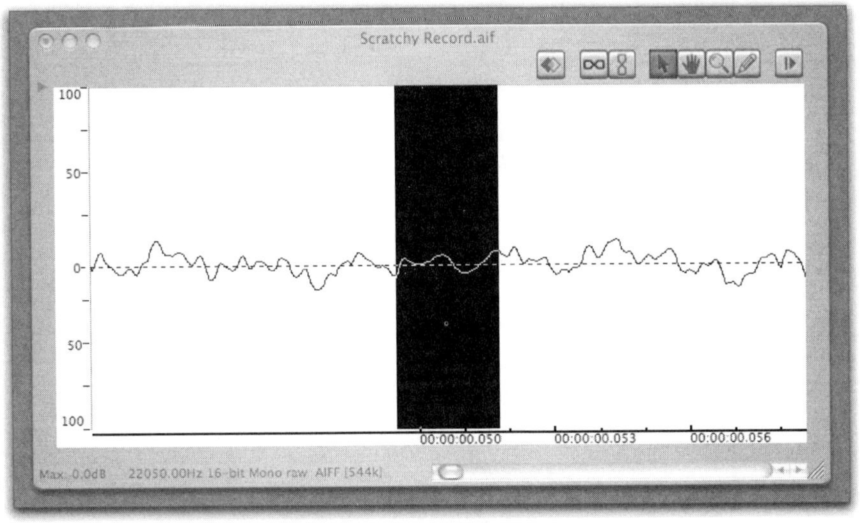

Figure 6-19
When you click the Repair button, Peak Pro constructs a new section of waveform to replace the original click.

For a quick-and-dirty repair of an entire document, just click the Repair All button. If you change your mind after the Repair All process gets underway, you can stop it by hitting the Command and Period keys together.

The Repair Clicks command is designed primarily to locate and smooth out multiple clicks in a recording, but you can also use it to repair a single click. Just make a selection that includes the unwanted spike and click the Next Click button. After auditioning and repairing the click in the usual way, click the Done button.

Repair Click

If you prefer detecting the clicks yourself on a case-by-case basis or you'd rather bypass the Repair Clicks dialog box, you can use an alternative command: Repair Click. To use it, place the insertion point directly on the spike and choose Zoom at Sample Level in the Action menu (or hit Shift-Left Arrow). With the click zoomed in and centered in the display, drag across the spike to make a selection of 1,000 samples or less. Then choose Repair Click from the DSP menu.

Tool Tips: SHORTCUTS

When searching for areas to repair, remember these handy keyboard shortcuts:

Command-]: zoom in
Command-[: zoom out
Control-Up Arrow: increase vertical zoom
Control-Down Arrow: decrease vertical zoom
Shift-Command-]: fit selection
Shift-Command-[: zoom out all the way
Shift-Left Arrow: zoom to sample level or zoom to sample level at the start of a selection
Shift-Right Arrow: zoom to sample level at the end of a selection

The repair is made using the Smoothing Factor setting from the Repair Clicks dialog box, so you'll have to do some experimenting to find a value that yields workable results. If the clicks that you're going after are similar and respond consistently, Repair Click can save time. Moreover, Repair Click does not rely on the Detection Setting algorithm to identify clicks, so you can decide for yourself which spikes get attention.

Repair Click and Repair Clicks can both have keyboard shortcuts and Toolbar buttons assigned to them (Peak > Preferences > Shortcut/Toolbar Preferences), but since Repair Click bypasses the Repair Clicks dialog box, it delivers faster results once a spike has been selected.

Peak Pro's click-repairing commands can work on a variety of anomalous spikes, but they're mainly designed to eradicate the kinds of clicks that occur as a result of the digital recording process. For example, they can help remove the spikes that result from clocking problems in a digital transfer.

The click-repairing commands don't work equally well in all situations. The clicks, pops, and scratches from vinyl records, for example, can be reduced and made less prominent but usually not completely eliminated. For heavy-duty noise elimination, including vinyl clicks and pops, you'll need a dedicated noise-reduction program, such as BIAS's SoundSoap 2 or SoundSoap Pro (see **Figure 6-20**). SoundSoap 2 can run as a standalone program or as a plug-in within Peak Pro. It has special algorithms that are specifically designed for cleaning up noise from old recordings.

Pencil Tool

Regardless of what kind of clicks, pops, or spikes you want to eliminate, Peak Pro's Pencil tool lets you dive right in and tackle them directly, one at a time. To use the Pencil tool, locate a click in the waveform display and zoom in for a close view (Shift-Left Arrow). Click the Pencil Tool button in the upper-right corner of the Audio Document window, and starting at the nearest zero crossing point at the left side of the spike, redraw the waveform through the click area.

Try to follow, as much as possible, the surrounding patterns of waveform undulations and end by creating a fluid transition into the waveform on the other side of the repaired area. Option-click the Pencil Tool button to open the Draw Tool dialog box (see **Figure 6-21**). It lets you control (or eliminate) the built-in smoothing function.

Using the Pencil tool can be tricky and sometimes unpredictable. Blending into the existing waveform takes a steady hand and a bit of patience. Waveform repairs that look smooth and natural may still leave an audible artifact. In some situations, however, the results are amazing and well worth the effort, especially if other approaches have failed.

Figure 6-20
Dedicated noise-reduction programs such as SoundSoap Pro have algorithms specifically designed for eliminating clicks and pops on old records.

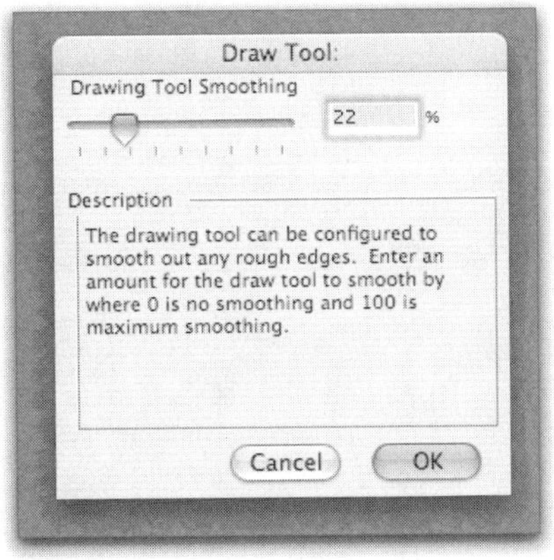

Figure 6-21
Option-click the Pencil Tool button to open the Draw Tool dialog box with its Smoothing control.

Unfortunately, drawing intricate waveform shapes with a mouse is like signing your name with a bar of soap. If your mouse-drawing skills are not up to snuff and you find yourself using the Pencil tool a lot, it might be worth investing in a graphics tablet. I have a small (4″ × 5″) Wacom Intuos 3 tablet, and it works great for redrawing waveforms as well as for making selections and performing other tasks.

Magic Pencil Tool

The Pencil tool is for people who like to have complete control over how a click repair is made. If you prefer speed and convenience to complete control, you will love the Magic Pencil tool. It is a variation on the standard Pencil tool, and it performs the repair for you automatically.

To use it, locate a click, set the insertion point on the spike, and zoom in close (Shift-Left Arrow). After selecting the Pencil tool, hold down the Option key to change into Magic Pencil mode. The pencil-shaped cursor turns into a magic wand. Click on the spike to replace it with a redrawn waveform based on a 96-sample area centered on where you click. The Magic Pencil tool is a lot like the Repair Click command. It offers instant click repair using the Smoothing Factor setting from the Repair Clicks dialog box (without the dialog actually appearing).

> **Tool Tips:**
> **POWER BLAST MODE**
> The Magic Pencil has a little-known variation called Power Blast mode. It works just like the standard Magic Pencil, except that instead of redrawing the waveform, it replaces the spike with silence. This may be the cleanest way to wipe out clicks that appear where little other audio signal is present.

Scrubbing

Having a large collection of editing tools is useless if you can't find the audio trouble spots in the first place. We looked at Peak Pro's many navigational functions in Chapter 3, and those will help you find your way through a waveform most of the time. For example, Peak Pro's recently improved waveform display shows clicks and other kinds of spikes even when it's zoomed all the way out (see **Figure 6-22**). As described above, you can take a close-up look by placing an insertion point on the line representing the click and hitting the Shift and Left Arrow keys together.

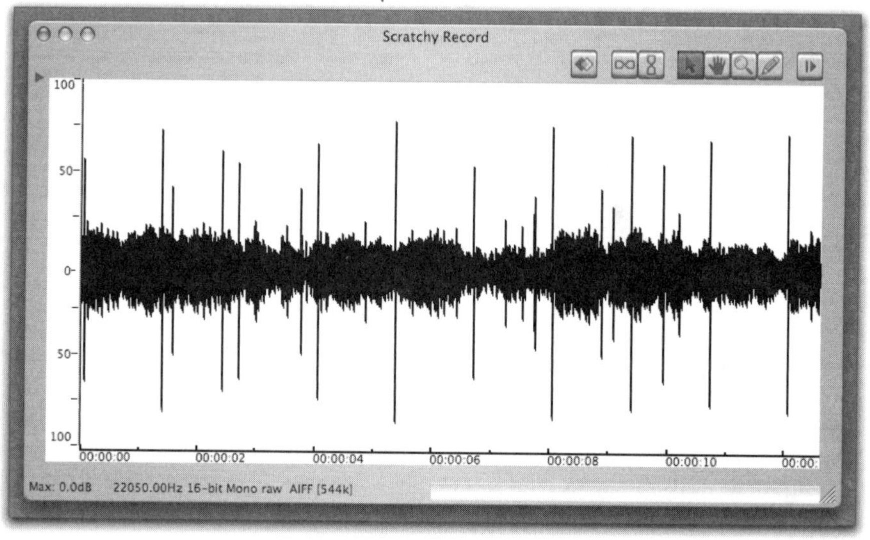

Figure 6-22
Peak Pro's waveform display shows clicks and other spikes even when it's zoomed out all the way.

But sometimes you need an audible Zoom tool, something that lets you examine a recording in great detail by listening to it "up close." That process is called scrubbing. Its name comes from the early days of tape-based editing, when the tape was dragged back and forth or "scrubbed" across the tape playback head to pinpoint problem areas and to find places for cutting and splicing. Peak Pro's main approach to scrubbing is called Dynamic Scrubbing and it's a bit more hi-tech than the old style.

The program actually has two types of Dynamic Scrubbing tools, and once you get used to them, you'll find them invaluable for locating problems that are impossible to identify by simply looking at the waveform.

Shuttle Scrubbing

With *shuttle-style* Dynamic Scrubbing you drag the mouse cursor forward and back through the waveform display. As you do, Peak Pro plays a very short user-definable loop (from 10 to 600ms) at the cursor location. If you drag quickly through the waveform you'll hear a kind of robotic-chipmunk rendition of the file. It sounds weird, but it's usually more or less recognizable. If you move very slowly through the waveform, however, you can hear the recording as a series of slices, kind of like an audio MRI scan. The slower you drag, the more the details and transitions begin to emerge. It takes a little getting used to, but it's worth the effort.

Open a recording and zoom all the way out on the waveform. Go to Dynamic Scrub Time in the Options menu, and for starters, choose 300ms (see **Figure 6-23**).

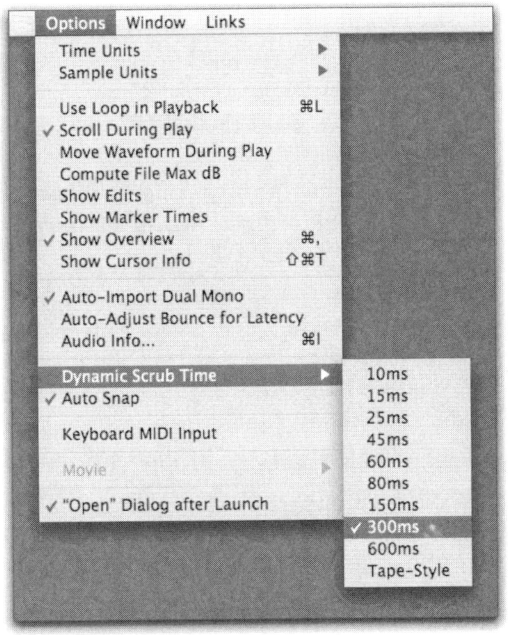

Figure 6-23
Peak Pro lets you set the size of the loop that it uses for Dynamic Scrubbing.

Returning to the waveform display, hold down the Control key and the mouse button together. (The insertion point jumps to the cursor position.) You'll hear a short slice of audio repeating over and over. As you move the cursor/insertion point (while holding down Control) the slice changes to reflect the audio that is centered under the cursor. Move the cursor quickly through the waveform to get a broad sense of the recording; move very slowly to explore the waveform in microscopic detail.

When you find the desired edit location, release the Control key and mouse button to leave the insertion point at that place. You can then zoom in with the trusty Shift-Left Arrow combination or move the cursor to the left or right of the insertion point and click the mouse button while holding down the Shift key. That instantly creates a selection that extends from the insertion point to the cursor position.

Once you get a feel for Dynamic Scrubbing, go back to Dynamic Scrub Time in the Options menu and choose a shorter loop size, such as 60 ms. That has the effect of increasing the scrubbing resolution. Shorter scrubbing loops sometimes make it a bit harder to stay oriented in the waveform, but they let you nail down specific events and transitions much more precisely. Peak Pro makes it easy to match the loop sizes to your current needs.

Jog Scrubbing

The other variety of Dynamic Scrubbing is called *jog-style* scrubbing. It uses the same loop settings from the Options menu. With jog-style scrubbing you don't directly drag the playback loop through the waveform as in shuttle-style scrubbing. Instead you control the direction and speed of playback by moving the cursor within the waveform display. If you have experience using a jog wheel for editing, you may find that this option has a familiar feel.

> **Tool Tips:**
> **SCRUB SWITCHING**
> Both types of Dynamic Scrubbing are based on the same Dynamic Scrub Time settings in the Options menu. And for both types, you have to hold down the Control key to activate them. For jog scrubbing, however, you also have to hold down the Option key, which means that you can easily toggle between the two scrubbing modes by simply holding or releasing the Option key.

To activate jog-style scrubbing, hold down the Control and Option keys and click the mouse. The cursor turns into a small horizontal arrow, the insertion point jumps to the cursor position, and Peak Pro begins playing a loop (based on the Options menu setting) at the current insertion point. Move the arrow slightly to the right, and the insertion point begins to move slowly to the right. Move it a greater distance to the right, and the playback speed increases.

You can change the playback direction by dragging the arrow to the left of where the insertion point started out. (This becomes a kind of reference point for establishing direction and speed.) When you cross the original line, the arrow points in the opposite direction to indicate reverse playback. Keep the arrow close to the original line position for slow playback, move it farther away for progressively faster playback.

By making very small mouse movements you can scrub back and forth over a potential edit point. To scrub over a different area, release the Control and Option keys and move the cursor to a new location. When you press the keys again, that insertion point location becomes the new forward/back reference.

If you locate a possible edit point as you're scrubbing, release the keyboard keys and mouse button to leave the insertion point where it is. You can then zoom in as described earlier or create a selection extending from the cursor (now appearing as an I-beam) to the insertion point by holding the Shift key and clicking the mouse.

Tape-Style Scrubbing

Peak Pro offers one other type of scrubbing, called *tape-style* scrubbing. It accurately emulates the sound of tape being scrubbed forward and backward over a tape playback head. With the loop-based Dynamic Scrubbing, the audio stays at the original pitch regardless of the direction or speed of scrubbing. With the loopless tape-style scrubbing, on the other hand, the pitch drops as the speed slows down and speeds up when the speed increases, just as it would on an actual tape player. Moreover, the audio plays backwards when it's scrubbed in reverse. If you're a long-time tape editor, you'll appreciate this option, both for its functionality and for its nostalgic appeal.

To activate tape-style scrubbing, go to Dynamic Scrub Time in the Options menu, and choose Tape-Style. Next, hold the Control key and click in the waveform display. As with jog-style scrubbing, the cursor turns into a small horizontal arrow. As you drag with the mouse, a vertical green line indicates the current playback position (see **Figure 6-24**). The insertion point remains in the original location for reference.

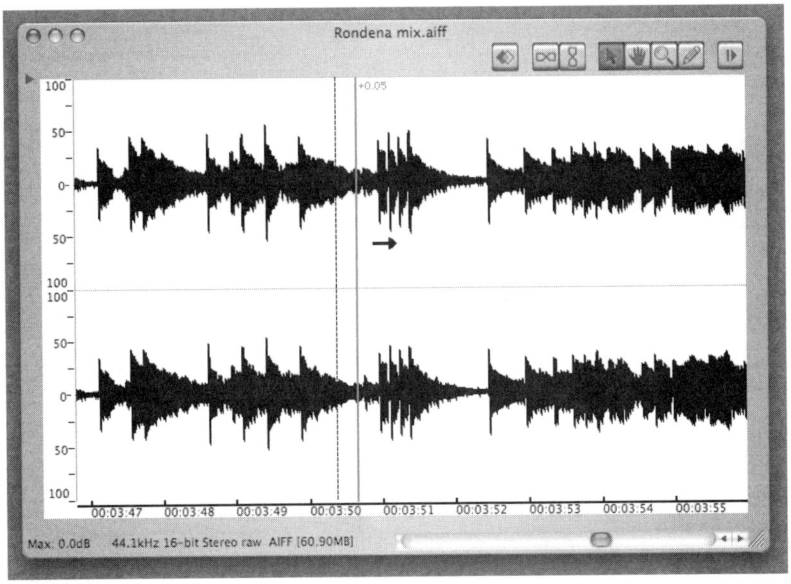

Figure 6-24
With tape-style scrubbing, the Insertion Point stays in the original position while a vertical green line shows the current playback position. A small arrow indicates the playback direction; the playback speed appears at the top of the line.

The scrubbing technique is essentially the same as for jog-style scrubbing: dragging to the right of the insertion point plays forward, dragging to the left plays backwards. The farther you move the mouse from the insertion point, the faster the playback speed. At the top of the green playback indicator, a small readout shows the current scrubbing speed: from –4 to +4 times the original speed.

What's Next?

In Chapters 5 and 6 we looked at the basic tools and techniques for preparing and fixing audio files for a variety of uses. In the next chapter we'll explore Peak Pro's essential collection of tools for manipulating, adjusting, enhancing, and solving problems in music and dialog recordings.

Chapter 7

Fine-Tuning Files: Essential Adjustments for Music and Dialog

In the last chapter we looked at Peak Pro's tool kit for editing, repairing, and preparing audio files of all kinds. Once a recording has been properly trimmed and unwanted noise and artifacts have been removed (or at least minimized), it's time to address other issues, such as maintaining consistent amplitude levels, placing the sounds within the stereo field, adjusting the overall timbre and ambience, and modifying the pitch and duration of the recording.

These tasks must be confronted to some extent in almost every recording, so it's important to familiarize yourself with the available tools and their capabilities. Of course, the commands in this chapter aren't just for working with music and dialog; they could work with many kinds of recordings. It's just that when used conservatively, they're ideally suited to improving music and dialog files. When used with more extreme settings, on the other hand, some of these same commands can become highly creative tools for sound design and other sonic endeavors.

In the next chapter, I'll focus on an assortment of powerful and exotic sound design tools. In this chapter, however, we'll explore a collection of commands that most often come into play when working with music and dialog. Just keep in mind that many of the following tools may also serve you well when developing unusual textures and sound effects.

Change Gain

One of the most common problems that you'll encounter when working with audio files is that the amplitude levels may vary when they shouldn't. For example, if a voice-over artist or narrator moves away from the mike, the sound may suddenly drop; if he or she moves in too close, the volume may suddenly jump. Sometimes, adjusting the levels becomes more of a creative decision. In an orchestral recording, for example, you might feel that the diminuendo doesn't get soft enough for your taste or that the crescendo doesn't have quite enough power. If the original recording quality is otherwise good, you can address these variations with the Change Gain command.

Select the area in the waveform that needs to be adjusted and choose Change Gain from the DSP menu. (If no selection is made, Peak Pro automatically selects the entire waveform.) The Change Gain dialog box (see **Figure 7-1**) provides a slider, a value field, and a drop-down menu for specifying whether the change should be in decibels or as a percentage of the original. If you want to double the volume, you can select 200 percent with the slider (or type in the amount) or you can set the amount to just over 6dB.

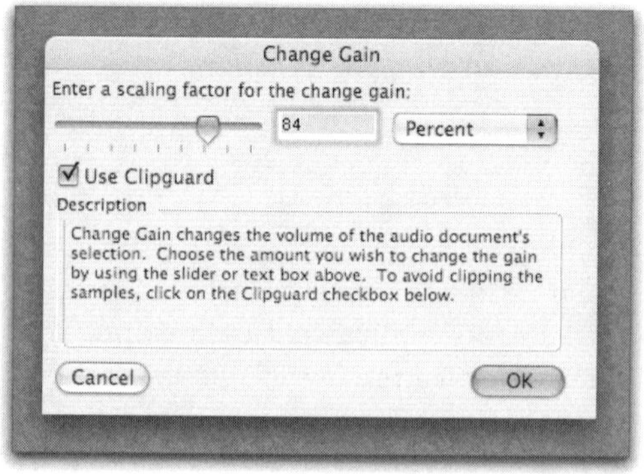

Figure 7-1
The Change Gain dialog box lets you increase or decrease a waveform's amplitude in decibels or as a percentage of the original.

Try this: With the drop-down menu set to Percent, type in 200. Then change the menu to dB and notice that the amount has changed to a little over 6dB. To lower the amplitude of a selection, enter a negative dB value instead.

You have to be careful when using the Change Gain command because it's easy to push the levels so high that clipping occurs. (This is especially risky if you aren't viewing the entire waveform at once.) Fortunately, Peak Pro provides a handy Clipguard feature in the Change Gain dialog box. When activated, Clipguard scans through the waveform or selected area and locates the highest amplitude point. It then limits the upper range of the Change Gain slider to an amount that will avoid clipping.

Try this: Open a waveform and choose Change Gain in the DSP menu. Set the drop-down menu in the dialog box to Percent and move the slider back and forth. Notice the available range (you can type in any amount). Now click the Clipguard box. After a brief pause for processing, Peak Pro moves the slider to the right and indicates your new upper limit.

With Clipguard active, the Change Gain command is a lot like the Normalize command. Its main advantage is that the slightly more flexible user interface makes it easier to use when adjusting sections of a recording.

Gain Envelope

The Change Gain command is a great tool for working on clearly delineated areas in a waveform. It can be a bit dicey, however, when the adjusted area is contiguous with the rest of the waveform. Blending in and out of the adjusted selections can sometimes be tricky. You could, of course, use the Fade In and Fade Out commands to smooth out the transitions, but that's a pretty awkward approach. Thankfully, there's a much better tool for making continuous level changes throughout a waveform: the Gain Envelope command.

Gain Envelope lets you create an amplitude envelope and apply it to all or part of the waveform. To use it, select a waveform to process and choose Gain Envelope from the DSP menu. When the Gain Envelope Editor appears (see **Figure 7-2**) you'll see the selected audio with a straight graph line superimposed over it at the zero-percent level. Click anywhere along the line to create a new grab handle and drag it up (above zero) to increase the amplitude or down (below zero) to decrease the amplitude in that part of the waveform. You can create as many breakpoints as you want, and as you drag them into position you'll see the waveform redrawn in real time to reflect the changes. When you like what you see, click the Change button to process the audio.

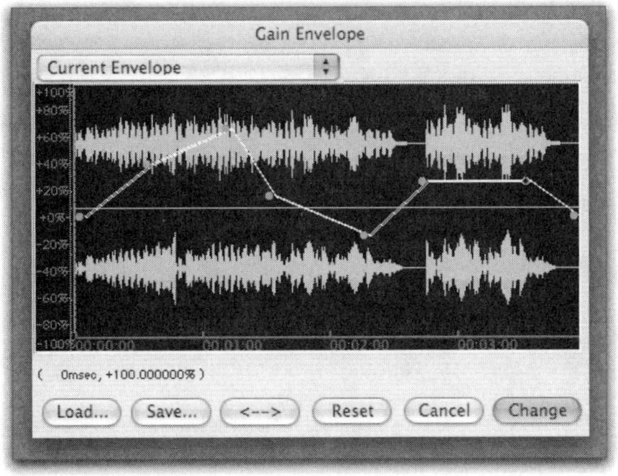

Figure 7-2 With the Gain Envelope Editor, you can create a custom envelope for increasing and decreasing the amplitude in specific areas throughout the waveform.

The drop-down menu at the top of the display lets you quickly apply any fade in/out envelope or custom envelope that is currently in the Peak Envelopes folder. The buttons at the bottom let you save new envelopes or load others.

Panning

There are many ways to create panning effects in Peak Pro. The simplest is to use the Swap Channels command (DSP > Swap Channels), which is covered in Chapter 6. For sparse recordings with occasional solos, for example, you could select a solo on the left and use Swap Channels to move it to the right.

For mono recordings that have been converted to stereo (that is, stereo files in which all of the audio is the same in the left and right channels), you can use the Fade In and Fade Out commands on a single channel to create a sense of movement across the stereo field.

Try this: Open a short mono recording and choose Mono To Stereo from the DSP menu. In the dialog box that appears, leave the Pan slider at zero and click OK. You now have a stereo file with the same audio on each track. Select only the left (upper) channel and choose Fade Out from the DSP menu. Now select only the right (lower) channel and choose Fade In from the DSP menu (see **Figure 7-3**). When you play your recording, you'll notice that the sound appears to travel smoothly from the left speaker to the right. This is a great trick for adding movement to sound effects such as cars, jets, and motor boats, and it can also come in handy for dialog and music.

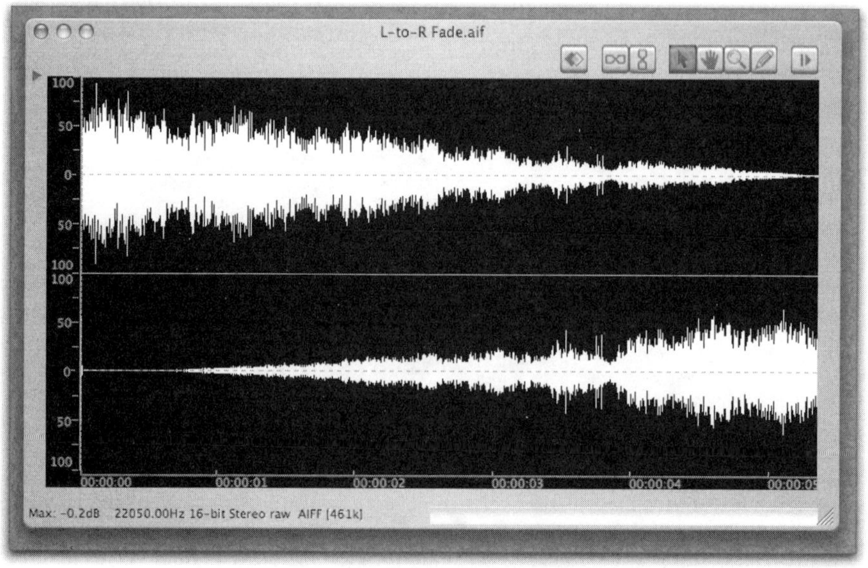

Figure 7-3
By using the Fade In and Fade Out commands on different channels, you can create the illusion of movement across the stereo field.

For situations in which your panning needs are more complex, Peak Pro offers a powerful tool for moving sound around the stereo field. The Panner command uses the same kind of envelope with breakpoints that we just saw in the Gain Envelope. This time, the envelope controls the left/right balance of the audio (see **Figure 7-4**).

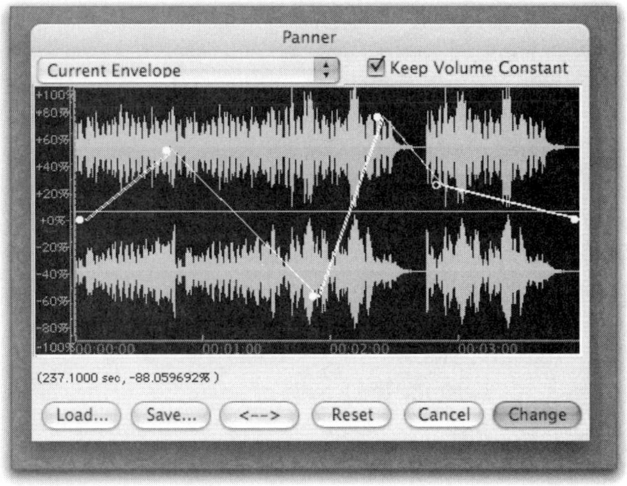

Figure 7-4
The Panner command uses an envelope graph to control the panning position and movement between channels for complex panning effects.

The percentage scale on the left indicates how much the sound is shifted from the original balance: above zero moves the sound to the left, below zero (negative) moves the sound to the right. (The waveform display in the Panner Editor doesn't change in real time as it does in the Gain Envelope Editor.)

The Keep Volume Constant checkbox lets you apply a logarithmic rather than a linear panning algorithm. It's designed to reduce the volume dip that would otherwise occur as audio is panned across the center of the sound field. (Most mixing consoles use linear panning.) As with the Gain Envelope Editor, you can also save and recall custom envelopes using the buttons at the bottom of the Editor.

Change Duration

Peak Pro's Change Duration command makes it possible to lengthen or shorten a recording by increasing or decreasing the playback speed. Unlike mechanical devices, however, Peak Pro's Change Duration command does not change the pitch when it changes the length. In some cases, that can be a lifesaver when working with music and dialog, especially when working to picture.

For example, let's say you're scoring a jingle for a TV ad. The director asks for exactly 30 seconds of music, so you deliver the perfect piece with a cadence that ends at exactly 30 seconds. You like it, the director likes it, everyone's happy. But then the editor, in an effort to tighten things up a bit, shortens the ad to 28.5 seconds. Suddenly your score ends in the wrong place. You could rewrite it and rerecord it; or you could just turn to Peak Pro's Change Duration command on the final mix.

> **Audio Lingo:**
> **CALLING ALL CHIPMUNKS**
> When a piece of audio is shortened by increasing the playback speed, the frequency also goes up. When the overtones in a vocal track are at higher frequencies, we perceive the voice as coming from a smaller head (because the resonances known as vocal formants are generated within the mouth and sinus cavities). This was the basis for a series of novelty hits in the late 1950s recorded by a group known as Alvin & The Chipmunks. The vocals on these records were created by singing to a slowed-down tape, after which the tape was returned to normal speed, leaving the "chipmunks" an octave higher and also comically tiny-sounding.
>
> Ever since, the speeding up of vocals has been referred to as "the chipmunk effect." Another common term is "Munchkinization," after the Munchkins in the movie *The Wizard of Oz.* The ability to change the speed or pitch of vocals without introducing the chipmunk effect is one of the strengths of modern digital audio processing.

Change Duration can shorten the piece without changing the overall structure and—when working with dialog—without introducing the dreaded "chipmunk" effect. There are limitations, of course. You can only expect reasonable results if you stay within about 10 or 15 percent above or below the original speed. For complex music, like orchestral pieces, the limits are more severe. I'd recommend staying within five percent. Change Duration is a little more forgiving when applied to dialog, rhythm tracks, and music with a little air space around the notes. Smooth, continuous sounds can be difficult to change without introducing artifacts. Because each piece is different, you'll have to experiment to see how far you can push the boundaries.

To change the length of an audio file, select all or part of a waveform and choose Change Duration from the DSP menu. That opens the Change Duration dialog box, which includes four radio buttons (see **Figure 7-5**). The buttons let you choose the unit of measurement for changing the duration: seconds, percent of original length, or beats per minute (for rhythm-based loops and other files). In the beats per minute section, you specify the original tempo and then the new tempo. Peak Pro crunches the numbers and makes the appropriate change.

If you choose the percentage option, remember that the number refers to the duration and not the speed, a common source of confusion. For instance, 50 percent means the new file will be half as long as the original. In other words, it will go twice as fast. By the same token, 200 percent makes the file twice as long (or half the original speed). To keep things simple, just think duration and not speed.

The Seconds field is the best option when you have to fit a piece into a specific time slot. It's especially handy when working with QuickTime movies. Remember to keep the changes modest for the best results.

If you're working on a drum or percussion track, click the Transient Mode button to preserve the attacks by not stretching or smearing the peaks. For many audio files, Transient Mode can yield a cleaner, more precise sound.

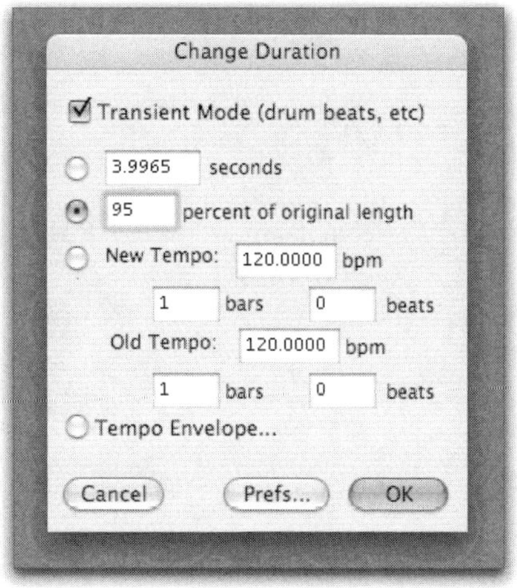

Figure 7-5
The Change Duration command enables you to change the duration (speed) of an audio file without changing the pitch. To accommodate different types of audio, it offers several different units of measurement to work with.

We'll get to the fourth button in a moment, but first take a look at the Prefs button at the bottom of the dialog box. Clicking it opens the DSP Preferences dialog box (see **Figure 7-6**). In this box, you can choose one of ten quality levels for the conversion. The lower the number, the faster the processing but the lower the quality. (Low settings make sense if you're working on a long file and you just want to get a quick idea of how the change will turn out.) If processing time is not an issue, choose 10.

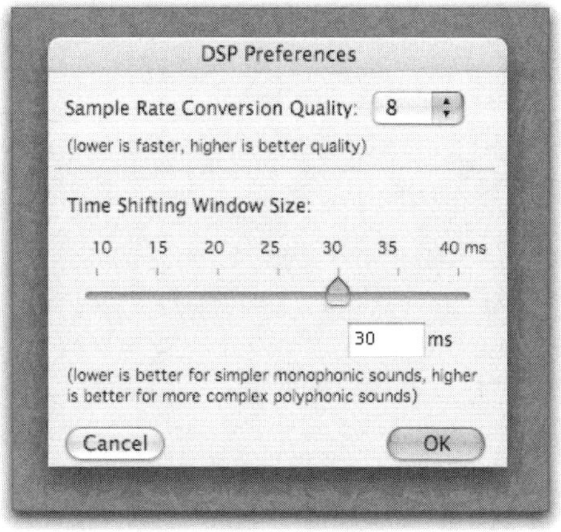

Figure 7-6
In the DSP Preferences dialog box, you can specify the quality level for the sample-rate conversion to be used when changing the duration or pitch of a waveform.

The fourth radio button is labeled Tempo Envelope. Clicking it opens the Tempo Envelope Editor, which includes a familiar-looking waveform display with a horizontal graph line superimposed on it (see **Figure 7-7**).

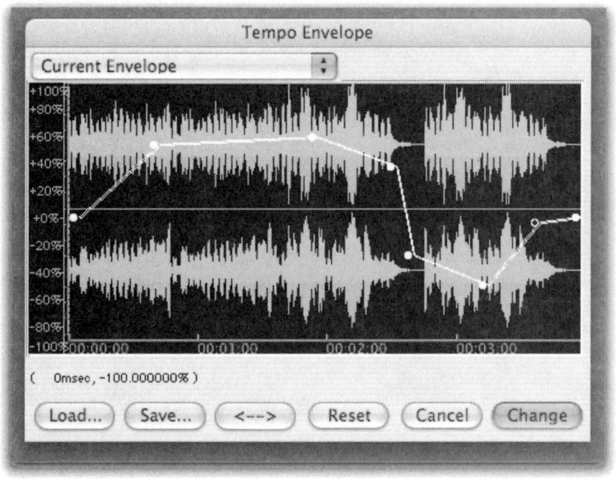

Figure 7-7
The Tempo Envelope Editor uses the same interface as the Gain and Panning Envelope Editors. It lets you create continuous changes in duration throughout the waveform or selected area.

As with the Gain Envelope and Panning Envelope Editors, the Tempo Envelope Editor lets you create a custom graph with moveable grab handles. Just click anywhere along the line to add a new breakpoint. In this Editor, the envelope graph represents changes in duration. When the graph moves above the zero line it increases the duration (slows the speed); when it moves below zero it decreases the duration (speeds things up). This Advanced Change Duration mode lets you create smooth, continuous changes in the duration within the range specified in the Max Stretch Factor field in the Advanced Tempo Options dialog box (the default is two times).

> **Tool Tips: SPEED BUMPS**
> The Tempo Envelope Editor can be confusing if you're used to working with tempo envelopes in MIDI sequencers. In most of those programs, when the graph line moves up, the speed (tempo) increases. When the graph moves down, the tempo slows. That's exactly the opposite of Peak Pro's Tempo Envelope Editor. Because it's related to the Change Duration command, its graph represents duration. When the graph moves up, therefore, the duration increases and the speed slows down. When the graph moves down, the reverse happens. It's best to think in terms of duration rather than speed to keep things straight.

Change Pitch

Just as Peak Pro lets you change a file's duration without altering its pitch, the program also lets you change the pitch without altering the duration. Although this command could certainly be useful when working with dialog and sound effects, it's mainly designed for music files. For example, you might have to fine-tune a recorded solo or move it into a different key to match the other parts in an arrangement. Or you might have to change an accompaniment to better accommodate a singer. You can also select a word or phrase in a vocal part and apply some manual pitch correcting to bring it into line. In any of these cases, you typically wouldn't want to change the tempo or duration, only the pitch.

Peak Pro makes the process easy. Select an audio document or an area in the waveform, and choose Change Pitch from the DSP menu to open the Change Pitch dialog box (see **Figure 7-8**). There you'll find two sliders. The Interval slider lets you alter the pitch up or down by as much as an octave. It's marked in standard musical intervals such as M3 (major third) and P5 (perfect fifth). The minor intervals fall between the labeled intervals. As you move the slider, a value field beneath it shows the corresponding change in cents (hundredths of a semitone). You can also type a number in directly to make the change.

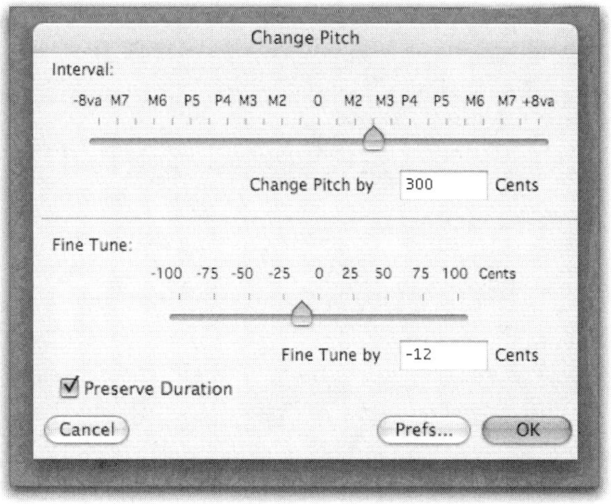

Figure 7-8
The Change Pitch command lets you raise or lower a waveform's pitch without changing its duration. The two sliders allow you to make changes by musical intervals and in fractions of a semitone.

The second slider is labeled Fine Tune. It lets you make more precise adjustments up or down by up to 100 cents (one semitone). As with the other slider, a value field gives a numerical readout of the change or allows you to type in a number directly. You aren't restricted to using only one of the sliders at a time; you can use them in combination. For example, you could raise the pitch by a major sixth and lower it by 13 cents.

By default, the Preserve Duration checkbox is selected so that only the pitch changes. But if you prefer, you can have the playback speed (duration) change up or down in relation to the sliders the way it would with a variable-speed tape deck. The Prefs button at the bottom of the dialog box opens the same DSP Preferences box dialog that is used with the Change Duration command (see **Figure 7-6**). It lets you adjust the sampling rate that is used in the Change Pitch process. As before, choose 10 for the best results.

Convert Sample Rate

Peak Pro's Convert Sample Rate command is another tool that allows you to change one parameter in a file without altering the other parameters. In this case, the command lets you raise or lower the sample rate without altering the pitch or duration. Its main use is for matching a file's sample rate to the rates of other files for smoother integration into other programs. Or it can prepare a file for use with platforms that demand specific sample rates.

For example, many audio/MIDI sequencers require that all of the audio files in a project have the same sample rate for proper playback. Game platforms and cell-phone ringtones often have very specific sample-rate needs, and Web sites impose a number of restrictions.

To change the sample rate, choose Convert Sample Rate from the DSP menu. This command can only be applied to the entire audio document. In the Convert Sample Rate dialog box (see **Figure 7-9**), type in a new sample rate or use the drop-down menu to select from a list of typical options for CD, DVD, DAT, and other formats.

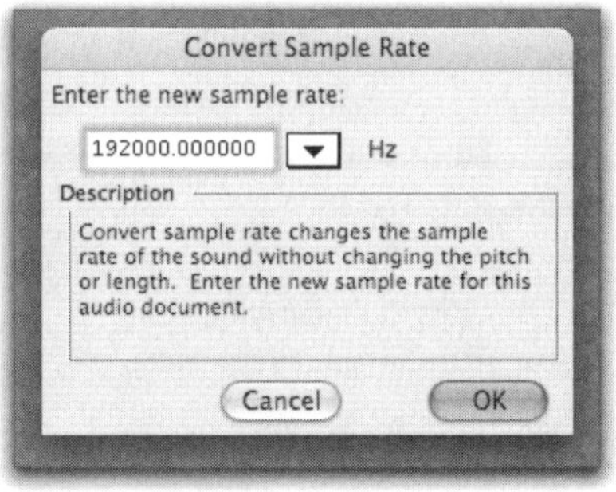

Figure 7-9
With the Convert Sample Rate command, you can change the sample rate without altering the duration or pitch.

Converting to a higher sample rate will not improve the audio quality of a low-sample-rate, low-resolution recording. The original lack of quality will remain the same, although the file size will increase.

Freq

In addition to its built-in DSP commands, Peak Pro now includes a number of high-quality plug-ins that greatly expand the program's capabilities. We'll explore plug-ins and how to use them more closely in Chapter 9, but for now I want to examine two plug-ins that are especially important when working with music and dialog: Freq and Sqweez.

Freq is a pro-quality 4-band parametric equalizer that is derived from BIAS's high-end SuperFreq plug-in. With Freq you can increase or decrease (attenuate) the signal at specific frequencies by as much as 18dB. This is an essential tool for brightening a dull recording, controlling a boomy bass, eliminating hum, or emphasizing specific areas in the audio spectrum. It can also come in handy for creating special effects when editing dialog. For example, you can simulate the sound of a voice coming over a telephone by cutting out the high- and low-end frequencies, leaving only the midrange. In addition, a good EQ is indispensable when mastering music.

Fortunately, Freq is not only powerful and highly flexible, it also has a wonderfully intuitive interface. To use Freq, select all or part of an audio file and choose BIAS Freq-4 from the drop-down BIAS plug-in menu (Plug-Ins > Insert 1 > BIAS > BIAS Freq-4). All of Freq's functions are accessible from a single "front-panel" display (see **Figure 7-10**).

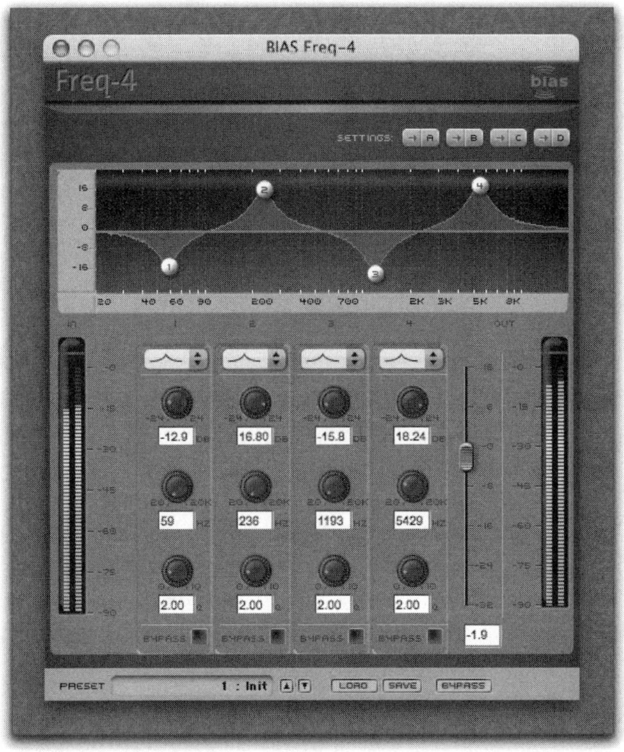

Figure 7-10
Freq is a high-quality four-band parametric equalizer plug-in with a graphic display and a flexible, intuitive interface design.

The graph area at the top shows where and by how much Freq is altering the audio spectrum. The horizontal axis shows the audible frequency range from 20Hz to 20kHz. The vertical axis shows the amount of increase or decrease with markings every 8dB. The horizontal blue line through the middle of the graph represents the unaltered (dry) signal. The blue-shaded areas in the graph above the center line are frequencies that have been boosted; below the center line are attenuated frequencies. The four numbered dots in the graphic display correspond to the four filter bands that form the EQ. Each band has its own set of controls that appear below.

A drop-down menu lets you choose one of five filter types to apply to that filter band: peak, lowshelf, highshelf, lowpass, and highpass.

A peak filter is the standard kind of filter used in parametric equalizers. It lets you increase or decrease a specific frequency range. With a peak filter, you set the center frequency of the range and specify how wide the range should be. It offers a great deal of control over where the filter is applied.

Highshelf and lowshelf filters increase or decrease the frequencies above or below a specified frequency. A lowshelf filter, for example, makes it easy to boost the bass frequencies below a particular note. A highshelf filter would be a logical choice to brighten or tone down all the treble frequencies, much like the treble knob on a hi-fi system but more flexible. Highpass and lowpass filters let frequencies pass unfiltered when they're above or below a specified frequency.

Each band has three knobs for adjusting its parameters. A readout beneath each knob shows the exact values, and the envelope in the graphic display changes to reflect the current setting.

The first knob (labeled dB) is the Boost/Cut control. It affects how much a given frequency range is increased or decreased. It goes from –24dB (all the way counter-clockwise) to +24dB (all the way clockwise).

The next knob (labeled Hz) is for the Frequency. You use it with a peak filter to set the frequency at the center of a peak (a boosted range) or a notch (an attenuated range). With the rest of the filter types, the Frequency knob lets you control the transition at which the filter takes effect.

The third knob controls the Q (bandwidth) of the filter. With the peak filter, it affects the width of the peak or notch, ranging from a narrow spike (a setting of 10.0) to a broad hill or valley shape (a setting of 0.05). With the other filter types, the Q control determines how steep the filter's transition is: from a gradual slope (a setting of 0.05) to a much steeper transition (a setting of 2.00). If you're not sure what you want, start out with a setting between 0.7 and 1.0, and see how you like the results. You can experiment from there.

Try this: With Freq open, click on the Bypass buttons for Bands 3 and 4 to turn them off, leaving only Bands 1 and 2 active. Set the first two bands to the peak filter type, using the drop-down menus. In the graphic display, click and drag the small number 1 dot straight up as high as possible. Notice that the Boost/Cut dial reads 24dB.

Next, go down to the Q knob at the bottom, and set it to 10.0 (all the way to the right), creating a tall narrow peak. Set the Frequency dial between 6.0 and 7.0kHz; the peak sweeps across the graph to the right. Notice that the Band 2 dot now appears to the left of the Band 1 dot in the graph. With Q set to 10.0, drag it straight up to create a second peak, and then drag it to the right past the Band 1 peak.

This simple exercise illustrates a couple of important features in Freq. First, you can make adjustments directly in the graphic display or with the knobs; whichever you prefer. (You can also type directly into the number fields.) And second, the four bands are completely independent. They don't have to appear in a particular order, nor are they restricted to a particular range. That makes Freq incredibly flexible, offering total control over how you create your EQ graphs. Combine that flexibility with the different filter types, and the possibilities are endless.

> **! Caution: INVISIBLE EDITS**
> Unlike most of Peak's edit commands, plug-ins such as Freq are real-time playback effects, which means they operate even when their window is not open. In order to apply the plug-in to the file, use the Bounce command in the Plug-Ins menu, as explained in Chapter 9.

You can save your custom EQs as presets by clicking the Save button at the bottom of the window. Load presets from any location by clicking the Load button. You can save relevant presets with a particular project, so that they're always available whenever you open that project. The last button on the right is a Bypass button, which lets you make before-and-after comparisons if you're listening to the file while making adjustments. Looped playback is often useful in this situation; Peak's looping features are explained in Chapter 10.

The Output Gain slider on the right affects the signal after it has left the EQ section. In most cases, you can leave it set to zero unless the filters have lowered the output levels too much. You can then use the slider to bring up the levels so they're back where they started.

However, if you've set one or more EQ bands to boost the signal, especially if you've boosted it a lot, there's a good possibility that the signal level has increased to the point of clipping. If the red clipping indicator at the top of the meter lights up, use the Output Gain slider to bring the signal level down a bit. The indicator will stay on if any clipping has occurred even briefly; you don't have to stare slavishly at the meter. Reset the clipping indicator by clicking on it.

Sqweez

Sqweez is a high-quality BIAS plug-in that only works within Peak Pro. As its name suggests, Sqweez is a compressor, and its controls mimic those on a typical hardware unit (plus a few extras). To use Sqweez, select all or part of an audio file and choose BIAS Sqweez from the drop-down Plug-Ins menu (Plug-Ins > Insert 1 >

BIAS > BIAS Sqweez). As with Freq, all of Sqweez's functions are accessible from a single front-panel display (see **Figure 7-11**).

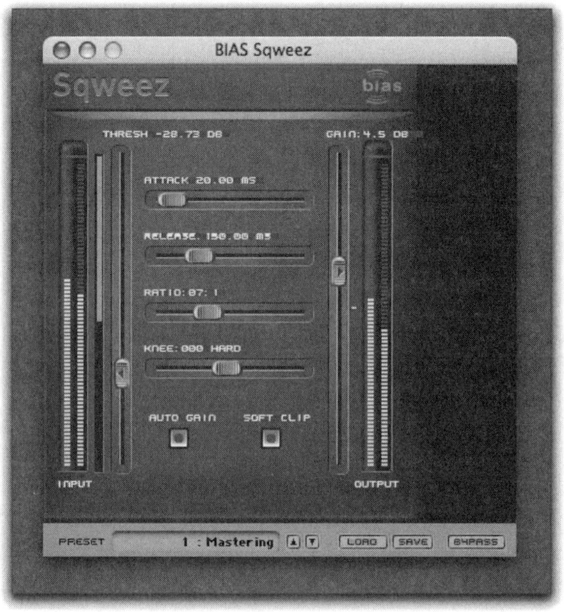

Figure 7-11
Sqweez is an easy-to-use compressor plug-in with controls that mimic many hardware units.

Compressors reduce the overall dynamic range of a recording by preventing sudden loud hits and passages from exceeding a specified level. The result is that the loud parts become quieter, and the soft parts become louder relative to the total sound. With the dynamic range more restricted and evened out, the signal can be boosted as a whole without clipping, allowing it to sit more prominently in a mix.

Compressors serve a number of important functions. For example, in popular music recording and radio broadcasting, compressors enable quiet passages to be more intelligible (by bringing them out more), especially when heard in noisy listening environments like cars and nightclubs. Compressors can also be used to slow a signal's decay rate, so they're often employed to add more sustain to electric guitars and basses. And compressors are particularly popular for tightening up and adding punch to drum parts.

As with Freq, Sqweez has Input and Output meters on the left and right. They have clipping indicators, although these go off automatically after a couple of seconds. Next to the Input meter, a long Threshold slider lets you set the amplitude level (from zero to –40 dB) at which the compressor kicks in. As an audio file plays, you can watch the Input meters to see how high the peaks are, and then move the Threshold slider down to that level to compress the necessary parts of the audio.

Moving the slider down increases the amount of audio that passes the threshold and thereby triggers compression. In other words, as the slider is moved down, more of the recording gets compressed.

Between the Input meter and the Threshold slider, a red Reduction Indicator shows in real time how much compression is being applied. If the compression gets too heavy, the changes in dynamics can produce an effect called *pumping* (or *breathing*). It's caused when the compressor's activities become unpleasantly obvious. (The sound was popularized as an intentional effect in many of Led Zeppelin's drum parts from the '60s and '70s.)

> **Tool Tips: NOT TOO TIGHT**
> Unless you're going for a particular effect, be careful not to over-compress your music. Dynamics are an essential element in the total sound of a recording, and too much compression can make a piece sound dull, artificial, and overly constricted.

The Input Gain slider lets you adjust the incoming signal level to get the best processing results. The Output Gain slider enables you to compensate for the reduced signal level that can occur as a result of compressing the audio. This *makeup gain* enables you to have the same level going in to and coming out of the compressor, although the nature of the sound will have changed.

In the center of its panel, Sqweez provides four horizontal sliders to control how the plug-in processes the audio. The Attack slider controls how quickly the compression takes effect once the signal passes the threshold. Its display is labeled from 0.10 to 200.10 milliseconds. Keep the setting slow for a subtle effect; use a faster setting to produce a more obvious compression. The faster settings are especially useful for controlling percussion instruments and other sounds with sudden, wide dynamic changes.

The Release slider determines how quickly the compressor lets go of the signal after the signal drops below the threshold. Its control ranges from 0.10 to 500.10ms. As with the Attack slider, a slower setting yields less obvious transitions; faster settings make the transitions more apparent.

The Ratio slider lets you set how much compression takes place each time the signal passes the threshold. It's expressed in whole numbers from 1:1 to 20:1. The higher the ratio, the more the audio is reduced. For example, a 5:1 ratio means that for every 5dB that the input signal rises above the threshold, the signal will be compressed so that it rises only 1dB above the threshold. In other words, it will be reduced by 4dB. Lower settings such as 2:1 or 3:1 yield gentler compression that is suitable for mastering and controlling acoustic instruments and vocals. Higher settings are often used with percussive sounds. Ratios higher than about 8:1 turn Sqweez into a *limiter*, a device that prevents the signal from ever getting much higher than the threshold.

The final control is the Knee slider. Its range is from –10 to 10 with the transition from Soft to Hard at the zero point. The knee setting determines how hard (abruptly) or soft (gently) the compression will begin as the signal nears and crosses the threshold point (see **Figure 7-12**). A soft knee provides a smoother and more subtle effect. A hard knee is more apparent but also a bit tighter in its action.

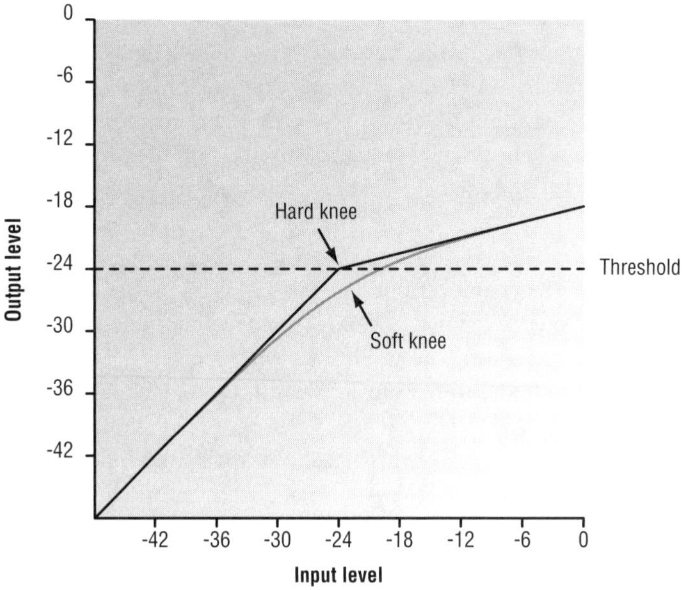

Figure 7-12
A hard-knee compressor applies compression abruptly as soon as the incoming signal reaches the threshold level. A soft-knee setting applies compression more gradually, typically beginning just below the threshold level.

Sqweez also includes two buttons beneath the sliders. The Auto Gain button automatically applies output makeup gain to compensate for any lost level due to the compression. And with the Soft Clip button activated, Peak Pro ensures that the signal won't overload.

The drop-down menu at the bottom of the window includes more than a dozen presets for processing electric instruments, vocals and dialog, drums, and other sounds. The up and down arrows let you cycle through the presets. The Load, Save, and Bypass buttons are the same as in Freq.

Strip Silence

Peak Pro's recently added Strip Silence command completes the program's trinity of standard studio fix-it tools (compressor, EQ, and noise gate) for working with music and dialog. To eliminate the noise floor or other unwanted background sounds from a recording, select all or part of a waveform and choose Strip Silence from the DSP menu. That opens the two-part Strip Silence dialog box (see **Figure 7-13**). Click the Noise Gate checkbox to activate the Noise Gate controls. Peak Pro provides sliders for the typical Threshold, Reduction Ratio, Attack, and Release parameters.

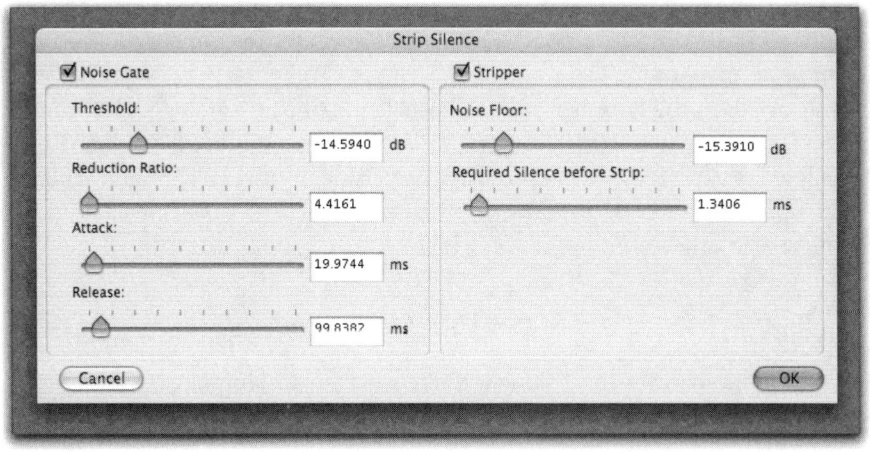

Figure 7-13
Peak Pro's new Strip Silence dialog box includes a full-featured noise gate on the left and an auto-delete silence stripper on the right.

The Noise Gate section lets you replace low-level background noise with lower-level background noise or silence, depending on how you set the controls. The Attack and Release controls establish how quickly the gate responds (opens and closes). The Threshold setting determines the level that divides the good (wanted) audio from the bad (unwanted) audio. Setting the Threshold lower (to –30dB, for instance, as opposed to –15dB) will cause larger segments of the audio to pass through the noise gate without being affected. The Reduction Ratio sets how much the gated audio is to be reduced. A setting of 5 reduces the gated audio a great deal, while a setting of 1 produces no effect. (For some recordings, partially reducing the background noise makes the noise-gate process less obvious.) The Noise Gate doesn't change the audio file's timing. It simply eliminates the noise floor by reducing its level.

But suppose you have a recorded phone conversation or a live music performance or a narration with long pauses in it, and you want to literally eliminate the silent portions of the recording? In that case, click the Stripper checkbox in the right half of the Strip Silence dialog box. Based on your settings for the Stripper's two parameter sliders, Peak Pro automatically finds and deletes all of the "silent" sections or pauses in the recording and consolidates the remaining audio into a shorter audio file.

The Noise Floor slider lets you specify how quiet a pause must be before it's considered "silence." Set this parameter carefully to avoid accidentally removing sections where the music or dialog has gotten relatively quiet for a awhile, but hasn't actually stopped. The second slider lets you specify how long a pause must be to be considered a candidate for removal. This slider is important, because in most situations you don't want to remove every brief pause in the dialog or every half-measure rest in the music.

If you're working with a recording that has a rather prominent noise floor, it may be difficult to set the Stripper section to yield the results that you want. For those situations, click both the Noise Gate and Stripper checkboxes. The Noise Gate can then silence the noise floor before the auto-delete Stripper section does its thing.

The Stripper shortens the recording, so it's not a good choice for cleaning up a drum loop. Use the Noise Gate instead, and experiment with the Threshold slider to avoid wiping out shakers, hi-hats, and other quiet percussion instruments (unless, of course, that's the sound you're going for).

ImpulseVerb

First introduced in Version 4 along with Freq and Sqweez, ImpulseVerb is arguably one of Peak Pro's most important new additions (see **Figure 7-14**). It's a sophisticated professional-quality impulse-response-based reverb that leverages Peak Pro's existing convolution DSP algorithm. (More on convolution in Chapter 8.)

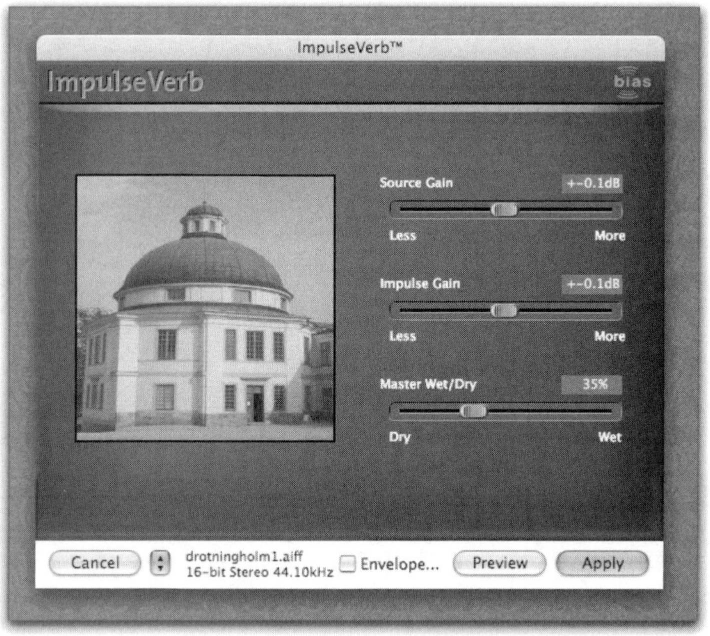

Figure 7-14
ImpulseVerb is a professional-level impulse-response-type reverb effect that is based on Peak Pro's Convolve DSP algorithm. The included presets offer a wide range of natural and man-made environments.

Impulse response files are derived from short percussive sounds (such as balloon pops or pistol shots) that are used to generate natural reverb in an acoustic space. The resulting sampled reverb (impulse response) can then be convolved with a "dry" recording (such as one made in a studio) to "place" the dry recording in the sampled space.

To use ImpulseVerb, select all or part of an audio document and choose ImpulseVerb from the DSP menu. Select a reverb preset by clicking the small arrow button in the lower-left corner of the dialog. It reveals a cascading drop-down menu with a variety of impulse responses. In most cases, a picture of the building or natural environment will appear on the left. Use the Master Wet/Dry slider on the right to adjust the relative amounts of processed and unprocessed audio.

The Source Gain slider functions much like an input gain control: It adjusts the level of the audio file before the reverb is applied. The Impulse Gain slider enables you to boost the level of the impulse response file, in case the reverb effect seems a bit too weak. Each of the presets has the two sliders set to the best overall value for many situations. But audio file characteristics can vary greatly, and you may need to fine-tune the sliders to avoid causing clipping or to achieve the best effect. The Preview button lets you make real-time adjustments as you audition the file.

The Altivec-optimized ImpulseVerb comes with a huge library of impulse response files, offering sampled reverb that captures a wide range of environments from bedrooms, bathrooms, elevators, and corridors to full-blown Italian cathedrals.

Peak Pro's impulse response files were developed by several companies, including Cyber Kitchen Sound Design Enterprise (www.cksde.com) and Numerical Sound (www.numericalsound.com). You can purchase additional impulse response files from these developers, and you can find other impulse response files at a number of Web sites. ImpulseVerb currently supports AIFF and SDII format files.

Peak Pro stores the impulse response files in a separate Peak Impulses folder (Macintosh HD > Library > Application Support > BIAS > Peak > Peak Impulses). The impulse files then appear in the drop-down menu in the ImpulseVerb window. Folders within the Peak Impulses folder appear as cascading submenus.

Peak Pro's impulse response files have either a 44.1 or 48kHz sample rate. You can tell which one, because the sample rate is included in the label that appears at the bottom of the window when a preset is selected from the drop-down menu. For the best results, always match the impulse-response sample rate to the sample rate of the recording; otherwise you may notice a bit of graininess in the reverb tail. If you really love a particular preset, but it's at the wrong sample rate, copy and resample the impulse response file and save it as a separate preset.

ImpulseVerb provides a real-time Preview button so you can find the best setting before actually processing the waveform. To use the real-time preview effectively with 16-, 24-, and 32-bit audio files at 44.1 and 48kHz sample rates, you'll need a 400MHz G4 CPU or faster. If you lose the "wet" portion of the preview, or the playback becomes choppy, your CPU is probably not fast enough for previewing.

Tool Tips: IMPULSIVE MATCH

BIAS does not recommend using the included impulse response files with audio documents that have a 96kHz or higher sample rate, because it may degrade the sound. You can, however, resample the needed impulse response files at a higher sample rate and save them alongside the other presets. Keep in mind that employing a higher sample rate will demand more processing speed if you want to use the real-time preview function.

Tool Tips: SIZE LIMIT
If you decide to add some of your own impulse response files to ImpulseVerb, you must limit the impulse response file size to no more than 524,287 samples.

One other ImpulseVerb feature is worth noting: When you click the Envelope button, a familiar-looking envelope editor appears (see **Figure 7-15**). It offers all of the same envelope shapes that we've seen with other DSP commands, and also lets you create your own custom shapes. The Impulse Response Envelope Editor enables you to control the reverb's length, attack, and decay characteristics independent of the Wet/Dry slider and the qualities that are inherent in the reverb itself. This is a handy tool if, for example, you like the fullness of a particular cathedral reverb but you need to reduce the length of the reverb tail to prevent it from overlapping another sound.

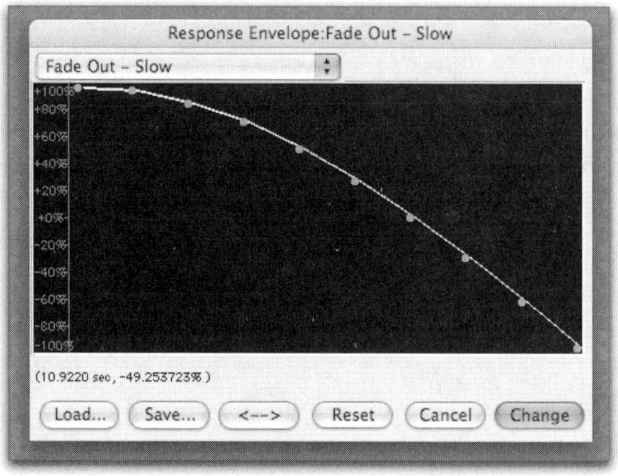

Figure 7-15
ImpulseVerb's Impulse Response Envelope Editor lets you create custom graphs to control the reverb's characteristics, such as length and decay.

Tool Tips: PICTURE THIS
If you create your own impulse response files, you can also add your own picture to appear in ImpulseVerb. However, you must use a resource editor, such as Mathemaesthetics' Resorcerer (www.mathemaesthetics.com), to accomplish the task. ImpulseVerb pictures are PICT resource #4500 files, and they need to be scaled to fit the 220 × 220-pixel picture area. You can paste photos into the resource editor by copying and pasting them from Adobe Photoshop or a similar program.

ImpulseVerb isn't limited to using impulse response files. Because it's based on Peak Pro's Convolve effect (see Chapter 8), ImpulseVerb can generate its effects from any file that is copied to the Clipboard, yielding an infinite palette of sound-design possibilities. For example, I used a recording of a mantle-clock chime and applied it to a recording of a nylon-string guitar. The resulting guitar track acquired metallic, ethereal sounds as if small bells were in the room and were responding to the playing.

To convolve sounds with ImpulseVerb, open an audio document, select an area in the waveform, and choose Copy. Next, open a second document and select an area to combine with the first sound. Choose ImpulseVerb from the DSP menu, and then choose Apply. You can preview the convolution first while adjusting the mix with the Master Wet/Dry slider.

Tool Tips: CONVOLUTION FAVES

You can add your favorite convolving audio files to ImpulseVerb's drop-down menu. Just save the audio clips as 24-bit Sound Designer II files and drag them into the Peak Impulses folder (Macintosh HD > Library > Application Support > BIAS > Peak > Peak Impulses). You'll then have them readily available (along with the impulse response files) to convolve with any selected waveform area in any open audio document.

What's Next?

ImpulseVerb's dual-use capability makes it especially versatile for creating sound effects as well as for working with music and dialog. And it provides a convenient segue into the next chapter, where we'll take another look at convolution and explore Peak Pro's arsenal of unusual sound-creation and audio-mangling tools.

Chapter 8

A Joyful Noise: Tools for Creative Sound Designing

Peak Pro is generally described as being an "audio editor," which for many people suggests a program that specializes in cutting, copying, pasting and otherwise fixing and manipulating pieces of sound. As we've seen, Peak Pro does all of those things, and it does them quite well. But a large and growing part of the program is devoted specifically to creating new and unusual sounds from existing material.

Of course, you can use cutting, copying, pasting, blending, fading, inserting, trimming, and all of Peak Pro's other editing tools to create new sounds. But sound designers are ever on the hunt for strange new timbres and unusual textures to use in their next project. To feed their dreams, BIAS has assembled a sonic laboratory of audio-twisting tools that would make any mad scientist proud. As you might expect, most of these tools reside in the DSP menu because they rely on complex, sophisticated DSP (digital signal processing) algorithms to work their alchemy. Peak Pro has also added the SFX Machine Lite plug-in from The Sound Guy, which greatly expands the program's sound-altering options.

Before we get to that and other related topics, however, let's pick up where we left off in the last chapter with convolution.

Convolve

As I pointed out in Chapter 7, Peak Pro's powerful ImpulseVerb effect is based on the program's Convolve algorithm. The Convolve command itself is fast and easy to use, and the results that you get from it are often surprising and sonically interesting. To put it simply, Convolve applies the spectral characteristics of one sound to another sound.

To use Convolve, you must first select a section of a waveform (with the characteristics that you want to apply), and copy the selection to the Clipboard. Then open the file that you'd like to modify, and select all or part of the waveform as the target area. When you choose Convolve from the DSP menu, Peak Pro modifies the target audio by applying the "spectral character" of the Clipboard material. Hit the Spacebar to hear the results.

In essence, Convolve multiplies the spectrum of the Clipboard audio with the target audio, thereby reinforcing the frequencies that the two have in common. You don't actually have to use two different audio documents; you can convolve different parts of the same file. For example, you could convolve the piano intro to a song with the guitar solo in the middle of the piece.

You'll get the best results, however, if you choose sounds that are distinctly different and if the Clipboard signal has plenty of harmonic content. I convolved a section of bluegrass banjo playing with a short section of dialog and got a vocal part with a distinctly musical quality. The same banjo part when applied to a didgeridoo yielded a dark, throbbing sound that might have served as the background to a horror film.

If you need more control over the Clipboard-to-target mix, you can use ImpulseVerb to do your convolving (see Chapter 7).

Tool Tips:
THANKS FOR THE MEMORY
Because Convolve relies on the Clipboard for its operation, it's important to have plenty of free RAM. Large, high-quality stereo files can easily consume all of your available memory. Keeping the Clipboard files relatively short reduces the memory requirements and the processing time, and it may yield better results with some waveforms.

Modulate

Modulate works like a ring modulator: it multiplies two audio signals, producing sum and difference tones of their frequency components. The results can include a range of complex timbres that sometimes add a metallic tinge to the original audio. Using a relatively simple tone, such as a flute or vibraphone phrase, as one of the sources usually yields the most listenable results.

In many ways, using the Modulate command is much like using the Convolve command. You first select a section of a waveform and copy it to the Clipboard. Then you select the target audio (typically in another audio document), and choose Modulate from the DSP menu. Unlike Convolve, Modulate provides a dialog box with a slider that lets you adjust the level of Clipboard material that will modulate the target audio (see **Figure 8-1**).

Tool Tips: MOD TIME
Because Modulate (unlike Convolve) works in the time domain, the Clipboard audio must match the target audio in length. For example, if you copy a five-second selection to the Clipboard and apply it to a one-minute file, only the first five seconds will be affected. The rest of the waveform will go unchanged.

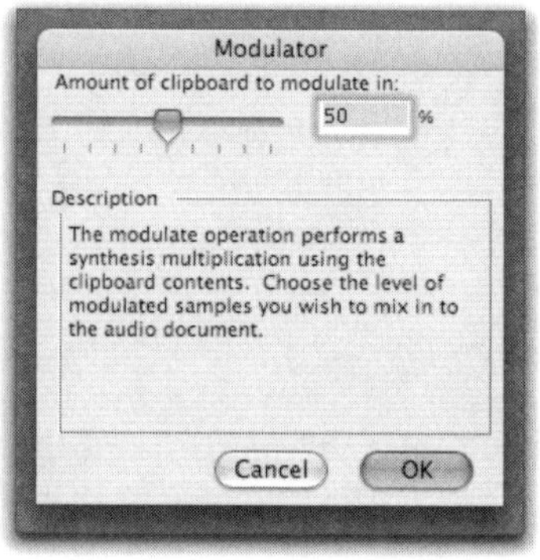

Figure 8-1
The slider in the Modulator dialog box lets you adjust the level of the Clipboard material that modulates the target audio.

I've often found that the slider must be set well above 50 percent before I can hear the character of the Clipboard audio in the modulator mix. If your results seem too subtle or bland with a particular sound, try boosting the slider to around 85 or 90 percent and try again. As with Convolve, experimentation is the name of the game.

Rappify

Ever want to take a nice high-fidelity audio file and make it sound as if it were coming out of a cheap transistor radio with a blown speaker? Well, Rappify is the tool for you. It lets you apply "extreme dynamic filtering" to a recording to transform it from hi-fi to lo-fi to very lo-fi.

To use the Rappify command, select all or part of a waveform and choose Rappify from the DSP menu. The Rappify dialog box (see **Figure 8-2**) includes a slider that lets you adjust how much of the rappified signal is blended with the original audio. It's like the wet/dry control on a reverb unit. At 100 percent, you'll hear only the rappified audio; at zero percent, you'll hear only the original (unchanged) audio. Hit the Spacebar to hear the results.

Figure 8-2
The slider in the Rappify dialog box is like a wet/dry control. It allows you to specify how much of the "rappified" signal is blended with the original waveform.

Rappify offers an interesting and unconventional way to thin out heavy drum tracks and could come in handy for sound designers who need to simulate the sounds of antediluvian audio equipment. You can set the slider to 50 percent as a starting place, but you may find that settings around 75 to 85 percent do a better job of capturing the Rappify spirit. It all depends on the type of music that you're using and on how "bad" you want it to sound.

Reverse

The Reverse command has been a staple of audio editing programs for decades. When you make a selection and choose Reverse from the DSP menu, Peak Pro rearranges the selection's sequence of samples in reverse order. The result during playback is the digital equivalent of playing an audio tape or record backwards.

Reverse has no dialog box; it's a simple all-or-nothing command. However, Reverse is a handy tool to have for creating a number of useful effects, such as backward cymbal swooshes, alien-sounding dialog, and dramatic orchestral hits. Try splicing forward (original) and reverse versions of a sound, such as a guitar-string pluck, to create a mirror-image with an attack and fade-out followed by a fade-in and an abrupt end (see **Figure 8-3**). Or reverse a sound, apply reverb, and then reverse the result for a backwards reverb effect.

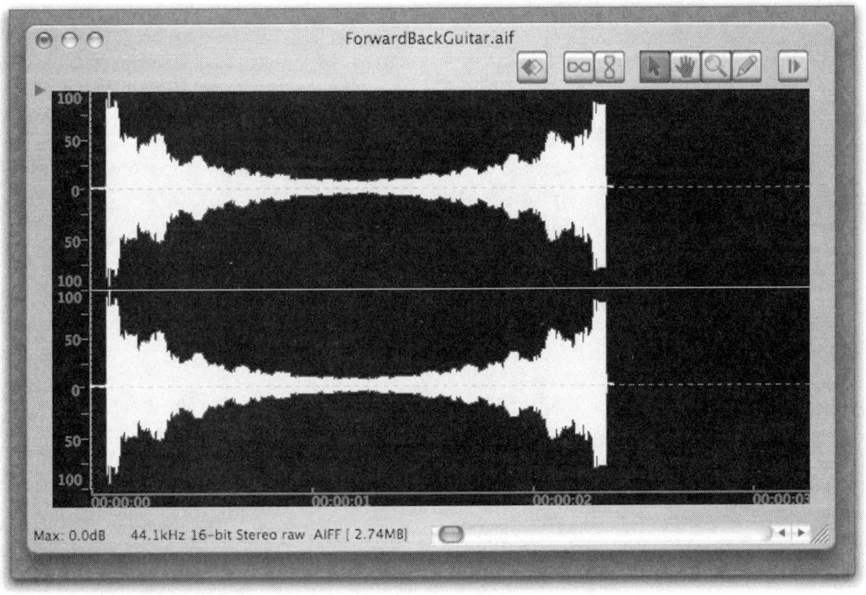

Figure 8-3
In this example, a guitar pluck sound was followed immediately by a reversed version of the sound, creating a mirror image that begins and ends abruptly.

Reverse Boomerang

The Reverse Boomerang command takes the Reverse command to the next level by allowing you to mix a reversed copy of the selected audio with the original (unreversed) waveform. After selecting all or part of a waveform, choose Reverse Boomerang from the DSP menu to open the Boomerang dialog box (see **Figure 8-4**).

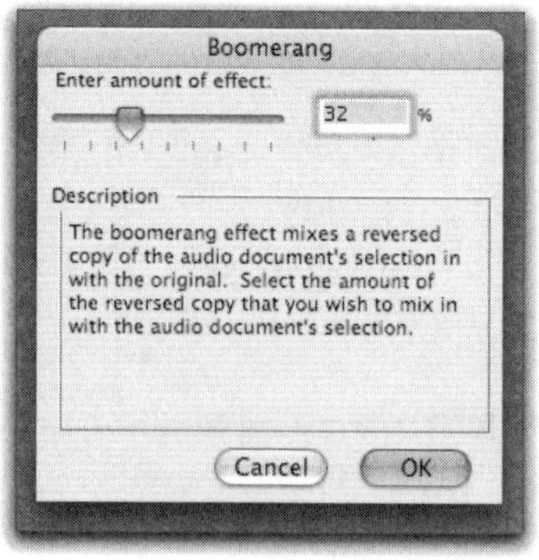

Figure 8-4
The Reverse Boomerang command enables you to mix a reversed copy of the selected audio with the original (unreversed) waveform.

A slider in the dialog box lets you adjust how much of the reversed audio is mixed with the original audio. A setting of 100 percent yields a completely reversed waveform. Zero percent leaves the original sound unchanged. Hit the Spacebar to hear the results.

Reverse Boomerang produces a variety of potentially useful effects—sometimes with a vaguely montage-like quality. Apply it at 85 percent to a section of dialog to transform it into an unidentifiable foreign-sounding language. Use it with sound effects to generate new variations.

Reverse Boomerang is especially effective when applied to drum loops and rhythm tracks. With the slider set to 50 percent, the drums and cymbals acquire a distinctly new sound without losing the overall beat. With the slider set to 25 percent, you can add new character to a drum track while maintaining the attack and prominence of the original instruments.

Harmonic Rotate

One of Peak Pro's newer DSP effects, Harmonic Rotate alters the frequency spectrum of a selected region by shifting the frequencies along the horizontal axis and assigning them to amplitudes from different parts of the selection. Harmonic Rotate lets you control how far the frequencies are shifted (independent of the amplitude values) from their original position. It isn't easy to conceptualize what's going on, and it's even harder to predict the results. If you're in the mood for a little experimentation, though, you might generate some worthwhile new sounds.

Select all or part of a waveform and choose Harmonic Rotate from the DSP menu to open the Harmonic Rotate dialog box (see **Figure 8-5**). The user interface consists of a single unmarked slider (to increase the effect) and two mysterious checkboxes, labeled Rotate Real and Rotate Imaginary, that affect the phase of the spectrum in different ways. You can have one or both checkboxes selected; with neither box checked, the effect is essentially inactive.

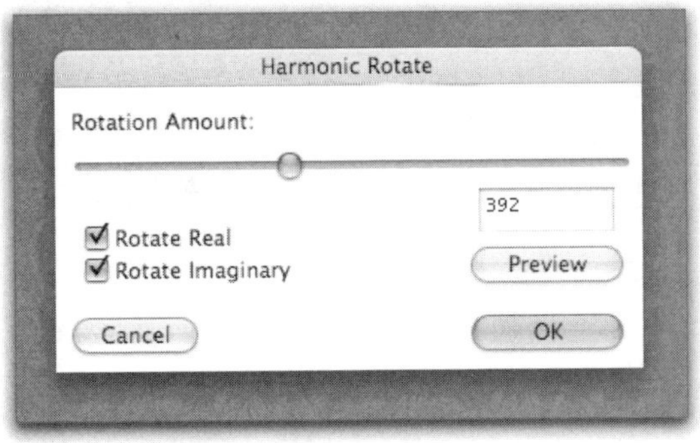

Figure 8-5
As you drag the Harmonic Rotate slider back and forth while listening to the preview, you'll pass through "sweet spots" that produce usable alterations of the selected audio.

Click the Preview button and, starting with the slider all the way to the left (zero in the value field), slowly drag the slider to the right. As you do, you'll typically pass through one or more "sweet spots" where the sounds are interesting and potentially usable. When you land on a setting that sounds good (or at least distinctive), click the OK button to process the waveform.

Harmonic Rotate works in strange and mysterious ways that often produce unexpected results. A Dobro guitar solo, for example, might be transformed into a tweety bird or a wild gamelan orchestra. A plucked string might become a clock chime or a finger cymbal. The resulting sounds are usually unlike anything familiar. It's always a bit of a surprise.

Amplitude Fit

The Amplitude Fit command is an unusual tool that may take a bit of trial and error before it starts to make sense. In essence, Amplitude Fit is a type of normalize command, but unlike the usual normalize found in most audio editors, Amplitude Fit first divides the waveform into a series of micro-chunks called grains. According to BIAS, these small groups of samples are typically around 10ms in size. Amplitude Fit applies its calculations to each grain in succession, changing the amplitude of each slice according to an amplitude envelope that you create.

Select all or part of a waveform and choose Amplitude Fit from the DSP menu to open the Amplitude Fit Envelope Editor (see **Figure 8-6**). You'll notice that this is the same Envelope Editor dialog box that we've seen many times before with other DSP commands such as Gain Envelope.

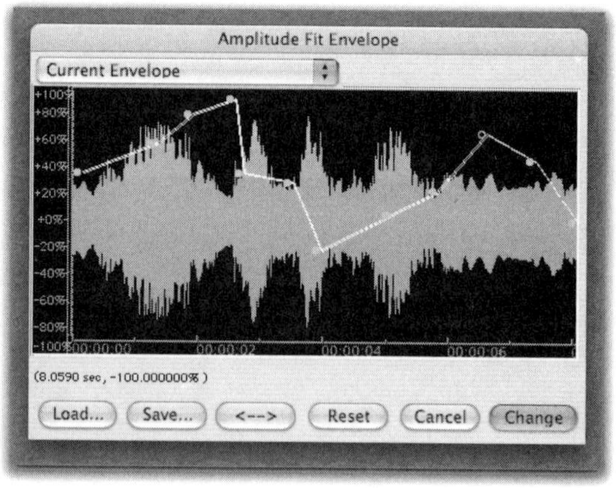

Figure 8-6
Amplitude Fit divides the selected audio into small grains and normalizes the grains based on the amplitude envelope that you create.

The dialog box has a drop-down menu with several standard fade in/out shapes, and buttons for saving and loading others. The waveform display shows the selected audio, and you can drag the graph line up or down and add as many breakpoints as you want. The graph determines the level of normalization (from zero to 100 percent), but remember, this normalization is being applied on a grain-by-grain basis, not to the waveform as a whole.

The processed audio is not simply made louder or softer overall; the nature of the waveform is changed as the amplitude relationships are changed throughout the selected audio. If you're still a little confused, it might help to compare the Gain Envelope and Amplitude Fit commands.

Try this: Open a short sound effect or other audio clip (something around five to ten seconds long will be fine), and choose Gain Envelope from the DSP menu. In the Gain Envelope Editor, choose Fade Out—Linear from the drop-down menu. When you click the Change button, the waveform acquires the expected fade-out. In the Edit menu, choose Undo Gain Envelope to return to the original state.

Now, choose Amplitude Fit and apply the same Fade Out—Linear preset envelope. This time the waveform looks dramatically different (see **Figure 8-7**). Notice that the waveform decreases in amplitude to the point where the envelope graph crossed the zero point and increases again from there to the end. That's because the values below the zero line cause the same degree of normalization as those above zero.

Remember, the values represented by the graph are applied individually to each corresponding grain. The normalized grains are then crossfaded from one to the other to form a smooth result. (Choose Undo Granular Operation in the Edit menu to return to the original state.)

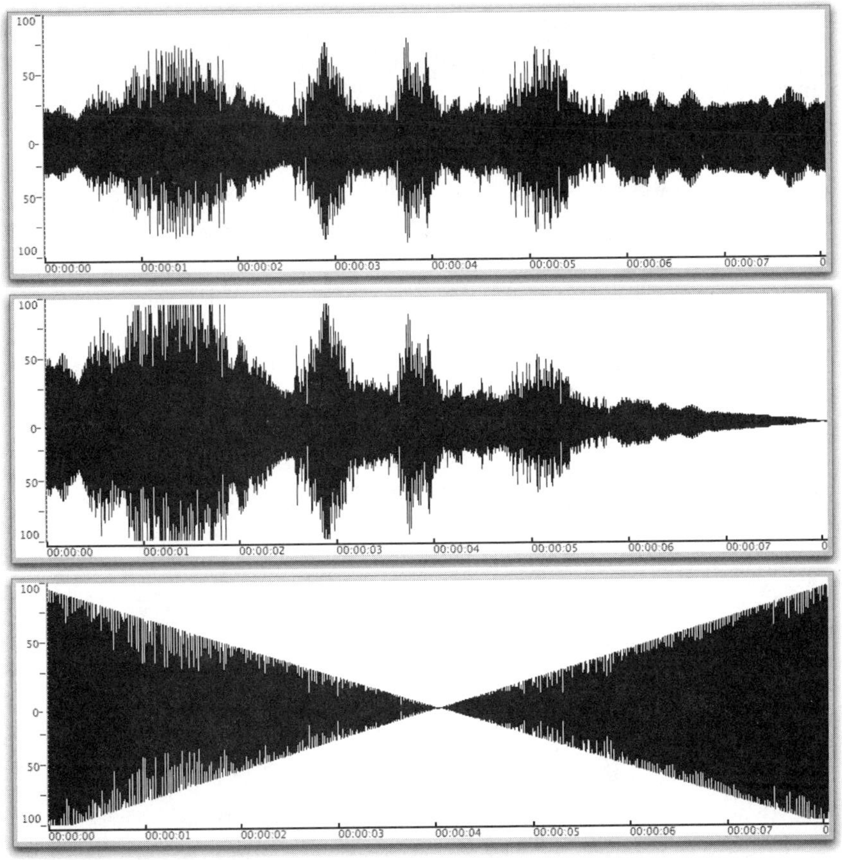

Figure 8-7
The waveform at the top is the original waveform. The middle waveform shows what happens when the Gain Envelope command is applied with the Linear Fade-Out preset. The bottom waveform shows the effect of using the same Linear Fade-Out preset with the Amplitude Fit command (on the same waveform).

Amplitude Fit could be used for adjusting the volume throughout an audio file, but there are better and more predictable tools for that task. The reason that Amplitude Fit is covered in this chapter instead of in Chapter 6 is because it's really a sound-design tool rather than a tool for fixing audio problems. It offers a novel way to add amplitude-based distortion to a recording in order to warp it in unexpeced ways. By creating unusual custom envelopes, you can twist and mangle an audio file in some interesting ways, changing its character as well as its amplitude.

Phase Vocoder

Surprisingly, the phase vocoder (not to be confused with the original "channel" vocoder) has been around for more than 35 years. Peak Pro's version is based on more recent algorithms that provide similar kinds of complex analysis-based time-scale and pitch-scale modifications to speech and audio signals.

The Phase Vocoder command analyzes the frequency content of an audio file and then resynthesizes the sound, changing the pitch and/or duration according to your settings. After analyzing a waveform's audio spectrum, Phase Vocoder uses the resulting series of frequency-spectrum snapshots to drive its oscillator-based resynthesis. In addition to the pitch and duration parameters, you can also control (in a limited way) the analysis process.

To use the command, select all or part of a waveform and choose Phase Vocoder from the DSP menu to open the Phase Vocoder dialog box (see **Figure 8-8**). The Change Duration field at the top of the dialog shows the current selection length in seconds; you can enter a new length by typing it in. The Change Pitch section lets you raise or lower the pitch by typing in a number of cents (hundredths of a semitone) or by using the drop-down menu on the right to choose one of several common musical intervals, such as minor third or octave.

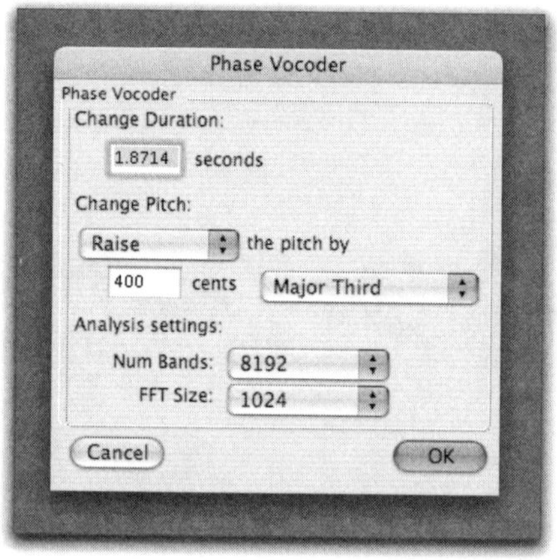

Figure 8-8
With the Phase Vocoder you can change the duration and pitch of a recording at the same time by applying an analysis-based resynthesis algorithm.

At the bottom of the dialog box, two drop-down menus let you control the FFT (Fast Fourier Transform) analysis process. The upper menu determines the number of bands used in the analysis (from 1024 to 8192). The lower menu controls the size of the FFT bands (from 512 to 2048 samples).

Smaller FFT Size settings produce less audio "smear" but may not capture the frequency resolution and bass frequencies as accurately. Try starting with a setting of 2048 and adjusting down if needed. A greater number of bands can better represent the harmonic content and may reduce the appearance of artifacts. The worst combination is when the FFT Size is larger than the number of bands. Setting the FFT Size to 2048 and the band size to 1024 usually yields a conversion with noticeable artifacts.

Phase Vocoder offers a unique alternative for stretching the pitch and frequency of audio files without using the Change Pitch and Change Duration commands. Although you can use it on any type of audio content, you'll most likely get the cleanest results with conservative settings applied to continuous monophonic sounds like solo instruments and voice.

Of course, if you're looking for more unusual sounds, try pushing Phase Vocoder to its limits. For example, stretch a vocal recording to two or three times its length while raising or lowering the pitch one octave. You can generate some very colorful robot sounds and outer-galactic musical textures with different combinations. Also, try experimenting with different analysis settings to see how they affect the results.

Envelope From Audio

With Peak Pro you aren't limited to combining actual audio data in various ways from different sources, you can also apply just the dynamics of one sound to another sound.

Find a sound with an interesting waveform shape, select all or part of the waveform, and choose the new Envelope From Audio command in the DSP menu. That opens the Envelope Resolution dialog box (see **Figure 8-9**), which lets you specify how closely the new envelope will follow the waveform shape. In the low range (slider to the left), you get a finer resolution and therefore a more accurate tracing of the waveform shape. With the slider to the right (larger slices of time), you get a more approximate rendering of the waveform shape.

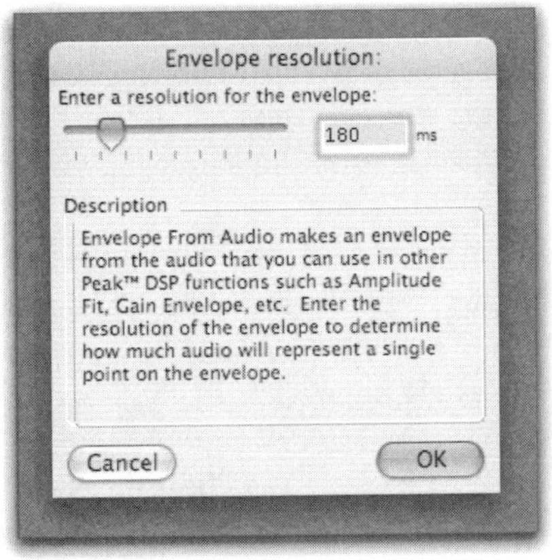

Figure 8-9
Peak Pro's new Envelope From Audio command lets you copy a waveform shape as an envelope that you can apply to other sounds. The resolution slider specifies how closely the resulting envelope follows the original waveform shape.

When you click the OK button, a Save As dialog box asks where you want to save the new envelope. Save it in the Peak Envelopes folder (Mac HD > User > Library > Preferences > Peak Envelopes) to add it to the existing collection of envelope shapes. It will then appear in the drop-down menu for any command that relies on one of the envelope dialog boxes.

The Envelope From Audio command could be used in a number of ways, but it will likely appeal most to sound designers, because it enables you to quickly generate a variety of unique sounds. For example, I took a recording of a guitar string being plucked in a slow rhythm and captured its envelope. I then applied that envelope with the Amplitude Fit command to a recording of a didgeridoo, producing a buzzy, growling plucked-instrument sound.

SFX Machine LT

One of the many new features that Peak Pro debuted in version 4.1 was the inclusion of a VST multi-effects plug-in called SFX Machine LT from The Sound Guy (www.sfxmachine.com). SFX Machine LT is a specialized "lite" version of the company's award-winning SFX Machine RT (real-time) VST and Audio Units plug-in. It includes around 300 effects, and an upgrade is available at a discounted price by clicking a built-in Upgrade button.

To use SFX Machine LT, select all or part of an audio file and choose SFX Machine LT from the drop-down VST plug-in menu (Plug-Ins > Insert 1 > VST > SFX Machine LT.vst). As with most plug-ins, all of the processing adjustments take place in a single multipurpose window (see **Figure 8-10**).

If you had the full RT version of the plug-in, the Category list on the far left would let you choose any of 21 types of effects, each with its own collection of presets. In the LT version included with Peak Pro, however, only the top category, labeled LT Collection, is active. The Preset list to the right of the Category list offers 21 effects that you can choose from by simply clicking on any of the titles.

The right side of the plug-in, with its parameter sliders and value fields, changes according to the effect. Some effects have as few as two sliders, others have as many as six. Each parameter is identified in the Parameter Description section beneath the sliders.

You can change a parameter setting by dragging its slider, or you can double-click in the Value field above the slider, type in a number, and hit Return (Enter). The slider instantly jumps to the new position. You can also adjust the range of any parameter in the same way: Double-click in the Maximum or Minimum field (above and below the slider), type in a new number, and hit Return.

As soon as you've chosen a preset, you can hear the effect by hitting the Spacebar (or clicking the Play button in Peak Pro's Transport window). As the audio file plays, you can change the parameters or skip from one preset to another. The changes take effect immediately.

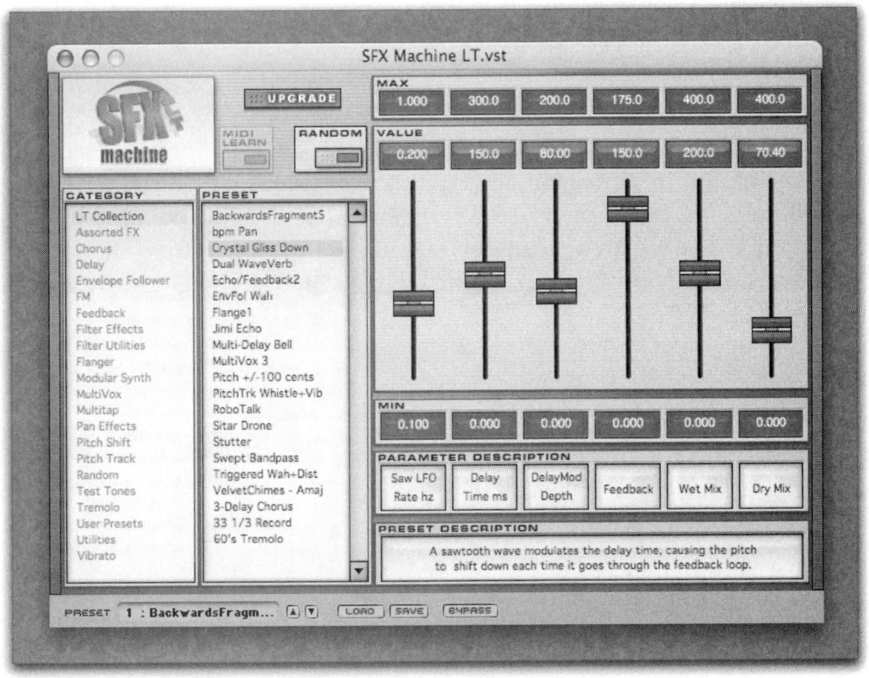

Figure 8-10
SFX Machine LT from The Sound Guy offers 21 unique effects in a fun and easy-to-use plug-in.

SFX Machine LT is a blast to play around with. The user interface is so simple, it just begs you to experiment. If you're looking for unusual ways to twist your audio files into new sounds, this plug-in is a goldmine. Just start the audio playing and try out different presets and settings. If you like playing games of chance, try out the Random button. Each time you click it, the parameter sliders of the current preset jump to a different combination of settings.

SFX Machine has a good assortment of echo, delay, feedback, chorus, flange, and reverb options, each with its own unique character. I especially like the Crystal Gliss Down effect, which adds downward glissandos to notes and phrases and bathes it all in reverb. Sci-fi fans will appreciate such presets as Robo Talk, Stutter, and Swept Bandpass. Nostalgia buffs will welcome the 33⅓ Record preset, which adds adjustable amounts of LP-style surface noise—pops, clicks, and hiss—to your audio files.

Other noteworthy presets include two great envelope-controlled wah-wah effects (EnvFol Wah and Triggered Wah+Dist), the spacey Pitch Trk Whistle+Vib, and the often-surprising MultiVox 3. There are no rules when using SFX Machine LT; just start the audio playing, grab some sliders, and start sliding until you find something you like.

Aside from the Parameter Description section, the only other help in understanding the effects appears in the Preset Description area in the lower-right corner.

Some descriptions are quite minimal, while some may take a bit of head-scratching before they start to make sense, such as this entry for BackwardsFragment5: "Backwards Fragmenter deglitched using sine-wave crossfades. To preserve pitch Delay-ModDepth * Delay Time = 1/LFO Rate."

In the final analysis, understanding the technical underpinnings of each effect is probably less fruitful than good old trial and error, which shouldn't be a problem given the plug-in's built-in fun factor. At the bottom of the window, tiny buttons let you save your favorite effects settings as presets and load presets from other folders. As with Freq and Sqweez, the last button on the right lets you bypass the current effect.

Tool Tips: EARS TO YOU

SFX Machine LT's developer urges caution when setting the levels of sounds that are processed with the plug-in. He points out that "SFX Machine LT's modular synthesis architecture is derived from its ability to produce interesting feedback loops. However, sometimes a slider change or an increase in input signal can result in increased amounts of feedback." That could be bad news for your ears, especially if you're monitoring through headphones.z

I haven't encountered any excessive feedback problems during my experiments, but I always keep the volume turned low until I've settled on a sound that I like. As a general rule, whenever you use the Random button, change parameters or presets, or change the input level setting, start at a lower volume and raise it after the effect takes hold. If you're using the program in a live setting at high volume (not recommended), be sure to follow the plug-in with a compressor or limiter to provide some control over the level. Your audience will thank you.

What's Next?

In Chapter 9 we'll take a closer look at plug-ins and explore Vbox SE, Peak Pro's powerful plug-in matrix. With Vbox and a handful of plug-ins, you'll be surprised what you can do. We'll look at inserts, routing, and recording with Vbox and learn how to expand the capabilities of the plug-ins that we've already covered: Freq, Sqweez, and SFX Machine LT.

Chapter 9

Plug & Play: Working with Plug-Ins and Vbox SE

As with most audio-related software, Peak Pro supports plug-ins as an effective and open-ended way to expand its processing capabilities. Many plug-ins provide valuable tools that are essential for mastering music, modifying sound effects, and preparing dialog.

Since version 4, Peak has added support for Apple Computer's Audio Units (AU) plug-in format, in addition to the program's existing support for the VST (Virtual Studio Technology) format from Steinberg Media Technologies. Both formats have become *de facto* standards with widespread support throughout the audio industry. And both are real-time, host-based formats, which means that you don't need any additional hardware (other than your computer) to use them.

Initially, Peak only supported effects-type plug-ins, but with the introduction of Version 5, BIAS has added support for software instrument plug-ins (VSTi and Audio Units instruments) such as MOTU's Mach Five software sampler and Native Instruments' Absynth 3. The ability to use plug-in instruments greatly expands Peak Pro's music and sound design capabilities.

Using plug-ins with Peak Pro is easy and intuitive; I've already covered the two high-end effects from BIAS—Freq and Sqweez—in Chapter 7. We also looked at the endlessly entertaining SFX Machine LT from The Sound Guy.

But BIAS didn't stop there. To ensure that you have immediate access to a large library of plug-ins, the Peak Pro installation disc installs more than two dozen freeware plug-ins from Maxim Digital Audio (MDA). The MDA effects all have no-frills, sliders-only user interfaces (see **Figure 9-1**), that are as simple to use as they are uniform in appearance. (See the sidebar "VST from MDA" for a list of the included effects.)

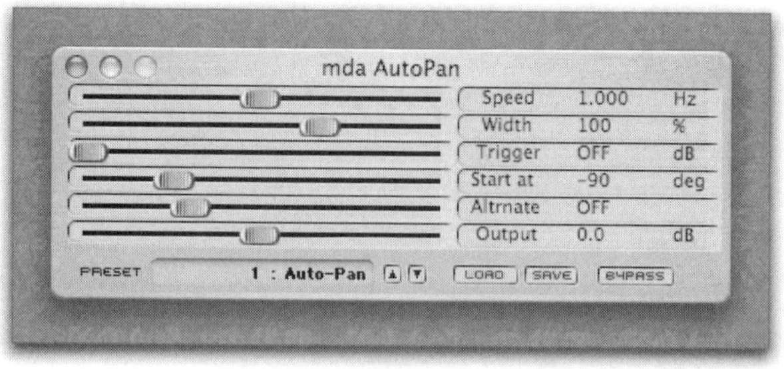

Figure 9-1
Peak Pro includes a large collection of freeware plug-ins from Maxim Digital Audio. The no-frills interfaces are straightforward and easy to use.

To get detailed descriptions of the MDA effects, go to the MDA Plug-In Reference Web site (http://mda.smartelectronix.com/vst/help/contents.htm). To find out what new plug-ins are available from MDA, check out the OS X Audio Web site (http://osxaudio.com/index.php?story=294) or the Maxim Web site (www.mda-vst.com) where you'll find some new VSTi freeware plug-ins.

The OS X installation disc itself adds about a dozen AU plug-ins from Apple (see **Figure 9-2**). The effects include a number of useful studio tools, such as a reverb, a multiband compressor, and several types of equalizers and filters. Altogether, the MDA, Apple, Sound Guy, and BIAS plug-ins comprise a substantial array of more than 60 plug-ins that Peak Pro lets you mix and match in myriad combinations, as you'll see.

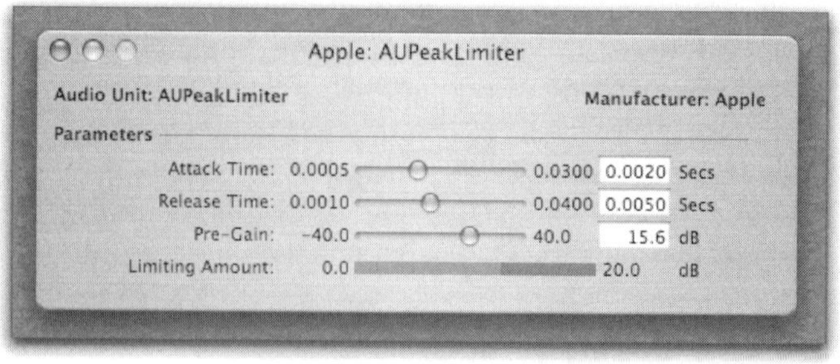

Figure 9-2
The OS X installation disc adds about a dozen Audio Units plug-ins from Apple Computer. They cover a variety of standard effects that you can combine with VST effects in Peak Pro.

Peak Pro provides two methods for applying plug-ins to Audio Documents: with inserts and with BIAS's Vbox SE plug-in matrix. Let's look at using inserts first.

VST from MDA

When you install Peak Pro, the installation disc also installs a large collection of freeware plug-ins from Maxim Digital Audio (MDA). Here's a list of the included VST plug-ins along with brief descriptions.

AutoPan: automatic panning
Bandisto: multiband distortion
BeatBox: drum replacer/enhancer
Combo: amp and speaker simulator
De-ess: reduces excessive sibilants in vocals and speech
Degrade: low-quality digital sampling
Delay: simple stereo delay
Detune: stereo pitch shifter
Dither: range of dither types for word-length reduction
DubDelay: simple delay with feedback saturation and delay time modulation
Dynamics: modern-sounding compressor/limiter/gate with low processor usage
Envelope: envelope follower and VCA
Image: stereo-image adjuster and MS matrix
Leslie: rotary speaker simulator
Limiter: simple "opto-electronic" limiter
Loudness: equal-loudness contours
Overdrive: simple distortion
RePsycho!: event-based pitch-shifter
RezFilter: VCF with LFO and EG
RoundPan (Round Panner): simple 3-D autopan
Shepard (Shepard Tone Generator): continuously rising or falling pitch
SpecMeter: spectrum analyzer and stereo VU meter
Splitter: 2-way signal splitter
Stereo: stereo simulator
SubSynth (Sub Bass Synthesizer): produces more bass than you could ever need
TestTone: test-tone generator
ThruZero (ThruZero Flanger): simulates tape-flanging and other "modulated delay" effects such as phasing and simple chorusing
Tracker (Pitch Tracker): tracks the frequency of the input signal with an oscillator, ring modulator, or filter
Vocinput: vocoder carrier signal
Vocoder: 16-band vocoder for applying the spectrum of one sound (the modulator, usually a voice or rhythm part) to the waveform of another (the carrier, usually a synth pad or sawtooth wave)

Inserts

Peak Pro's inserts appear as a drop-down list in the Plug-Ins menu. The program supplies five insert "slots," each of which can hold a single plug-in. To use the inserts, open an audio file and choose any insert in the Plug-Ins menu. As you move the mouse down the list, cascading submenus let you first specify the plug-in format (VST, BIAS, or AU) and then the list of available plug-ins in that format (see **Figure 9-3**).

> **Tool Tips:**
> **DISAPPEARING ACT**
> When using plug-ins with inserts, remember that a plug-in is still occupying an insert slot until you remove it by choosing None from the plug-in list. Just because you can't see the plug-in doesn't mean it isn't there. You could, for example, close a plug-in window to make it disappear, but the plug-in would still be active, and it would still be taking up an insert.
>
> If you're not sure of the current status, return to the plug-in list for the insert in question and look for a plug-in with a check mark in front of it. You can reopen the plug-in window by clicking on its name in the list.

As soon as you select a plug-in, its user interface pops up onscreen, ready for you to choose a preset and/or adjust the parameters. If you pick an insert slot that is already occupied, the existing plug-in is replaced by the new selection. To remove an existing plug-in from an insert slot, choose None from the top of the plug-ins list.

It's important to keep in mind that the signal flow follows the numerical order of the inserts. In other words, if you put Freq on Insert 1, Sqweez on Insert 2, and MDA Detune on Insert 3, the signal first enters Freq. The output from Freq then feeds the input of Sqweez, the output from Sqweez feeds the input of MDA Detune, and so forth down the line.

With the inserts configured the way you want, and with the plug-in windows onscreen, you can audition the audio file or the selected segment and hear the results of the processing. Changes made to onscreen knobs and sliders affect the audio immediately. These real-time changes don't actually alter the waveform itself, because the nondestructive processing occurs only during playback. You can, however, make the changes permanent with the Bounce command, which is also found in the Plug-Ins menu.

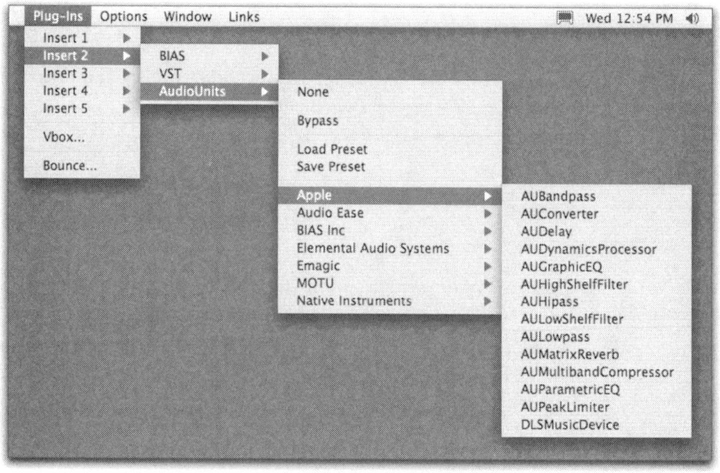

Figure 9-3
Use the cascading menus under the Plug-Ins menu to add effects to any Insert slot.

Once you've settled on the best combination of plug-ins and settings, select Bounce to apply the settings to the current audio file. (This could take a while, depending on the length of the audio file or the segment you've selected for processing, and on the number of plug-ins.)

After the processing is complete, the waveform changes to reflect the results, and a dialog box pops up asking if Peak Pro should now disable the plug-ins. If you only want to process one file, choose Yes. If you'd like to use the same insert/plug-in setup for additional files, choose No, and the current configuration will remain available.

Inserts offer a quick-and-easy way to process audio files with effects, especially if you only need a few plug-ins. But Peak Pro provides a much more powerful and versatile option for working with plug-ins: Vbox SE.

Tool Tips:

DOUBLE JEOPARDY

If you don't disable the plug-ins after using the Bounce command, and you play back the file with the current plug-ins still active, the file will sound as if it has been processed twice through the same plug-ins.

Vbox SE

For the utmost in plug-in flexibility, Peak Pro provides a special environment for combining and routing effects and software instruments. Vbox SE (henceforth referred to simply as Vbox) is actually a plug-in itself, and it holds other plug-ins in its compact, grid-like display. You can open Vbox by choosing it from the Plug-Ins menu (Plug-Ins > Vbox) or from the Inserts list (Plug-Ins > Insert 1 through 5 > BIAS > BIAS Vbox). Its most salient feature is its 16-box Matrix, where plug-ins can be loaded and connected in various combinations (see **Figure 9-4**).

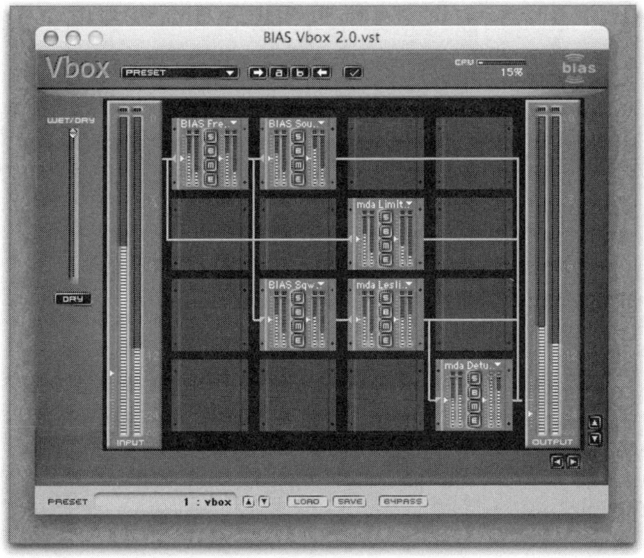

Figure 9-4
With the Matrix area in Vbox SE, you can create plug-in configurations ranging from simple to highly complex.

To load a plug-in into Vbox, click on an empty (dark gray) box to open a pop-up menu of available plug-ins. Choose a plug-in to have it appear in the box, which changes appearance from "inactive" to "active." The box now contains a miniature control panel (complete with miniature rackmount flanges and virtual screw holes) for the selected plug-in (see **Figure 9-5**). Each identical control panel includes a truncated plug-in name at the top and an assortment of controls and meters (which I'll get to in a moment).

Figure 9-5
When you load a plug-in into Vbox, it appears as a miniature rackmount-style front panel complete with input and output meters and faders and Solo, Mute, and Bypass buttons.

What's in a Name?

The name "Vbox" comes from a contraction of "Virtual box." The original Vbox was a standalone program that could also work as a plug-in. It was marketed by BIAS as a separate product for combining VST plug-in effects. The SE (Special Edition) designation was introduced when BIAS incorporated Vbox into Peak as a built-in part of the program.

To distinguish the plug-in-only version in Peak from the original separate version of Vbox, BIAS added the SE label. The only difference between the two versions is that the original version (now discontinued) could function as a standalone program, while the SE version only works as a plug-in and is only available in Peak.

You control the flow of the signal through the various plug-ins by choosing where in the Matrix to position the effects. Plug-ins placed in a horizontal row process the incoming signal in a serial pattern (see **Figure 9-6**). The signal—represented by the green line—travels from left to right through each effect in the chain, just as it would if you had placed a plug-in in each of the insert slots in the Plug-Ins menu.

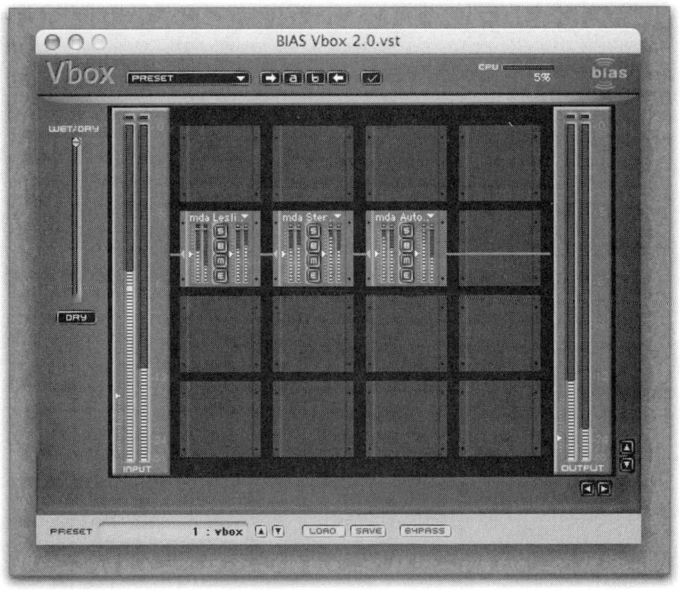

Figure 9-6
Plug-ins placed in a horizontal row function in series to process the signal.

Vbox, however, also lets you process the signal with parallel plug-ins, a trick that you can't do with the inserts. Plug-ins that appear in the Matrix above and below one another in columns process the signal simultaneously (see **Figure 9-7**). The signal is split as many times as necessary to feed the vertical stack of plug-ins and the results are mixed back together again before reaching the Vbox output.

You aren't only limited to using plug-ins in either serial or parallel configurations; you can create highly complex arrangements that include both serial and parallel processing. To better understand how that works, let's try a couple of simple setups.

Try this: With Vbox open and the Matrix empty, click on the box in the upper-left corner and choose BIAS Freq-4. After the miniature Freq panel appears, click the box to its immediate right and choose BIAS Sqweez. You now have two plug-ins arranged in series. The green signal line passes from the Vbox input (on the left) to Freq to Sqweez and on to the output on the right (see **Figure 9-8**).

Tool Tips:
PLUG-IN FLEXIBILITY

Because Vbox is actually a plug-in itself, you can combine it with other plug-ins when using the inserts. For example, you could have individual plug-ins on Inserts 1 and 2 and have Vbox on Insert 3. However, from a processing standpoint, there isn't any benefit to arranging your plug-ins in that manner. Putting all of the plug-ins in Vbox and working with them inside the Matrix display is much easier, and it adds greater control and more flexibility.

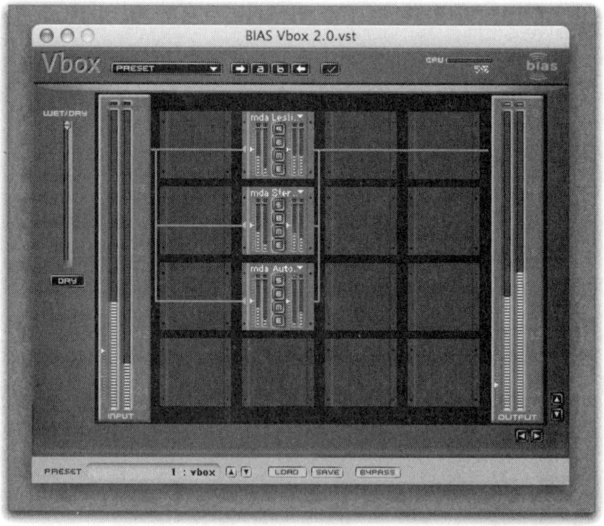

Figure 9-7
Plug-ins that are stacked vertically process the signal in parallel.

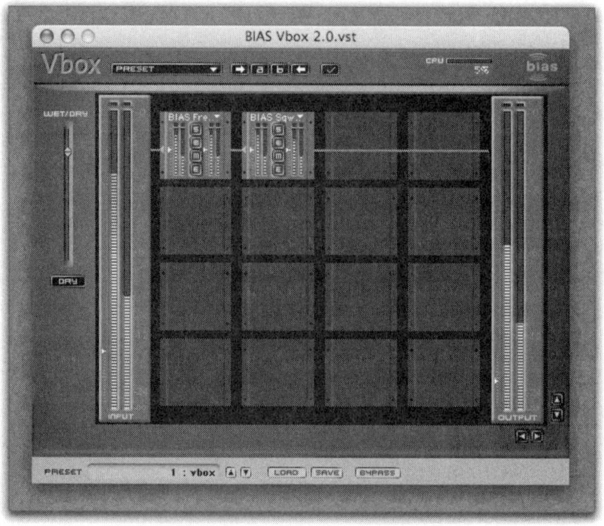

Figure 9-8
This is an example of a simple serial effects configuration. The signal passes from left to right through each effect in succession.

Now let's set up a parallel arrangement. Move the cursor arrow to the Sqweez panel and click and hold over the miniature VU meters to the right of the buttons (either side will actually work). When the arrow turns into a grab hand, you can drag the plug-in to any available box. Drag Sqweez into the box directly below Freq and release the mouse button. Notice that the green signal line now splits into two copies, each of which flows to a separate effect (see **Figure 9-9**). On the other side of the plug-ins, the signals join back together before reaching the output.

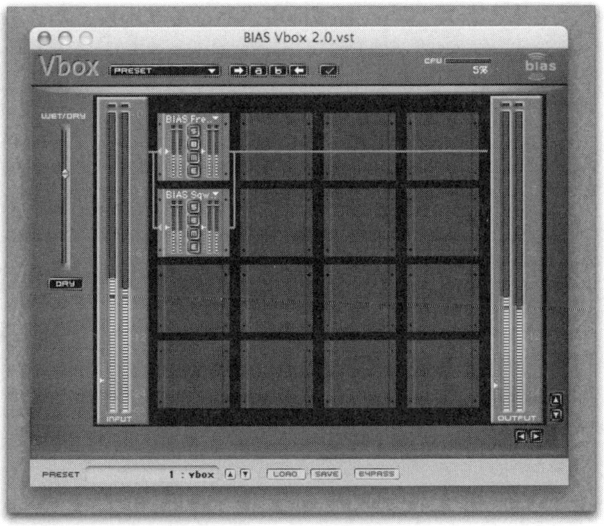

Figure 9-9
In this example, the signal is split before entering the effects, which then process the signal simultaneously. After processing, the two signal branches rejoin and proceed to the output.

For a slightly different arrangement, grab Sqweez and drag it one box to the right to form a diagonal configuration (see **Figure 9-10**). With only two plug-ins, the results of this processing will be the same as in the previous example, even though it looks different. Because two rows are involved, the signal is again split until after the last effect is reached. However, things get more interesting when a third plug-in is added.

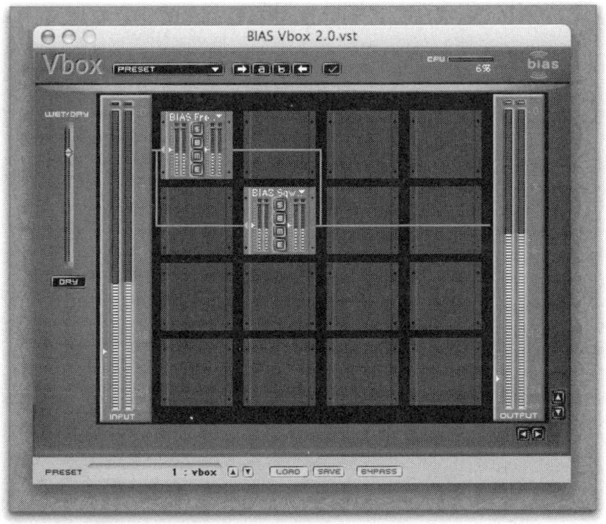

Figure 9-10
This configuration produces the same results as the preceding example, even though it looks different. That's because the signal is still split, processed in parallel, and then rejoined.

With the diagonal configuration still in place, click on the box directly above Sqweez and to the right of Freq, and choose SFX Machine LT. We now have a combination serial/parallel arrangement (see **Figure 9-11**). As before, the signal splits into an upper and lower path. In this example, the upper path travels through Freq and then into SFX Machine LT, while the lower path travels through Sqweez. The two paths are then joined together before reaching the output.

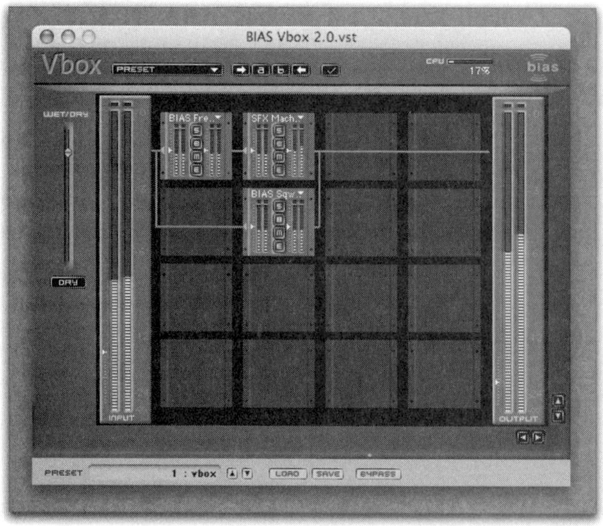

Figure 9-11
This is an example of a simple configuration that combines serial and parallel processing.

But what if you don't want the signal to split at the very beginning? What if you want the signal to be processed by Freq and *then* be split between SFX Machine LT and Sqweez? You can do that too. Look closely at the left side of the Sqweez panel where the green signal line enters the plug-in. Click on the tiny green arrowhead to reroute the signal upward (see **Figure 9-12**). The signal now enters Freq and *then* is split into two copies. The top passes through SFX Machine LT while the bottom goes through Sqweez.

If you're a real power user and you're starting to wonder whether 16 plug-in boxes are enough, don't worry. Vbox only lets you see 16 boxes at a time, but you can actually have as many as 9,801 boxes if you really need them.

At the top of the Vbox window, click the button with the checkmark on it to open the Vbox Preferences dialog box (see **Figure 9-13**). There you can enter as many as 99 rows and 99 columns. The checkbox at the bottom prevents playback from breaking down if you overload your CPU with processing (which would certainly

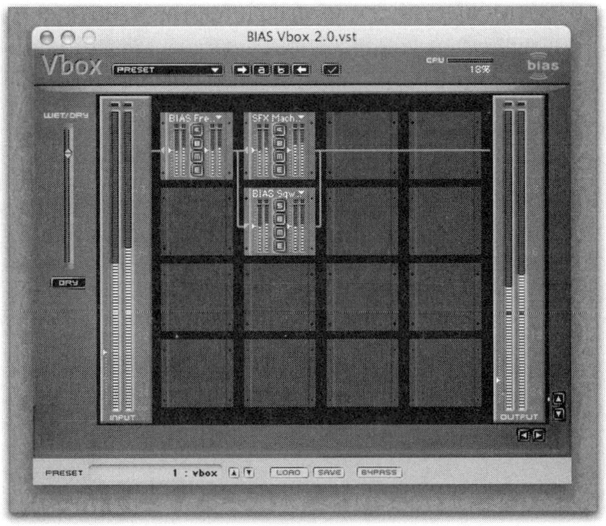

Figure 9-12
Using the setup in Figure 9-11, Vbox lets you reroute the signal so that the split occurs after some processing has taken place.

happen if you activated thousands of plug-ins at once). Combining multiple plug-ins can easily overtax your computer, so keep an eye on the CPU gauge in the upper-right corner of the Vbox window.

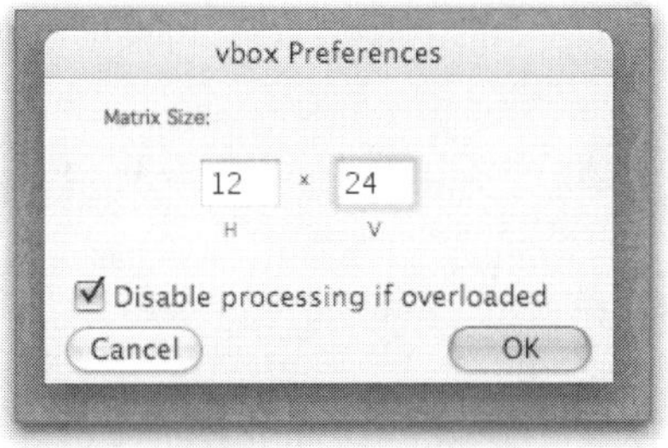

Figure 9-13
In the Vbox Preferences dialog box you can specify the number of available Matrix rows and columns.

To view all of the available boxes, use the left/right and up/down scroll arrows in the lower-right corner of the Vbox window. Other features in the Vbox window resemble those in the miniature control panels for the plug-ins. On the left, a set of master input meters shows the incoming signal level, which you can raise or lower by up to 6dB (+/–100 percent) with the small white slider at the bottom of the meters. The center position represents zero cut or boost. The same setup is provided on the right side of the window for monitoring and controlling the output.

The slider on the far left lets you adjust the wet/dry mix of the Vbox plug-in configuration as a whole. At the center position, you get an equal blend of Vbox processing and original (dry) signal. As you move the slider up, you'll hear more of the processed sound and less of the original. Dragging down accomplishes the reverse.

Tool Tips: SNAP TO IT
You can quickly return any Vbox master slider—Input, Output, and Wet/Dry—to its center position by clicking on the slider while holding down the Option key.

Click the Dry button under the slider to hear only the original source material without any Vbox processing.

The remaining buttons at the top of the Vbox window are for making A/B comparisons between different setups (see **Figure 9-14**). Click the arrow button on the left to assign the current arrangement to button A. Create a new arrangement and assign it to button B by clicking the arrow button on the right. You can then switch quickly between the A and B states by clicking the corresponding buttons.

Figure 9-14
Vbox makes it easy to compare two different configurations with its A/B buttons.

The drop-down Preset menu to the left of the A/B buttons lets you save and name any Matrix arrangement for later retrieval. Choose Load to open a standard OS X dialog box where you can navigate to your folder of presets to make a selection.

Plug-In Controls

As we've seen, each plug-in that is added to the Vbox Matrix acquires its own miniature front panel with its own independent set of meters and controls. The stereo meter on the left indicates the input levels; the meter on the right shows the output levels. As with the Vbox master meters, red indicators above the meters alert you to the presence of clipping. Next to each plug-in meter, a tiny white arrowhead serves as a fader for controlling the input and output levels.

Down the center of the plug-in panels, four buttons offer additional functions. Clicking the Solo button at the top (it turns red when active), bypasses all the other plug-ins in the same series (horizontal row). If the signal splits before reaching the soloed plug-in, however, the other (parallel) rows of plug-ins won't be affected.

To bypass an individual plug-in that is part of a series or parallel setup, use the Bypass button just beneath the Solo button. Clicking the Bypass button (it turns blue when active) allows the signal to pass unprocessed through the plug-in.

The third button down is the Mute button (it turns yellow when active). Clicking the Mute button turns off a plug-in's output and therefore shuts down the signal at that point in a series. Subsequent plug-ins in the same series with the muted plug-in are, in effect, muted as well because they don't receive an input signal. Other rows of plug-ins that are in parallel with the muted plug-in aren't affected, because they have a separate branch of the signal to process (see **Figure 9-15**). On the other hand, if the parallel row branches off from the first row after the muted plug-in, the parallel row will be muted too.

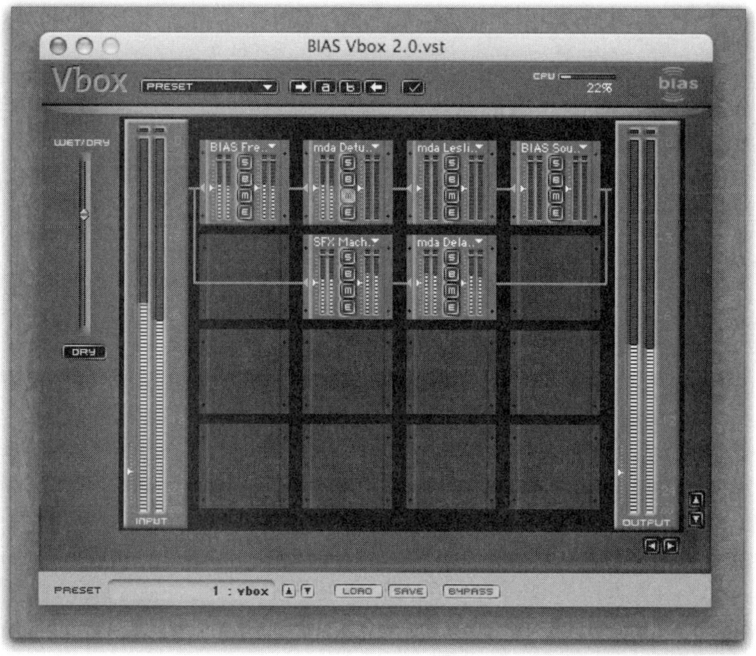

Figure 9-15
The Mute button shuts off the signal after the muted effect. (Notice that the top-row plug-in meters are inactive after the second effect.) Plug-ins on a separate parallel branch, however, are not affected.

The button at the bottom of the plug-in panel is the Edit button (it turns green when active). Click the Edit button to open the plug-in's full user interface whenever you need to make adjustments or change presets. Remember, you can insert the same effect in multiple Matrix boxes with each instance set differently. Click the Edit button for each instance of the plug-in to see them all at once. You can then compare settings and make adjustments.

When you click the Edit button on several plug-ins, the corresponding interfaces will appear in the order that you click the buttons. Because Peak Pro stacks the windows onscreen, large windows can completely cover smaller windows. You must drag the windows to spread them out and make them all visible at once. If you just want to look at one window that is covered up in the stack, double-click its Edit button in the Matrix. The first click closes the window, and the second click opens it again. When it reopens, it will be on top of the other windows.

You can freely move any plug-in panel from its current location in the Matrix to any other box. (Clicking on the plug-in's meters turns the cursor into a grab hand.) Dragging a plug-in to

> **Tool Tips: SWITCH HITTING**
> If you find that your plug-in displays are getting buried under a pile of panels or they're being covered up by various windows, hit the Command and tilde (~) keys together to bring a different window to the forefront. By hitting the key combination several times, you can cycle through all of Peak Pro's open windows until the one you're looking for appears.

Tool Tips: SWAP MEET
The plug-ins in the Vbox Matrix are "hot-swappable." You don't have to stop playback to rearrange them. Just grab a plug-in panel and drag it to a new location at any time. Playback may pause for a split second (depending on your CPU and how many plug-ins are active), but is often barely interrupted.

an empty box simply rearranges the signal flow. Dragging to a box where another plug-in resides replaces the existing plug-in with the new one. You can also replace a plug-in by clicking on its name in the Matrix panel and choosing another plug-in from the pop-up menu.

Plug-Ins Envelope

Peak Pro's Plug-Ins Envelope feature allows you to control the application of an effect or Vbox setup over time by creating an envelope graph. This could come in very handy if, for example, you wanted a Leslie speaker effect (such as MDA Leslie) to start out strong but then gradually diminish in intensity. Or you could use an envelope to have an effect, such as an echo or reverb, appear gradually as the audio file progresses. Of course, you can also create wild effects that disappear and then reappear with varying intensity. The possibilities are intriguing.

To use Plug-Ins Envelope, select all or part of a waveform and choose Plug-Ins Envelope from the Preferences dialog box (Peak > Preferences > Plug-Ins Envelope). The dialog box that appears should look pretty familiar by now, it's the same envelope display (superimposed over your selection) with the same drop-down menus and presets that we've seen in a number of editing commands (see **Figure 9-16**). You can use one of the presets or create a custom envelope by clicking on the graph to create moveable breakpoints.

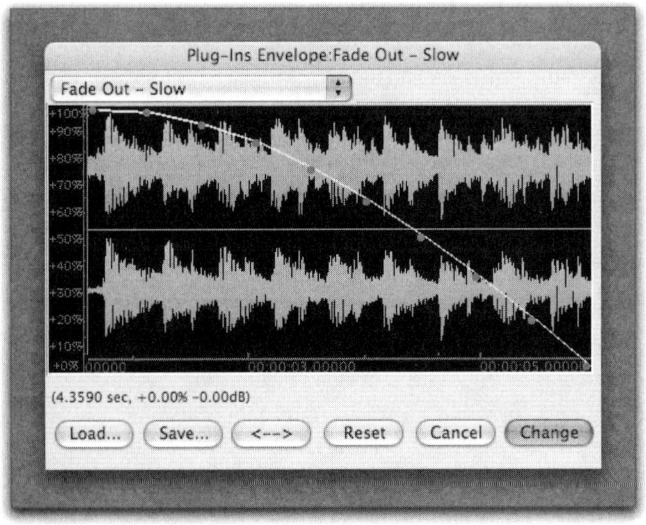

Figure 9-16
With the Plug-Ins Envelope dialog box, you can control how much of an effect is applied over time.

The scale on the left side of the display shows the amount of the effect that is applied to the audio file: the top represents 100 percent (wet); the bottom represents zero percent (dry). When you've devised an envelope that you're satisfied with, click the Change button. Open Vbox or the plug-in that you want to use and adjust the parameters to your liking. (Hit the Spacebar to audition the plug-in without the envelope to get a feel for the sound.) Then choose Bounce from the Plug-Ins menu to apply the changes.

Latency Compensation

Whenever an audio signal passes through one or more plug-ins, a small delay, which is called latency, is introduced as a result of the processing. Beginning with Version 5, Peak Pro automatically detects the latency as reported by the plug-in itself. The processed audio is then shifted in time to compensate for the delay. Although the delays are typically small (measured in samples), they could be significant if you're working, for example, in tight sync with dialog or sound effects and video. Or the delay could be a problem if you process a selection in the middle of a waveform.

In those few cases where a plug-in doesn't correctly report its latency, you can still manually compensate for it before applying the effects to the audio file.

The Auto-Adjust Bounce for Latency feature is on by default in the Options menu. To manually compensate for latency, you'll first have to uncheck the command. Then hold the Option key down *before* choosing Bounce from the Plug-Ins menu to open the Bounce Effects dialog box (see **Figure 9-17**). In the field at the top of the box, enter a number of samples to shift the processed audio, and then click the OK button.

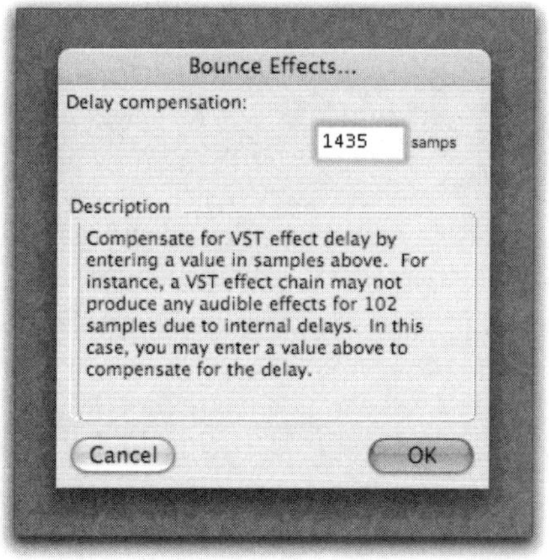

Figure 9-17
In a few cases where Peak Pro doesn't automatically compensate for plug-in latency, you can use the Bounce Effects dialog box. Enter a number in samples to counteract the latency caused by processing through one or more plug-ins.

Of course, the above instructions assume that you already know how much latency the plug-in (or plug-in combination) introduces. Most of the time, you probably won't know, so here's an easy way to find out how much of a shift is required. Before applying your processing for real, do a preliminary bounce.

Open the audio file and make sure that the Audio Document and Transport windows are clearly visible. In the Options menu, set the time units to Samples (Options > Time Units > Samples). Drag through the waveform to make a selection, but be sure to start the selection on a peak or some other high amplitude area and not in an area of silence. (Turn off Auto Snap.)

With the selection highlighted and your effects in place within Vbox or an Insert slot, choose Bounce from the Plug-Ins menu. If you aren't zoomed out too far, you may see the waveform jump to the right a bit as a small section of silence is added to the beginning of the selection (see **Figure 9-18**). That's the latency caused by the processing. When the Disable All Plug-Ins After Bounce dialog box appears, choose Yes.

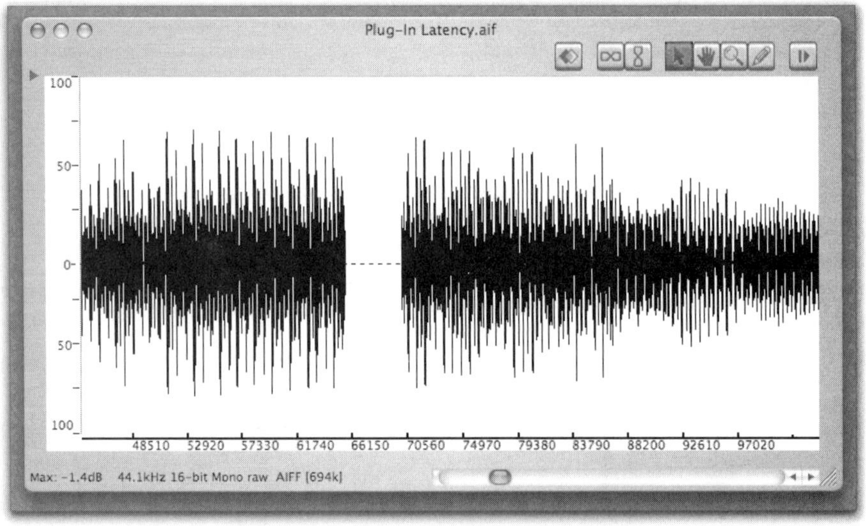

Figure 9-18
If you process a selection in the middle of a waveform, the latency will appear as a section of silence preceding the processed part of the waveform.

Next, drag through the short section of silence within the waveform, and look at the numerical display in the Transport window. You should see a readout, in samples, of the added latency. Write down the number and then undo the Bounce command (Edit > Undo Bounce Plug-ins). Now when you open the Bounce Effects dialog box during the actual processing, you'll have a number to insert.

You probably won't need to use this procedure if you have Peak Pro 5 or later, because as mentioned earlier, the program now automatically compensates for plug-in latency. However, you might run across a shareware plug-in or an older piece of software that needs to be adjusted. So it's a good idea to keep this capability in mind.

Recording Through Plug-Ins

As both a creative option and a handy time-saving feature, Peak Pro lets you record directly through any of your plug-in effects. The easiest approach is to open Vbox (Plug-Ins > Vbox) and insert the effects that you want to use by clicking on the Matrix boxes and choosing from the pop-up plug-in menu.

Once you have the appropriate setup, choose Record Settings from the Audio menu to open the Record Settings dialog box (see **Figure 9-19**). In the lower-left corner, check the box labeled "Record thru plug-ins" to make that function active. Look over the other Record Settings options and check the ones that apply to your needs; then click the OK button.

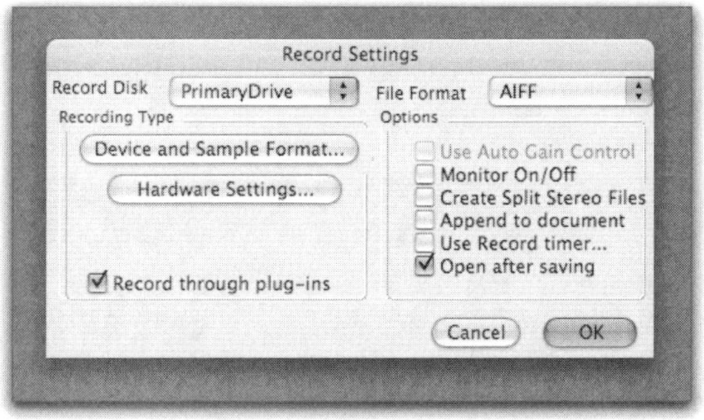

Figure 9-19
In the Record Settings dialog box you can configure Peak Pro to record through your plug-in effects.

Next, click the Record button in the Transport window or choose Record from the Audio menu to open the Record window (see **Figure 9-20**). Click the Record button in the lower-right corner to begin recording. (For more on recording in Peak Pro, see Chapter 4.)

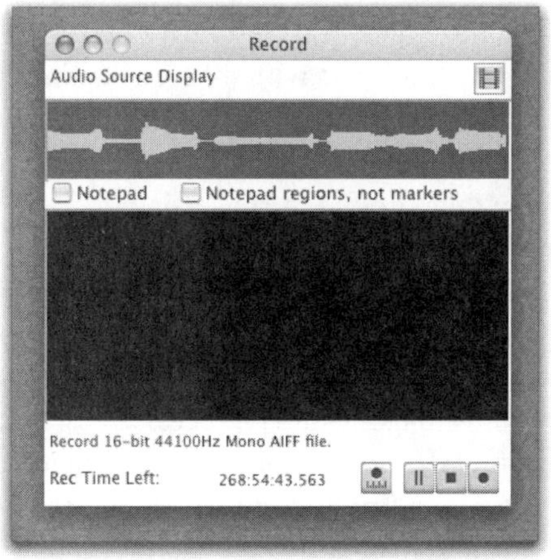

Figure 9-20
The Record window opens when you click the Record button in the Transport window.

Plug-In Instruments

One of the exciting new features introduced in Version 5 is Peak Pro's support for plug-in instruments: VSTi plug-ins and Audio Units software instruments, including synthesizers and samplers. This adds an entirely new dimension to the program and opens new creative possibilities.

If you want to use a MIDI keyboard, guitar, or other external controller, you'll need a separate MIDI interface or a digital-audio interface with built-in MIDI capability. For performing directly into Peak Pro, that's the best solution. You can activate the keyboard input function by going to the Options menu and choosing Keyboard MIDI Input. But if you don't have a MIDI interface or a keyboard controller, you can still trigger notes with your mouse by clicking on the virtual keyboard. To open the Keyboard window, go to the Window menu and choose MIDI (see **Figure 9-21**). Click any onscreen key to play it; hold down the computer's Shift key, and click to create chords.

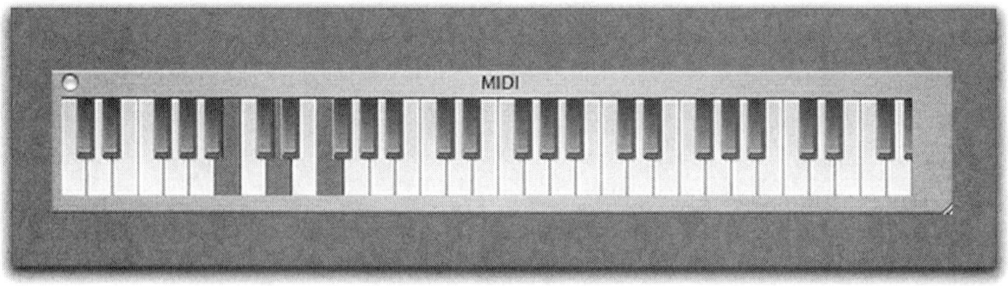

Figure 9-21
Beginning with Version 5, Peak Pro offers a virtual keyboard for triggering notes in plug-in samplers and synths.

To use a plug-in instrument, simply choose it as you would any other plug-in for an Insert slot, or add it to Vbox. In fact, in Vbox you can create parallel setups that enable you to stack instruments for a layered sound. You can also combine instruments with effects. For example, you could have a sampler followed in series by a compressor, an EQ, and a reverb. Or you could have two synth plug-ins in parallel, each feeding delays and resonant filters with different settings.

The great thing about working this way in Peak Pro is that you can record your performance to disk. Just follow the procedure outlined above for recording through plug-ins. You can then process the recording further with more effects and bounce the whole thing to disk again.

Keep in mind, however, that Peak Pro is primarily an audio editing program and is not intended to replace an audio/MIDI sequencer. For starters, Peak Pro's design and workspace is centered on individual Audio Documents rather than on multitrack projects. The big advantage to having access to software instruments lies mainly in the areas of sound designing, sample development, and loop processing.

Starting with Peak Pro 5, you can now create samples for a plug-in sampler and try them out in performance without leaving the program. You can also produce unusual sound effects by combining a synthesizer with Peak Pro's varied assortment of plug-ins and then bounce the whole thing to disk for some really impressive new sounds. That's something to keep in mind when developing sound effects for games, videos, and movies. (See Chapter 12 for more on working to picture.)

What's Next?

In the next chapter, we'll take a close look at Peak Pro's use of markers and the many things that they enable you to do. Markers are not only essential aids for organizing and editing audio, they're an important element in creating loops. And speaking of loops, Peak Pro has a number of powerful tools for producing and editing loops, all of which we'll explore in Chapter 10.

Chapter 10

On Your Mark: Working with Markers, Loops, and Regions

Peak Pro's implementation of markers is one of the program's most powerful features. Markers are colored indicators that you can place anywhere within a waveform to mark important spots. For example, you could use markers to identify the start of each verse, chorus, and bridge in a song or to flag parts of a recording that will need additional work. You can then return instantly to any marked location for playback and editing or skip easily from one marker to another, which speeds up your workflow and helps you stay organized. Markers are saved whenever Peak Pro saves a file.

But markers are much more than simple devices for playback, navigation, and organization. They're also valuable tools for performing a variety of editing tasks, offering alternate approaches in a number of situations. And for many users, the real power of markers lies in their essential role in creating loops and regions. Combined with Peak Pro's sophisticated looping tools, markers enable you to create and edit loops with precision and flexibility. When used as region boundaries, markers work hand-in-hand with Peak Pro's new Playlist window for preparing and mastering CDs.

As you can see, markers can assume a number of different roles, and although they may look similar (and can often be converted from one type to another), their functions are quite distinct. Understanding the different kinds of markers and how they work can unlock the secrets to many of Peak Pro's advanced capabilities.

In this chapter we'll examine the three types of markers—regular, loop, and region—and then delve into Peak Pro's many looping features. After covering region markers later in this chapter, I'll continue in Chapter 11 with a close look at playlists and CD burning. First, though, let's look at how to create and edit markers.

Adding Markers

Markers are simply indicators that appear in the waveform display allowing you to designate and label noteworthy locations in an audio file. They appear as colored vertical lines with small triangles at the bottom. Each marker also has a label, which appears next to the marker line (see **Figure 10-1**).

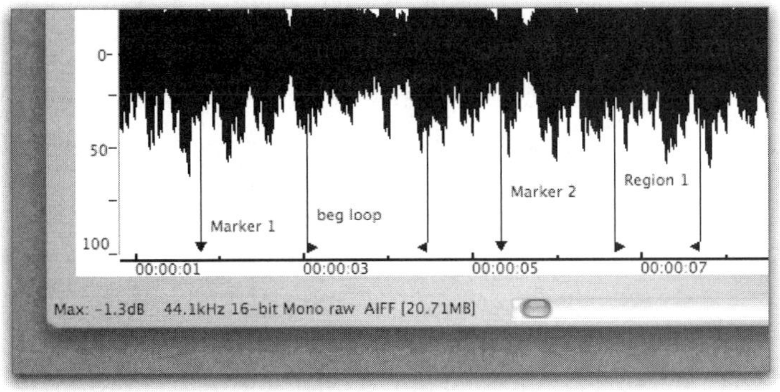

Figure 10-1
This waveform has all three marker types in it: regular (1 and 4), loop (2 and 3), and region (5 and 6). The small triangles at the bottom of the markers help to identify the different types and provide access to various editing capabilities.

There are several ways to add markers to a waveform, depending on the type of project you're working on and where you are in the editing process. The easiest and most accurate approach is to add the marker to the waveform while playback is stopped. Locate the desired location by examining the waveform. When you find a place to mark, click with the mouse at that point to set the insertion point. Then simply choose New Marker from the Action menu (or hit Command-M) to create a marker.

Peak Pro automatically labels the marker with a default name and number that you can change later if you want. If you'd like to have your markers always appear at zero-crossing points (handy if you're using markers as editing guides), be sure that Auto Snap is selected in the Options menu and that the Snap To command is set to Zero Crossings (Action > Snap To > Zero Crossings). You can also have the markers snap to CD frames or other units. On the other hand, if you want to have complete control over marker placement, deselect the Auto Snap command.

If you're having trouble finding the precise place that you want to mark, you can use Peak Pro's scrubbing tools to nail down the location. Hold down the Control key for dynamic scrubbing or the Control-Option keys for jog-style scrubbing, and drag the cursor through the waveform. (See Chapter 6 for a detailed look at Peak Pro's scrubbing features.) When you find the place that you want to mark, release the mouse button to

Tool Tips: MORE SNAP

You can always change the location of any marker by dragging it with the mouse. If you'd like a marker to snap to the nearest zero-crossing point, set the Snap To command to Zero Crossings (Action > Snap To > Zero Crossing), and hold down the Shift key as you drag. To have the Snap To command always on (without using the Shift key), choose Auto Snap in the Options menu. The Snap To command can also snap to a number of other units, such as CD frames.

place the insertion point at that location. Then hit Command-M to generate a marker.

In many cases, it's faster and easier to simply drop in markers on-the-fly during playback of an audio file. Just click the Play button in the Transport window, and then hit Command-M every time you hear something that you want to mark. You don't have to be too accurate when placing markers in this way, because you can go back later and adjust the positions. In fact, you can even make adjustments before the playback has ended, although it's easier to pinpoint locations by stopping playback and using the scrubbing tools.

Another potential time-saver is generating the markers during recording. Use the Notepad Cues feature in Peak Pro's Record window to drop in a marker (Cue) each time you hit the Return key. You can then type in a label for the marker as you wait for the next noteworthy event in the recording.

Notepad Cues are a great way to quickly identify the good and bad takes in a single recording or to label the parts of a song (chorus, verse, bridge, etc.). It can also be very helpful in later identifying different parts of a narration or the different actors in a dialog recording. (For more about using the Notepad feature, see Chapter 4.)

In addition to the general-purpose marker tools mentioned above, Peak Pro has a couple of specialized commands for automatically generating markers. The Markers From Tempo command in the Action menu creates a set of markers at regular intervals based on a specified tempo. The Threshold command in the DSP menu creates markers for peaks that exceed a specified amplitude value. These are covered more fully in the section on looping.

Marker Appearance

Because a regular marker is simply a time or location indicator, its triangle points down to the timeline beneath it. Loop and region markers represent the edges of an area in the waveform, so their triangles point inward to the waveform section that they delineate. Loop markers have a single label for each pair; region markers have separate labels for the beginning and end of the region.

Regardless of the type, you can reposition any marker by clicking and dragging its base. If you'd like to have Peak Pro automatically add the current time position after each label, choose the Show Marker Times command in the Options menu. The time is displayed in the format specified by the Time Units command in the Options menu.

Showing the times can be helpful if your markers have to be at specific points in time. But if your markers are close together, adding the timing info can cause labels to overlap, cluttering the screen and making the labels difficult to read. As a general rule, it's best to show the times only when there's plenty of space between markers. Remember, you can always view the current marker times in the slide-out Contents

Drawer. Just click the button in the upper-right corner of the Audio Document window. The three buttons inside the drawer let you view each type of marker separately.

With some color schemes, the markers and their labels can be hard to see clearly. It's a good idea to choose marker colors that contrast sharply with the waveform and background. To change the current colors, open the Document Colors dialog box (Peak > Preferences > Colors > Document Colors). There you'll find separate buttons for assigning different colors to the different types of markers (see **Figure 10-2**).

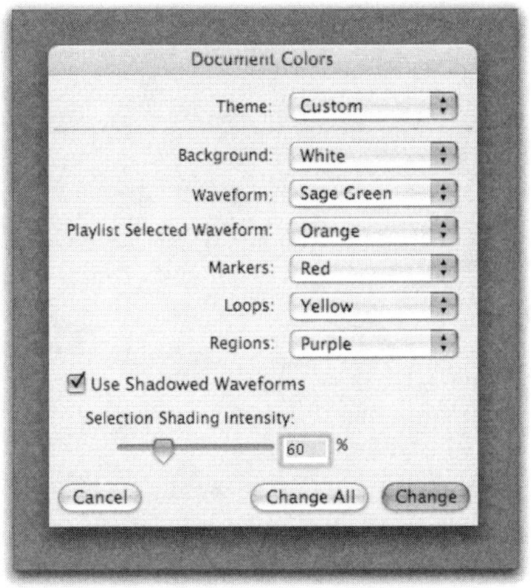

Figure 10-2
In the Document Colors dialog box you can assign different colors to the different types of markers. Be sure to choose a color scheme that is clear and easy to read even when the waveform is selected.

Editing Markers

After you have added some markers to an audio document, you can go back and individually change many of their characteristics. Just double-click on the small triangle at the base of any regular or loop marker to open its Edit Marker dialog box (see **Figure 10-3**). Region markers are different; I'll cover those a little later.

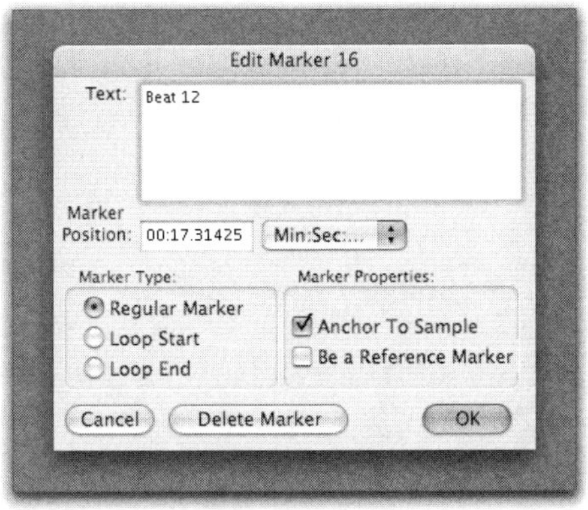

Figure 10-3
Double-click the base of any regular or loop marker to open its Edit Marker dialog box. It lets you change marker types, rename the marker, and precisely change its position.

Marker Labels

In the Text box at the top of the Edit Marker dialog, you can replace the default label by typing in a new label with up to 256 characters. That's long enough to add titles and subtitles, brief explanations or instructions, or even opening lines of dialog for later navigating and editing. However, only the first 29 characters will appear in the waveform display. To read a lengthy text message, you'll have to double-click the marker's triangle to open its Edit Marker dialog box, where you can then read the entire message.

Marker Positions

Beneath the Text box, the Marker Position field lets you specify an exact location for the marker. Use the drop-down menu on the right to select a unit of measurement, including minutes and seconds, several SMPTE timecode formats, bars and beats, and samples. The Marker Position field is especially useful when you know that a particular sound effect, music cue, or other audio event must occur at a specific elapsed time. It can also come in handy for spacing markers at precise intervals from one another.

Marker Attributes

The radio buttons on the left let you designate the marker as a regular marker or as the beginning or end marker for a loop. When you click one of the loop-related buttons, the marker changes appearance to reflect its new attributes.

By default, a marker is linked to a specific place in the waveform. For example, if you insert a marker at the snare drum attack in a rhythm loop, the marker stays aligned with the snare drum even if you delete the kick drum hit just before it. In other words, as you cut, copy, and paste within the audio file, the markers move so that they can stay aligned with the original samples in the waveform to which they were assigned.

However, sometimes it's better to have a marker linked to an elapsed time location even if the edited waveform content changes relative to the marker. If you'd rather have the marker tied to a time position instead of a specific place in the waveform, uncheck the box marked Anchor To Sample. That breaks the link between the marker and the waveform.

Reference Markers

The remaining checkbox lets you designate the marker as a reference marker. As the name suggests, a reference marker provides a reference point against which the cursor or another marker can be compared. (As with other markers, a reference marker can be linked to a specific waveform location or to an elapsed time position.) As you drag markers through the waveform to reposition them, the DTR (Distance To reference) field in the Contents Drawer automatically displays the distance to the nearest reference marker. (The time units are the same as those selected in the Time Units command in the Options menu.) Note that this display is only updated when the mouse is within the area of the waveform. If you drag the marker with the mouse below the waveform, the data display won't change.

Try this: Open any Audio Document but be sure that it doesn't already have any markers in it. Position the cursor somewhere in the middle of the waveform and click to place the insertion point. Then hit Command-M to drop in a marker. Do the same thing to add a second marker a short distance away, but not too close.

Double-click the base of the marker on the right to open its Edit Marker dialog box. Select Reference Marker and click the OK button. Open the Contents Drawer in the Audio Document window and locate the DTR (Distance To Reference) display. It shows the current distance from the cursor to the reference marker (see **Figure 10-4**).

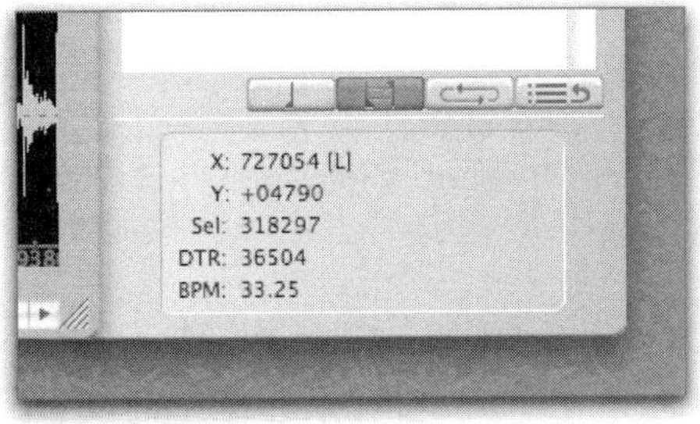

Figure 10-4
The DTR (Distance to Reference) display in the Contents Drawer of the Audio Document window shows the current distance from the cursor to the nearest reference marker.

To show the distance from the regular marker to the reference marker, click and hold the base of the regular marker. While holding down the mouse button, slide the cursor up into the center of the waveform display. Now, as you drag the marker to the left or right, you can read the distance to the reference marker in the DTR display. If you'd like the readout to be right next to the cursor, select Show Cursor Info from the Options menu before you click-and-drag.

Reference markers come in handy when you have to quickly edit an audio file so that certain events occur at specific places relative to another event. For example, let's say you have an audio file with a gunshot that is preceded by a cymbal crash. Your assignment states that the cymbal crash must occur exactly 3.5 seconds before the gunshot.

One easy approach would be to copy the cymbal crash to the Clipboard and place a reference marker on the gunshot. Then simply drag the cursor through the waveform until the DTR display shows 3.5 seconds, and click to place the insertion point. Choose Replace from the Edit menu and the job is done.

Why Replace? Because if you choose Paste, the Clipboard contents will be added to the existing material and the timing will change. Replace adds the new material without changing the overall timing, keeping the original measurement to the reference marker intact. Sounds occurring after the reference marker would not pose the same problem, unless there were other timing conditions that they had to meet. If you had wanted to blend the cymbal crash with the existing waveform, you could have used the Add or Mix command in the DSP menu. (See Chapter 5 for more on the Paste, Replace, Mix, and Add commands.)

Tool Tips:
PROPER REFERENCES

One of the most common problems when working with reference markers occurs when there is more than one reference marker in an Audio Document. Remember, the DTR display provides a real-time readout of the distance from the cursor to the *nearest* reference marker. With more than one reference in the waveform display, you may find yourself inadvertently reading distances to the wrong marker.

If you notice that the DTR display seems to be acting erratically or changing direction as you drag toward a reference marker, the problem may be that the cursor is trying to interact with too many markers. To keep things simple, I like to have only one reference marker at a time in the waveform. But if you need to have multiple references, be sure to keep them well spaced, and be aware of their positions as you drag the cursor around.

Finding Markers.

For situations where you're working on a long audio file with lots of markers, Peak Pro makes it easy to locate the various markers. Simply type in the first three or four letters of a marker's name and (after a brief pause) the marker jumps to the center of the screen. (This only works when your marker names contain no spaces, because the Spacebar will start playback.)

I like to add numbers to my marker names, such as verse01, edit02, marker13, or loop24. Then all I have to do to locate a particular marker is type the number from the numeric keypad (not from the QWERTY keyboard section). That makes it a breeze to skip from one marker to another with a minimum of typing, and it eliminates problems with duplicate names. (If more than one marker has the same name, Peak Pro jumps to the first one when the name or name-fragment is typed in.)

Tool Tips: ON POINT

If you hit the Enter key right after typing a marker's name or number, Peak Pro jumps the marker into view and places the insertion point at the marker position. That offers a convenient way to start playback from any marker; just hit the Spacebar.

Moving Markers.

As described above, you can move any individual marker by simply dragging its base. Or you can double-click on the base to open the Edit Marker dialog box, where you can type in a precise location in the Marker Position field. But what if you need to move several markers at once? Using the Edit Marker dialog could quickly become tedious.

Fortunately, Peak Pro provides the oddly named Nudge Markers dialog box for just that purpose. Don't let the name fool you. You can do much more than "nudge" a group of markers;

you can actually move them quite a bit if you have to. Here's how it works: Select an area in the waveform that includes several markers and choose Nudge from the Action menu to open the Nudge Markers dialog box (see **Figure 10-5**).

Figure 10-5
With the Nudge Markers dialog box, you can move several markers forward or backward as a group.

In the field provided at the top of the box, type in an amount (in seconds) by which you want to shift the markers. Positive numbers shift the markers forward; negative numbers shift them backward. Click the OK button to make the change. In addition to the markers, all of the loops and regions in the selection are moved as well.

Deleting Markers.
Peak Pro offers two ways to get rid of unwanted markers. To eliminate an individual marker, double-click its base and then click the Delete Marker button in the Edit Marker dialog box.

If you want to eradicate all of the markers in an audio document or in a selected area, choose Select All from the Edit menu (Command-A) or drag with the mouse to select part of the waveform. Then choose Delete Except Audio from the Edit menu or hit Option-Delete to expunge the unwanted markers. (You must use the Delete key that is directly above the Return key and to the right of the = key.)

This commandprovides a quick and easy way to get back to the basic waveform, but remember, in addition to markers, it also deletes all loop and region designations in the selected area.

Selecting with Markers

Peak Pro includes a number of convenient ways to use markers for making and modifying selections. For starters, you can select the audio between any two adjacent markers by clicking between the markers while holding down the Command key. Click in the center area of the waveform display (between the channels) to select both sides in a stereo document. Command-click above the zero line in the top, or below the zero line in the bottom waveform to select only one channel.

> **Tool Tips: EASY MARKS**
> Here are some easy-to-use key combinations for working with markers and selections:
>
> **Command-M:** adds a marker
> **Spacebar:** plays the current selection
> **Command-Click (between two markers):** selects the area between the markers
> **Shift-Command-Click (between two markers):** expands the current selection to include the new pair of markers.
> **Tab:** selects the area between the next available pair of markers
> **Shift-Tab:** adds the area between the next available pair of markers to the existing selection
> **Option-Delete:** removes all markers from the selected area

You can jump the selection from one set of markers to another set by clicking between the second set of markers with the Command key down. To extend a selection to include additional markers, hold the Shift and Command keys down together, and click between another pair of markers. The selection will then expand to include all of the waveform from the first selection through the new selection. Repeat the process again to expand the selection further.

Another nifty approach uses the Tab key. In an audio file with several markers, hit the Tab key to select the area between the first two markers. Hit the Tab key again to jump to the area between the next two markers, and so on. This is a great way to cycle through the different parts of a recording; you can quickly audition them by hitting the Spacebar.

If you hold down the Shift key while tabbing, you can add each successive selection to the previous one to expand the selected area. You can even switch from one mode to the other. For example, hit the Tab key to select the first area, then hit Shift-Tab to add the second area. Hit the Tab key alone to drop that first expanded selection and jump to the third pair of markers instead. You can then Shift-Tab from there to expand from that selection, and so forth.

Editing with Markers

As mentioned earlier, markers offer some alternative approaches to the basic edits covered in Chapters 5 and 6. For example, if you want to trim the dead air from the beginning and end of a long audio file, scroll to the beginning of the file and drop in a marker where you want the audio to begin. Then scroll to the end of the waveform and drop in a marker where you want the recording to end. You can then select the area between the markers by Command-clicking anywhere between them.

Audition the selection by hitting the Spacebar to make sure you haven't trimmed off part of the attack or reverb tail. If you have, you can drag the marker a bit as needed and Command-click between the markers again to update the selection. Then hit Command-apostrophe (Command-') or choose Crop from the Edit menu to keep the good part of the waveform and throw away the rest.

Markers are also commonly used for indicating trouble spots for later editing. If you go through an audio file and add a marker wherever you find a click, bad splice, unwanted noise, an out-of-tune note, or other editing issue, you can identify the problems in advance with well-labeled markers. That can help you better organize your tasks and improve your workflow when you finally get down to editing. Adding markers can be especially helpful if more than one person has to work on the file.

Creating Loops

Peak Pro offers a variety of powerful tools for creating and editing loops of all types, including music cues, drum loops, and files for exporting to hardware or software samplers. In Peak Pro, a loop is simply a section of audio that is bordered at the beginning and end by loop markers. As mentioned earlier, the small triangles at the bottom of loop markers point inward toward the selected waveform area to remind you that they're defining a segment of audio for playback.

Loops can be used to repeat large sections of audio, such as when a piece of music or an ambient sound-effects bed is played over and over again for background sounds. Or loops can be very short, such as when a brief section of an instrument sound is looped to create a sustained note when played by a sampler. One of the most popular uses for loops, however, falls in the middle range. Drum loops lasting from one to several measures are easy to create and edit in Peak Pro thanks to some dedicated tools for working with and fine-tuning rhythmic loops.

Tool Tips: LOOP LIMIT

It's important to understand that Peak Pro only supports one loop per Audio Document. After creating a Loop Start and Loop End marker in a document, you can't add another loop marker using the Edit Marker dialog box without replacing one of the existing markers. For example, if you attempt to create a second Loop Start marker, Peak Pro automatically converts the existing loop marker to a regular marker before adding the new Loop Start marker.

Peak Pro provides two ways to "manually" create loops. The first is to create some regular markers (you can drop in markers during playback or when playback is stopped), and then use the Edit Marker dialog box (double-click the marker's base) to change one of the markers to a Start Loop marker and another to an End Loop marker. The part of the waveform that lies between the two markers is now defined as a loop.

For a much faster approach, create a selection by dragging through the appropriate part of the waveform and then hit the Shift, Command, and Hyphen keys together. You can also choose Loop This Selection from the Action menu. Loop markers will then appear at the beginning and end of the selection.

You can play through the loop by hitting the Spacebar, but to hear the loop repeat, you must first click the Loop button in the Transport window (see **Figure 10-6**) or hit Command-L. You can also select the Use Loop in Playback command from the Options menu. Whichever approach you take, the Loop button will turn blue to show that it's active, and the Use Loop in Playback command will appear with a check next to it. Hit the Spacebar to begin playback, and when Peak Pro reaches the loop, it will repeat it indefinitely until you hit the Spacebar again or click the Stop button in the Transport window.

Figure 10-6
You can click the Loop button in the Transport window or hit Command-L to enable looped playback.

If you want to listen to the loop by itself, select the loop by hitting the Command and Hyphen keys or by choosing Select Loop from the Edit menu. If loop playback is enabled (see above), hit the Spacebar to hear only the loop.

As the loop plays, you can drag either of the loop markers independently and listen to the changes in real time. If the loop markers are scrolling in and out of view (making it tricky to grab them with the mouse), you can stop the movement by going to the Options menu and unchecking Scroll During Play. Depending on the zoom resolution and the size of the loop, you may also need to uncheck Move Waveform During Play. Dragging the markers enables you to increase or decrease the loop's length or move the transition point to create a smoother loop.

There are times, however, when you might want to move both markers in parallel to shift the loop to a different part of the waveform. To do that, hold down the Option key and drag either one of the markers. Both markers will move together as a set, maintaining the original distance from one another. You can also accomplish the same thing by clicking the Horizontal Lock button at the top of the Audio Document window (see **Figure 10-7**). Don't forget to turn off the Horizontal Lock feature if you later want to move either of the markers independently.

Tool Tips:
JUST A SMIDGEON
Peak Pro lets you shift a loop forward or backward through the waveform one sample at a time. Hit Option-Right Arrow or choose Nudge Loop Forward from the Action menu to move the loop markers to the right. Hit Option-Left Arrow or choose Nudge Loop Backward from the Action menu to move the loop markers to the left. You may have to zoom in a bit to see the changes.

Figure 10-7
You can drag both loop markers in parallel by Option-dragging either of the markers or by clicking the Horizontal Lock button (center) before dragging.

Loop Tuner

To create high-quality, natural-sounding loops, it's imperative that the transition from the Loop End marker to the Loop Start marker be as seamless as possible. That's especially true when the loop is in the sustain portion of an instrument sound. Otherwise your loop will be marred by an obvious click or pop each time the splice point repeats. Drum loops are a bit less problematic, but sustained instruments and continuous sound effects are notorious troublemakers.

Fortunately, Peak Pro provides Loop Tuner, a specialized tool for zooming in on the critical transition point. To use Loop Tuner, first create a loop in the Audio Document window and then select Loop Tuner in the DSP menu to open the Loop Tuner dialog box (see **Figure 10-8**). Loop Tuner's split display shows a close-up view of the loop end point on the left and the loop start point on the right. By using the scroll bars and arrows under each part of the display, you can precisely coax each of the markers into place until they land on a part of the waveform that forms a smooth and continuous shape.

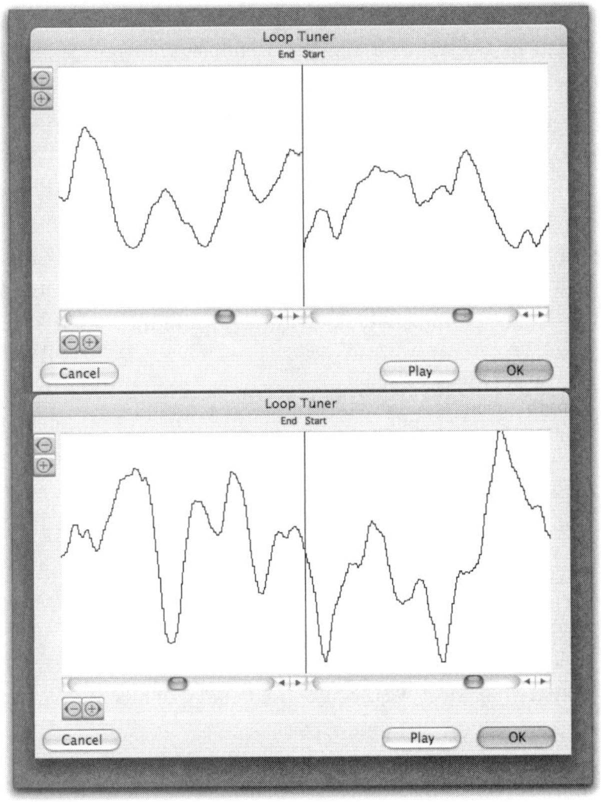

Figure 10-8
The Loop Tuner dialog box makes it possible to smoothly align the waveform across the loop transition. In the top example, the loop's splice point will cause a click because the waveform is mismatched across the transition. In the lower example, the loop will sound much smoother because the waveform is properly matched.

The Play button at the bottom of the dialog lets you set the loop in motion so you can hear the changes as you make them. Don't assume that just because you can make the left and right sides meet in the middle that your job is done. Producing a smooth transition often takes quite a bit of trial and error, and a smooth appearance onscreen may not necessarily provide the seamless transition that you expect.

You'll get the best results if you can find a place where a repeating pattern in the waveform on the left meets a similar pattern on the right. Look for places where the slopes in the waveform's hills and valleys are similar in each half of the display, and try to meld them into a continuous line with a consistent slope.

If you need some help, use Loop Tuner's zoom buttons. The buttons in the upper-left corner increase or decrease the vertical zoom, which could help out in quiet transitions. The buttons in the lower left zoom in or out horizontally to provide a closer look at the waveform. When you find a transition that works, click the OK button to set the changes.

Tool Tips: SHARPER LOOPS

Loop Tuner can be used equally well for finding matching loop points at the ends of a longer segment of audio, or for finding a *single-cycle loop.* A single-cycle loop contains only a single cycle of the waveform at the fundamental frequency of the note being looped. Single-cycle loops are guaranteed to sound smooth, but they also sound lifeless. They were used more often in an earlier generation of sample playback instruments, built in the days when memory was expensive and only small amounts could be devoted to a single sample. When used to find single-cycle loops, Loop Tuner does indeed change the pitch (tuning) of the loop. Fine adjustments of the loop start or end marker will cause the pitch to rise or fall, as well as adding or eliminating the buzzy artifacts caused by a waveform mismatch at the start and end of the loop.

Loop Tuner has no field for displaying the pitch of a single-cycle loop, but you can either do that by ear or use a calculator. To do the math, first choose Samples as the time units (Options > Time Units > Samples). Next, select the region of the loop by Command-clicking between the loop markers, and look at the Sel: field in the Contents Drawer. This will show the size of the loop in samples. To get the frequency of the loop in Hertz, divide this number into the sampling rate of the file. For instance, if the loop is 1,000 samples long and the sampling rate is 96,000 samples per second (96kHz), the frequency of the loop is 96Hz (96,000/1,000).

To create a loop with a given frequency, reverse the operation. Divide the sampling rate by the frequency in hertz to get the desired loop length in samples.

Crossfading Loops

Loop Tuner is a terrific tool for cleaning up rough transitions, but it can't always deliver a click-free splice. Although it can often make the transition noticeably better, it may not necessarily make it completely disappear. In most cases the problem lies in the nature of the loop itself: the beginning and ending may simply be too dissimilar to blend properly. But that doesn't mean you're out of luck. Peak Pro provides a powerful Crossfade Loop feature that offers another approach to smoothing out stubborn transitions.

After creating a loop in the Audio Document window, choose Crossfade Loop in the DSP menu to open the Crossfade Loop dialog box (see **Figure 10-9**). The dialog box shows a generic waveform display (not the one you're working on), with four yellow rectangles delineating the four potential areas where a crossfade could be applied: before and after the Loop Start marker and before and after the Loop End marker. Above each rectangle a checkbox lets you select the corresponding area for crossfading.

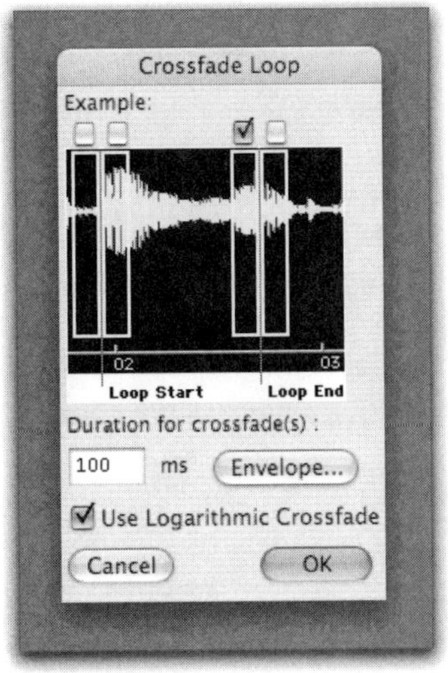

Figure 10-9
The Crossfade Loop dialog box offers several options for smoothing out the loop transition by applying a user-definable crossfade. Selecting the check-boxes above the outer two regions will cause a portion of the material in the loop to be cross-faded into an area before or after the loop, which is useful only in special circumstances.

Beneath the display, you can enter a duration in milliseconds for the selected crossfade areas; the same number applies to all. Crossfade Loop's default setting is 100ms applied to a single crossfade just before the Loop End marker. For most people most of the time that's the best setting; try it out and see how it works. If you need more blending, try experimenting with a longer duration. Be careful not to make the crossfade unnecessarily long, however, because in some cases it could muddy the loop a bit. An overly short crossfade, on the other hand, might be a little too abrupt to create the proper blend.

The other crossfade locations are more esoteric. They're offered mainly for the benefit of sound designers who are developing samples for toys, games, hardware samplers, and other proprietary devices with specific loop-transition needs. For example, some hardware samplers can play loops forward, backward, or in forward/backward combinations. And video-game audio engines may have specific loop requirements. Because of the different ways in which these devices trigger loops, crossfades may need to be started at different locations to be effective. If you're working with such a product, check the owner's manual and/or developer's documentation for specific loop playback parameters and crossfade requirements.

If you'd like to apply even more control over the crossfade process, click the Envelope button to open Peak Pro's Blending Envelope Editor (see **Figure 10-10**). This is the same Blending Envelope Editor that you can access through the Blending dialog in the Preferences window (Peak > Preferences > Blending > Edit Blending Envelope). You can use any of the existing crossfade-envelope presets, or create your own by dragging the breakpoints to form a custom shape. You can also add more breakpoints by clicking anywhere on the line. (For more on the Blending Envelope Editor, see Chapter 5.) When you're done designing your blending envelope, click the Change button. Peak Pro will then use the new envelope for blending until you change it again.

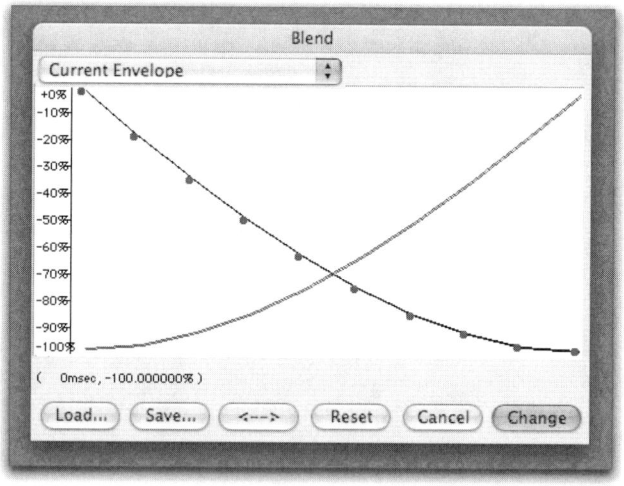

Figure 10-10
You can use Peak Pro's Blend Envelope Editor to customize the crossfade that is used by the Crossfade Loop command.

Loop Surfer

If you play a lot with drum and other kinds of percussion parts, you'll appreciate several of Peak Pro's tools for speeding up the workflow when creating rhythm-based loops. At the heart of this set of tools is Loop Surfer, which automates several of the steps in the loop-creation process and helps you establish "rhythmically correct" loops based on a specific tempo and number of beats.

To use Loop Surfer, place the insertion point just before one of the peaks in the waveform that represents a drum hit. You'll get the best results if you choose a downbeat to a measure. If you listen to the recording briefly, you should be able to identify the strong beats easily. Place the insertion point close to the attack of the beat, but don't worry about being too precise; you can make adjustments later.

Choose Loop Surfer from the Action menu or hit Command-J to open the Loop Surfer dialog box (see **Figure 10-11**). In the Tempo field, type in the tempo of the drum part. Most drum and percussion sample libraries indicate the tempo for each track, so if you're working with a track that you've imported, check the track list for the tempo. For imported sequencer or drum machine tracks, see if you can call up the original display information.

If you don't know the tempo, you can use Loop Surfer's built-in Tempo Calculator. In the Audio Document window, listen to the track and then drag through a section that represents one or two measures. (You can actually use an uneven number of beats, but you'll get the best results if you use exactly one or two measures as a selection.) In the appropriate boxes, type in the number of bars and beats and the time signature of the selected audio. Tempo Calculator instantly deduces the tempo and displays it at the bottom of the dialog box.

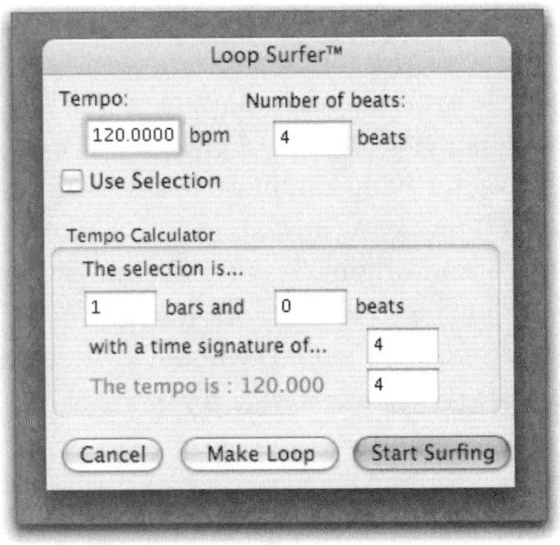

Figure 10-11
If you know a rhythm track's tempo, Peak Pro's Loop Surfer tool provides an easy-to-use method for quickly creating drum and percussion loops of various lengths. If you don't know the tempo, the Tempo Calculator section can help you figure it out.

Round off the number and enter it in the Tempo field at the top of the dialog box. Then enter the number of beats that you want the loop to have. When Loop Surfer refers to beats, it means quarter-note beats, so if you're in 3/4 time and you type in 6, you'll get a two-measure loop. In 4/4 time, 4 will get you a one-measure loop and so forth. You aren't limited to an even number of measures or beats. For a little variety, try typing in 5 or 7 beats and see how it works. Of course, the musical effectiveness of using an odd-length loop will depend largely on the nature of the drum track and the instruments used.

After specifying the tempo and number of beats, click the Start Surfing button. Peak Pro automatically closes the dialog box, creates a selection of the proper length starting at the insertion point, creates loop markers at the beginning and end of the selection, activates the loop playback function, and starts playing the loop. Clicking the Make Loop button instead of the Start Surfing button triggers all of the above actions, except that playback doesn't begin automatically. You have to hit the Spacebar or click the Play button in the Transport window to listen to the loop.

With the loop playing you can go in and fine-tune the loop markers. Option-drag one of the markers to shift both markers together; or drag either marker independently to reposition it. (To make small adjustments, you'll need to go to the Options menu and switch off both Scroll During Play and Move Waveform During Play.) You'll instantly hear the changes as you make them. Try dragging the loop onto a different set of beats to create an irregular pattern or generate some syncopation, all while maintaining the proper tempo and duration.

Tool Tips: ON THE BEAT

When working with loops and drum tracks, it may be helpful to change the unit of measurement in the Audio Document window timeline to Bars/Beats. Because Peak Pro doesn't know ahead of time what the tempo of the music is, you must provide it for each audio file. Otherwise, your Loop Surfer beats won't match up with your timeline beats and measures.

Choose Audio Info from the Options menu or hit Command-I to open the Audio Info dialog box. Enter the tempo and the meter (time signature), and then click the OK button. Next, go back to the Options menu and choose Time Units > Bars/Beats.

Once you've settled on a loop that you like, stop the playback and zoom in on the Loop Start marker. Adjust its position so that it's very close to the beginning of the beat, but leave a bit of air space to avoid trimming any of the attack. Now do the same for the Loop End marker. Allow the same amount of air space in front of its beat to ensure a clean loop of exactly the right length. Hit the Spacebar to hear the results.

Loop Surfer's greatest time-saving advantage is its ability to quickly find loops of different lengths based on your original result. For example, you can use Loop Surfer to create a one-measure loop and edit it until it's just right. Then (assuming your drummer was playing at a constant tempo) you can go back and generate 2-, 4-, and 8-measure loops by simply typing in a new entry in the Number of Beats field.

If you're not concerned about the tempo or time signature, you can drag through a section of the waveform to make a selection, and then click the Use Selection checkbox. When you click the Start Surfing button, Loop Surfer automatically turns the selection into a loop and begins playback. If you combine your selection with information about tempo and number of beats, you can also generate different-length loops as described above.

Guess Tempo

There may be times when the documentation of a loop library doesn't tell you the tempo of a rhythm track. Don't be discouraged; you can still take advantage of Loop Surfer's full feature set—as long as the music has a clear beat with distinct peaks on the drum hits. Peak Pro's Guess Tempo command can supply a pretty good estimate of the tempo. The advantage of Guess Tempo over Loop Surfer is that you don't have to select a region that starts and ends on the beat. As long as the track has prominent peaks, Guess Tempo will operate on any selected region, though it may do a better job if you select a metrically sensible region.

In the Audio Document window, drag through a section of the waveform to select it. Choose Guess Tempo in the Action menu. Peak Pro then analyzes the selected audio and calculates the tempo. After a brief pause, the answer appears in a dialog box (see **Figure 10-12**).

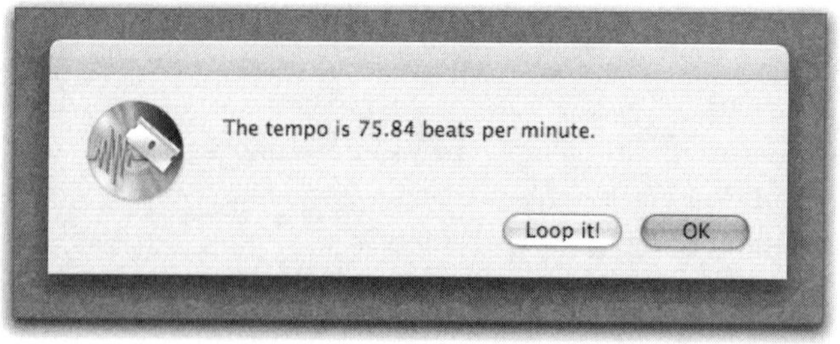

Figure 10-12
If you don't know a drum loop's tempo, the Guess Tempo command can make an estimate after analyzing a selected area in the waveform.

In spite of Guess Tempo's two-decimal-place readout, its algorithmic calculation can only provide a ballpark figure. If you choose another region in the same drum track, you'll likely get a slightly different number. Sometimes the results are reasonably accurate, with a variance of only 1 or 2 beats per minute. At other times the tempo may be off by around 5 or 6 beats per minute. It depends on the selection and the type of music.

Nevertheless, the Guess Tempo results are generally close enough to create a pretty good loop, which you can later adjust by dragging the loop markers into better positions. (If the tempo results seem questionable, try selecting two or three different one-measure areas to get an average before proceeding.)

> **Tool Tips: GUESSING GAME**
> If you're having trouble getting a reliable reading with Guess Tempo, try normalizing the audio file before using the command. With some drum tracks, normalizing can boost the attack peaks enough to give a clearer pattern for Guess Tempo to scan, yielding more accurate results.

Once you have a tempo to work with, you could manually type the number into Loop Surfer, but the most expedient approach is to simply click the Loop It! button in the Guess Tempo dialog box. That takes you directly to Loop Surfer, where the tempo is already filled in. Just enter the number of beats for the loop and click the Start Surfing button to generate a loop based on the selected audio.

Threshold

Another valuable tool for creating new loops or deconstructing existing loops is the Threshold command. It analyzes an audio file, looking for peaks in the waveform that represent the starting points of individual musical events. It then marks those events so you can save them as separate segments or regions.

Most of the time, the Threshold command is used to mark and separate the individual hits in a drum or percussion loop. But it can also be used to locate and isolate sound effects or the different notes from a melodic instrument after a sampling session. In either case, Threshold enables you to save the individual hits or events as separate files for exporting to a sampler, or as regions that you can reassemble in a playlist. Once they're in a playlist, you can rearrange the events in countless new nondestructive combinations. If you convert them to separate sampler files, each sound can be triggered from a different MIDI key.

To use the Threshold command, you must first select all or part of a waveform and then choose Threshold in the DSP menu to open the Threshold Regions dialog box (see **Figure 10-13**). If you don't make a selection, Peak Pro automatically selects the entire document for you.

As soon as the dialog box opens, you'll probably see that a number of markers have appeared in the Audio Document window. These show the results of the default Threshold settings on the current audio file. Notice that the Threshold Regions dialog consists of an upper and a lower part, each with identical controls.

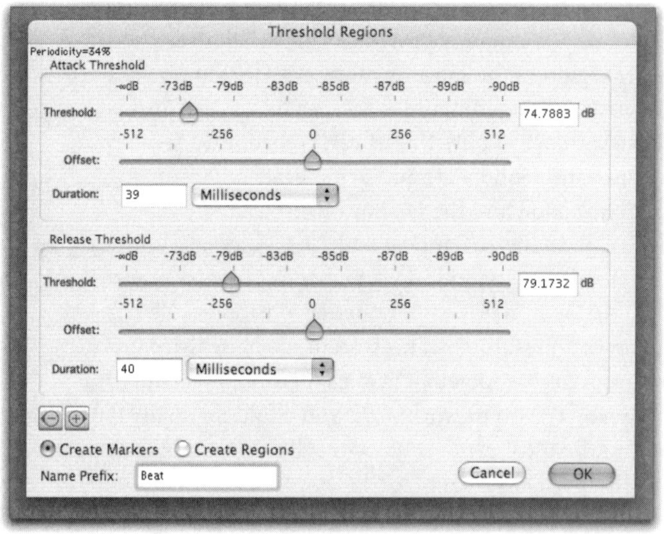

Figure 10-13
The Threshold command automatically divides up a rhythm track into separate beats by analyzing the waveform's peaks and laying down markers for the attacks that exceed the specified threshold levels.

The upper part controls the Attack Threshold parameters; the lower part controls the Release Threshold parameters when working with regions instead of regular markers. The Threshold slider at the top is perhaps the most important; it determines which peaks qualify for a marker based on whether they exceed the currently set amplitude level. As you slowly lower the threshold level by dragging to the left, you'll notice that more markers pop up, identifying additional peaks (see **Figure 10-14**). If you're only interested in marking the main beats in a drum part, slowly drag the slider left or right until only the loudest hits (the ones with the highest peaks) have markers.

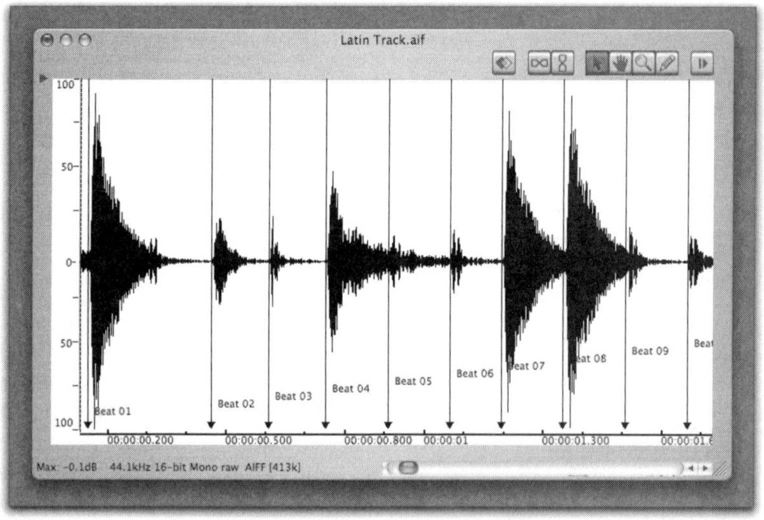

Figure 10-14
When set to use regular markers, the Threshold command leaves a marker in front of each qualifying hit.

The Offset slider lets you "nudge" the marker positions by as much as 512 samples in either direction, which can be useful for making sure you don't miss the low-level portion of an attack transient. The Duration field lets you specify how long a peak must remain above the threshold to qualify for a marker. That keeps sudden unwanted clicks or pops from getting markers and also lets you control which secondary sounds qualify for a marker.

The two radio buttons at the bottom of the dialog box are important. They determine whether regular markers are to appear at each qualifying peak (Create Markers), or whether each drum hit or other event should be marked as a region with beginning and end markers (see **Figure 10-15**). With the Create Regions button active, the Release Threshold set of sliders comes into play. (Regions are discussed in more detail below.)

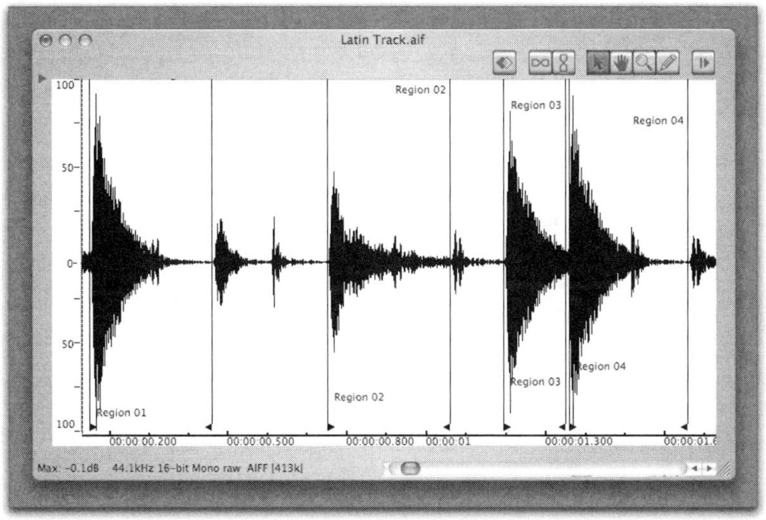

Figure 10-15
When set to use region markers, the Threshold command generates Start and End region markers to delineate each hit. You can then export the individual regions as separate audio files.

The Threshold slider lets you specify an amplitude level that triggers the placement of each region's end marker. If you drag the slider all the way to the right, the end (release) markers will seem to disappear because they will be overlapping the beginning (attack) markers. As you slowly drag the Threshold slider to the left, however, you'll see the regions grow from thin slices to larger sections. Adjust the slider until the regions encompass the selected drum hits without capturing any unwanted silence at the ends.

The release Offset slider lets you nudge the end markers by as much as 512 samples in either direction. The Duration field determines how long the amplitude level must remain at the current setting to qualify for an end marker.

Tool Tips:
REGIONAL MIGRATION

After creating a series of regions with the Threshold command, you can select each region in sequence from left to right by hitting your computer's Page Up key. To go in the other direction, hit the Page Down key. If a region is playing when you select a new one, the new region will be queued up to begin playing when the current region finishes.

After applying the Threshold command with regular markers, you can select individual beats by Command-clicking between markers. To create a loop, Command-click between a couple of markers and then Shift-Command-click between several other consecutive pairs of markers to extend the selection over several beats. Hit the Spacebar to audition the selection. If it includes the right number of beats and sounds fine, hit the Shift, Command, and Hyphen keys together, or choose Loop This Selection from the Action menu.

The Threshold command offers a great alternative approach to creating rhythm loops and can deliver precise combinations of attacks when used with regular markers. You can also employ it to create accurate selections to use with Loop Surfer's Use Selection feature.

However, when the Threshold command is used with region markers instead of regular markers, it becomes even more powerful. For example, after marking out the individual hits in a drum track, you can use the Export Regions command in the File menu to export each drum hit as a separate file for use in a hardware or software sampler. (We'll get to Export Regions in a moment.) Or you can export the regions to a playlist in Peak Pro (see Chapter 11) in order to assemble endlessly novel rhythmic loop recombinations.

If you select the "Output to new windows" radio button in the Export Regions dialog box, you can even have Peak Pro convert the individual drum-hit regions into a stack of separate windows that are ready for editing, processing, and copying and pasting (see **Figure 10-16**).

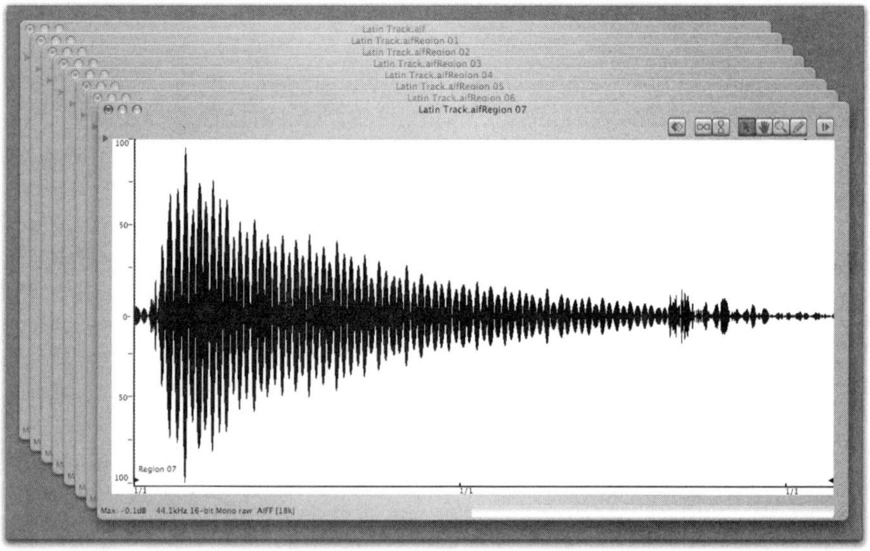

Figure 10-16
With the Export Regions command, Peak Pro can convert the individual drum-hit regions into a stack of separate windows.

Markers From Tempo

Peak Pro has one other handy marker tool for working with drum loops. If you know the tempo and time signature of a drum or other percussion part, you can automatically mark all of the measures or beats in a waveform by choosing Markers From Tempo in the Action menu.

The Markers From Tempo dialog box (see **Figure 10-17**) provides fields for entering the tempo and time signature, along with a drop-down menu for selecting whether the markers should appear only at the beginning of each measure or on every beat.

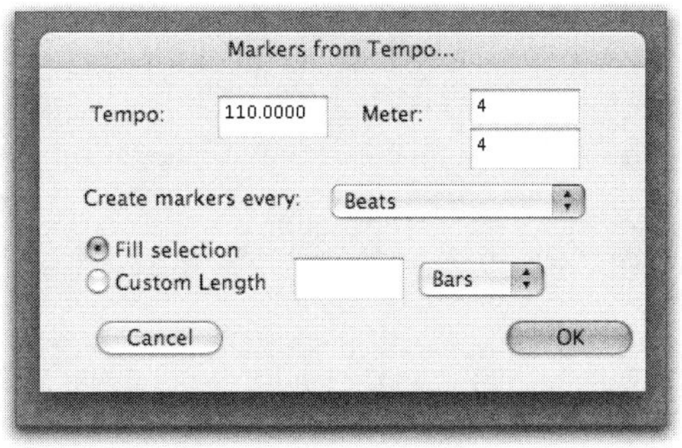

Figure 10-17
If you know a drum track's tempo and meter, you can use Peak Pro's Markers From Tempo command to generate markers at every measure or beat.

Click the Custom Length radio button in the dialog box, and then place the Insertion Point right at the attack of the beat where you'd like the markers to begin. Alternatively, you can click the Fill Selection button, and select the part of the waveform that you want marked.

When you click the OK button, Peak Pro instantly lays down a series of markers (see **Figure 10-18**). These are mathematically correct markers and probably won't align perfectly with the beats in the actual recording. Nonetheless, the markers give a good idea of how steady the rhythm is and which notes are early or late. You can also select the areas between several pairs of markers, as described above, and create a loop with the Loop This Selection command in the Action menu. If you don't know the tempo, you can always try using the Guess Tempo command, but the results will only be approximate and might not be satisfactory.

Regions

Regions are specially designated parts of an audio file that can be imported into a playlist as audio events and combined in many interesting ways. Just as loop markers define a loop, region markers define a region by establishing its beginning, end, and length. (See Chapter 11 for a closer look at using regions with playlists.)

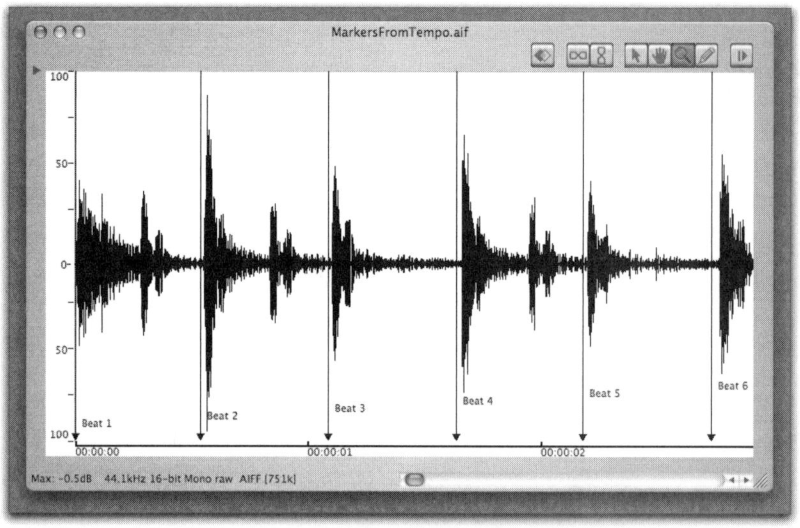

Figure 10-18
The markers that are created by the Markers From Tempo command are based on Peak Pro's calculations from the provided tempo information. They won't, therefore, reflect any tempo changes that occur naturally during a live recording, although it's easy to adjust individual markers as needed.

To create a new region, drag through the waveform to make a selection, and choose New Region in the Action menu (or hit Shift-Command-R) to open the Edit Region dialog box (see **Figure 10-19**). Type in a name (or leave in the default name) for the region and click the OK button. Start and End region markers will immediately appear in the waveform display. You can change the name, region length, and marker positions at any time by double-clicking the triangle on either of the two region markers. This reopens the Edit Region dialog box, where you can enter the changes. You can also rename any marker by clicking its name to highlight it in the Contents Drawer or Contents window. Then simply type in another label and hit Return.

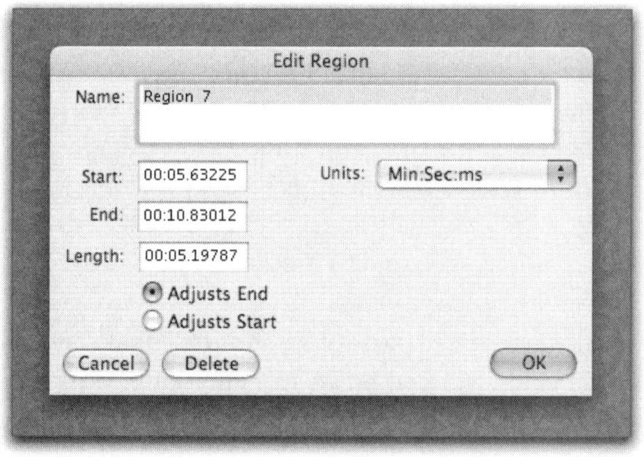

Figure 10-19
In the Edit Region dialog box you can name a region, change the Start and End marker positions, or change the region's length.

Although regions have several unique features, region markers and loop markers share several common characteristics. For example, you can move a region marker to a new position by dragging its base with the mouse. And you can move both the Start and End markers together through the waveform by Option-dragging either marker, or by clicking the Horizontal Lock button in the Audio Document window and dragging one of the markers. (Don't forget to deactivate Horizontal Lock when you're through moving your regions around.)

You can locate region markers in the same ways that you locate loop markers. Open the Contents window (Window > Contents) or slide open the Contents Drawer in the Audio Document window. Quickly double-click a region name and the region will jump into view with its section of the waveform selected. If neither display is open, you can accomplish the same thing by simply typing part of the region's name. Peak Pro will locate the region and bring it into view.

Markers to Regions

Another way to create regions is to convert existing regular or loop markers into region markers. All you have to do is select an area of the waveform that has two or more markers in it, and choose Markers to Regions in the Action menu.

If your selection has only two markers in it, they will be turned into a Region Start and a Region End marker. If your selection has more than two markers, Peak Pro converts the audio into a contiguous series of regions.

For example, if you select an area with three markers in it, Peak Pro converts it into two regions: The first marker becomes a Region Start marker (for Region 1), the third marker becomes a Region End marker (for Region 2), and the second marker becomes both an End marker for Region 1 and a Start marker for Region 2 (see **Figure 10-20**).

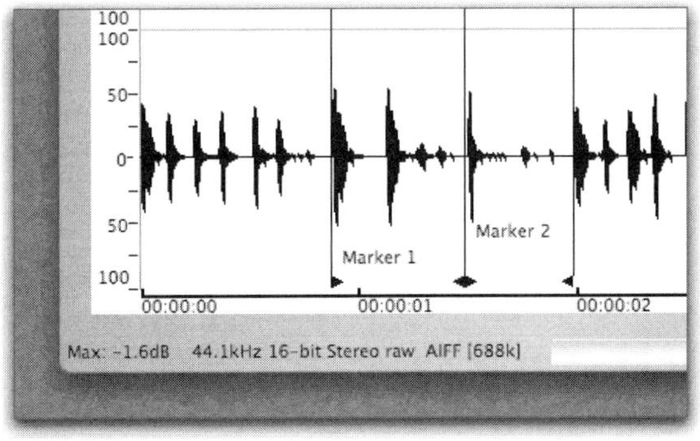

Figure 10-20
The Markers To Regions command converts a selected group of regular markers into regions. In this example, three markers were selected and converted into two regions. The center marker is now actually two overlapping (but independent) markers: an End marker for Region 1 and a Start marker for Region 2. The names come from the original markers.

> **Tool Tips:**
> **REGIONAL PRESERVATION**
> Peak Pro lets you save regions in either AIFF or Sound Designer II (SDII) format and it can usually read regions from other programs if the files are in SDII format. When Peak Pro saves regions in AIFF format, however, it uses a proprietary method that most other applications can't read. If you're working with other programs that need to import and export regions, it's a good idea to save your Peak Pro files in SDII format to maximize compatibility.

The region marker names are taken from the original marker names. The double triangles at the bottom of the second marker indicate that it's actually two overlapping (and independent) markers. You can grab either triangle with the mouse and drag it into a new position. Or you can separate one pair of markers from the other by Option-dragging one of the triangles to move that region to a different location.

Exporting Regions

If you have a document with several markers or regions in it (such as the Audio Documents that are created with the Threshold command), you can use Peak Pro's Export Regions command to automatically divide and export any or all of the audio segments and save them as separate files.

This is an especially powerful capability if you're preparing audio files for use with samplers. For example, you can divide up a drum track into its component instrument sounds (kick, snare, cymbal, cowbell, etc.) or into one- or two-measure fragments for looping and send them to a sampler for mapping across the keyboard range.

What's more, you can combine the Export Regions command with Peak Pro's Batch File Processor (see Chapter 13) to process the files with a variety of built-in DSP effects or third-party plug-ins as the files are exported. Here's how it works.

Select the regions that you want to export or hit Command-A to select the entire audio file. Choose Export Regions in the File menu to open the Export Regions dialog box (see **Figure 10-21**).

The dialog box is divided into three parts. At the top you can specify which areas in the selected waveform are to be exported: regions, the audio between other types of markers, or the audio between markers that either have (containing) or don't have (not containing) specific words in the labels. For example, you could export only audio segments with markers that have "new" in the label. Or you could skip over any marker with "old" in the label. (If you'll be using Export Regions a lot, it will pay to plan ahead when creating labels for your markers.)

In the middle, the Output Format section lets you determine the parameters that the exported files will have, including whether they'll be in mono or stereo and whether they'll have regions or other markers in them. The Output Directory section, in the bottom third of the dialog, lets you specify what will happen to the exported files. If you want each file to appear in its own Audio Document window, click the "Output to new windows" radio button.

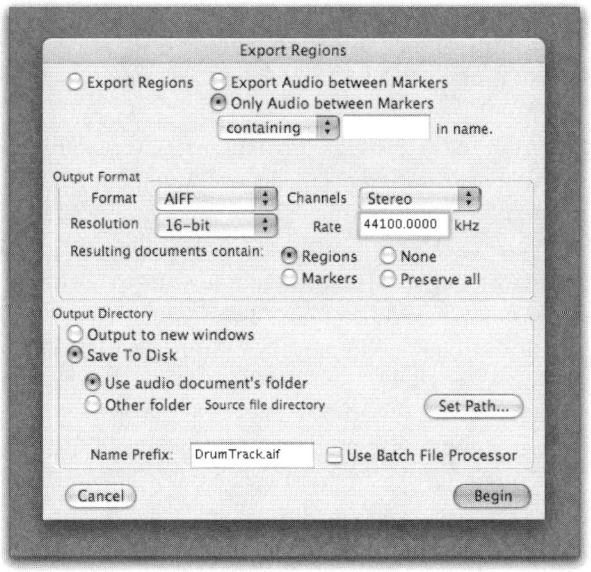

Figure 10-21
The Export Regions dialog box lets you open individual regions in separate windows or save them directly to disk in a number of formats.

If you just want the files to be written directly to the hard drive without being opened, click the Save To Disk button. That option lets you choose between saving the new files to the original file's folder or to another folder that you specify. You can use the Name Prefix field to add a prefix to each of the new files.

If you'd like to process the files as they're exported, configure and then turn on the Batch File Processor *before* opening Export Regions. With the Batch File Processor active (a check will appear next to it in the File menu), open the Export Regions dialog box. In the Output Directory section, click the Other Folder button and navigate to a folder (other than the original file's folder) where you'd like the exported files to end up, and click the Choose button. Then click the Use Batch File Processor checkbox in the lower-right corner of the Export Regions dialog box, and click the Begin button. (For more on using the Batch File Processor see Chapter 13.)

Tool Tips: DUE PROCESS
When using the Batch File Processor, remember to turn it off as soon as the processing is complete. (Open the dialog box and click the Off button at the top.) Otherwise, whenever you try to open a file in Peak Pro, it will automatically be sent to the processor.

Auto Define Tracks

If you've ever had to transfer a taped demo or album to CD, you'll appreciate Peak Pro's new Auto Define Tracks command. It automatically locates and marks the individual tracks within a recording, making it much easier and less time-consuming to prepare a recording for working with playlists. For example, if you have an old studio tape with numerous takes on it and you want to archive the session on CD with separate tracks, this command can streamline the process. It also comes in handy for transferring old 78s, LPs, or live performances to CD. Here's how it works.

Record (or load) the audio into Peak Pro, and make sure that the Audio Document window is in the foreground. Next, choose Auto Define Tracks in the DSP menu to open the Auto Define Tracks dialog box (see **Figure 10-22**). The dialog box lets you set several parameters that determine how Peak Pro will identify the tracks. The slider in the middle establishes a threshold (in dB) for defining "silence." Set this too low, and the noise floor might prevent you from getting the proper separation of tracks. Set it too high, and occasional dips in the amplitude will trigger unwanted markers for new "tracks."

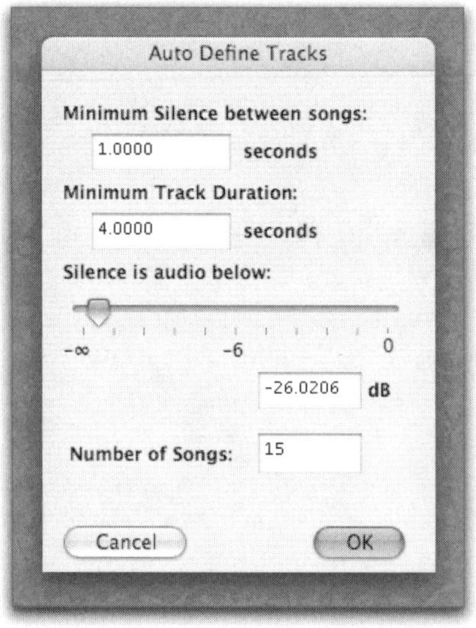

Figure 10-22 Peak Pro's Auto Define Tracks command automatically marks recorded segments within an imported vinyl record or tape recording as regions based on several settings.

In most cases, the slider will end up on the left side but not all the way to the left. As you move the slider, you can watch as region markers pop up throughout the waveform. Adjust the slider gradually until Peak Pro picks up the beginning of each track without adding any extra markers (see **Figure 10-23**). The Number of Songs field at the bottom of the dialog box shows how many tracks have been identified.

At the top of the dialog, you can specify how much silence must exist before Peak Pro sees it as a pause between tracks. Use this field to prevent having every little pause in the music marked as a new track. The Minimum Track Duration field enables you to set a minimum track length, so for example, a noise during a pause in a live recording won't be treated as a separate track. The slider control uses these two parameters in determining where to place the region markers.

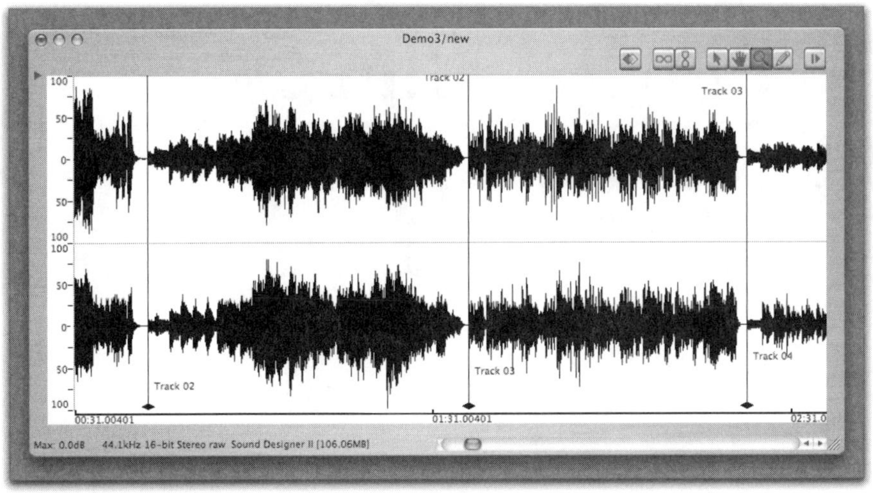

Figure 10-23
With the proper settings, the Auto Define Tracks command can accurately identify the beginning of each track.

When you get the results that you want, click the OK button to add the markers to the waveform. The region markers at the beginning of each track are actually double (overlapped) markers. Notice the double triangles at the bases. Drag a left-pointing triangle (it marks the end of the preceding region) to the left if you want to trim the silence at the end of a region. Label the regions to identify the tracks, and you're ready to import the regions into a playlist where they can be arranged in any order, processed, and burned to a CD. For an even quicker and simpler solution, you can burn your CD directly from the Audio Document window as soon as the region markers have been entered.

What's Next?

Now that you know how to create, edit, and manipulate regions, it's time to explore Peak Pro's newly redesigned Playlist window. The powerful Playlist window is packed with features that let you combine regions in a variety of ways with nondestructive crossfading and processing. Playlists are also essential for mastering and burning CDs, so the next chapter will cover those topics and several others as well.

Chapter 11

Burning Desires: The Playlist Window and Mastering CDs

Without a doubt, Peak Pro's new Playlist window is one of the program's most powerful features (see **Figure 11-1**). Its great power lies not only in its full-service CD mastering capabilities, but also in its versatile, nondestructive editing functions, which allow you to combine and recombine audio segments in myriad ways. To create a playlist, select File > New > Playlist Document or hit Command-Shift-P.

In effect, the Playlist window becomes a kind of audio sketchpad where you can try things out before committing to a final version. For example, you could string together a series of sound effects to see how they work in context with one another. Or you could assemble a sequence of music clips to see if they lead appropriately from one to another. Rearranging the order of Playlist entries is easy, and you can edit the transitions along with many other parameters.

Playlists are comprised of regions. When a region is added to a Playlist, it's called a Playlist Event. At its basic level, a Playlist is simply a list of Events that Peak Pro plays in order from top to bottom. When you rearrange, add, or delete Events, it doesn't alter the waveform sections associated with those regions. That's because the Playlist doesn't actually hold any audio waveform data. Instead, it consists of a series of reference pointers or flags (based on the region markers) that tell Peak Pro which part of the original waveform or waveforms to play.

When you click the Play button in the Playlist window, Peak Pro jumps around in the waveform as needed to play back the various regions in the specified order. You can repeat the same Event several times throughout the Playlist, crossfade between adjacent

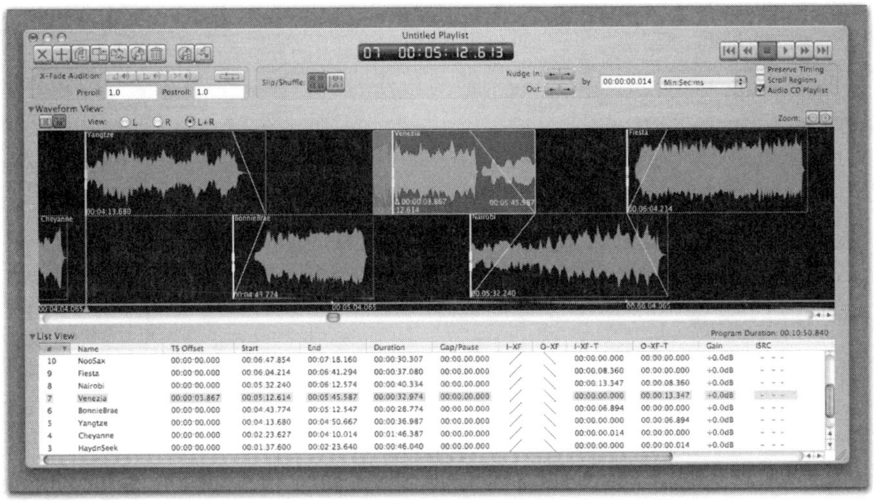

Figure 11-1
Peak Pro's Playlist window consists of three parts: a counter, a toolbar, and several audition tools are at the top; the Waveform View is in the center; and the List View is at the bottom.

Events, process individual Events with plug-in effects, and change the length of Events without altering the original material. This nondestructive editing capability is what makes the Playlist such a powerful tool for CD mastering, soundtrack preparation, and dialog editing.

Because Playlists are constructed from regions, you must first understand how to create, name, and edit regions. Those topics and more were covered in Chapter 10, so if you aren't comfortable with how regions work, it would be a good idea to review the previous chapter before going on.

The Playlist Window

The Playlist window consists of three sections. In the very top section on the left, the Playlist Toolbar offers several shortcut buttons that let you quickly accomplish common operations, such as adding or deleting regions, changing crossfade types, or burning CDs (see **Figure 11-2**). At the top in the center, a large LED-style counter shows the current position of the playback cursor. At the top on the far right, a set of Transport controls lets you (from left to right) jump to (and select) the previous region, scan in reverse, stop, play, scan forward, and jump to (and select) the next region (see **Figure 11-3**).

Figure 11-2
The Playlist Toolbar provides shortcuts to common operations such as adding or deleting regions, changing crossfade types, or burning CDs.

Figure 11-3
The Playlist window includes a set of standard CD-style playback controls.

Beneath the Toolbar, Counter, and Transport controls, two narrow recessed areas provide tools for, among other things, auditioning crossfades and nudging regions forward or backward in time. The second Playlist section includes the prominent Waveform View, which displays regions as waveform segments. It offers two display modes, which are explained below. The Playback cursor appears in the Waveform View as a vertical green line with a triangular base. You can hit the Spacebar to start and stop playback instead of using the Play and Stop buttons in the Playlist Transport controls. Drag the base of the Playback cursor to start playback from another location, or simply click anywhere along the timeline and playback will automatically begin from that point.

> **Tool Tips:**
> **PLAYLIST "SCRUBBING"**
> To scrub (scan) forward or back through the Events in a Playlist, click in the Counter display and drag the mouse forward and back.

The large List View section at the bottom of the window provides a traditional Playlist layout, showing Events and their related timings and other parameters. Both the Waveform View and List View sections have small triangles in front of their labels (on the left side of the window) that let you hide or reveal those sections. When you hide one section, the other section expands to fill the window, so you could, for example, get a much closer look at the waveforms and crossfades by hiding the List View section (see **Figure 11-4**). On the other hand, if you have a Playlist with a great number of Events, you can see more of them at once by hiding the Waveform View (see **Figure 11-5**).

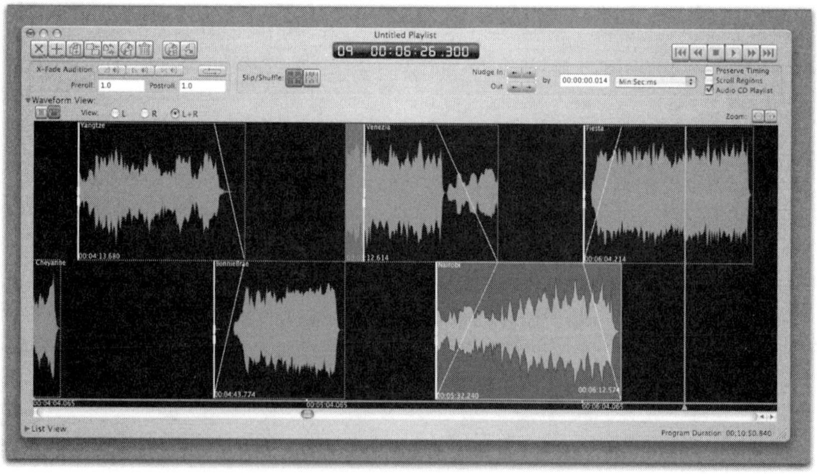

Figure 11-4
Hiding the List View section fills the window with the Waveform View area.

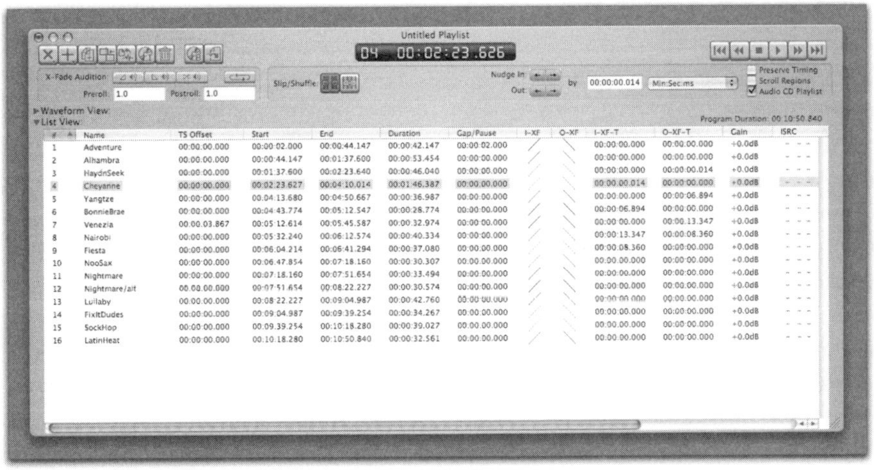

Figure 11-5
If you're working with a long list of Events, you can hide the Waveform View section to enlarge the List View area.

Unlike the Audio Document window, the Playlist has no buttons for selecting different mouse tools. Instead, the mouse changes to a different tool depending on where it's positioned in the Playlist window.

Creating a Playlist

To create a new Playlist, as mentioned earlier, you can choose Playlist Document from the File menu (File > New > Playlist Document) or hit Command-Shift-P (see **Figure 11-6**). The white List View section at the bottom of the window is where you'll assemble your regions into a sequential list. In the Waveform View area in the middle of the window, you can view the waveform segments (regions) that correspond to the Events in the list below.

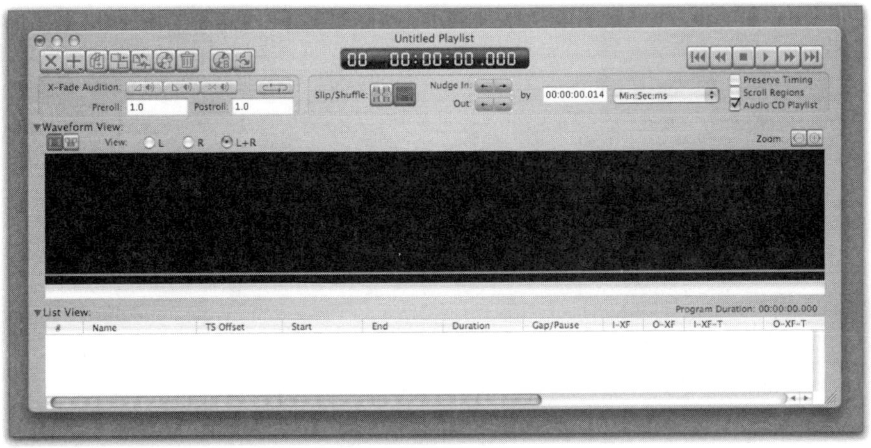

Figure 11-6
Hit Command-Shift-P to open a new, empty Playlist window.

There are a number of different ways to assemble a Playlist. If the Playlist is to consist of several regions from a single audio document, one approach is to first create, name, and edit all of the regions that you want to use. Then open the slide-out Contents Drawer in the Audio Documents window by clicking the button in the upper-right corner of the window. The Contents Drawer shows all of the regions in the audio file when you click the Region button (second from the left) beneath the list. With the Contents Drawer clearly visible, open a new Playlist window (Command-Shift-P), and drag the region names from the Contents Drawer into the List View area. (A thin border appears in the List View section if it can accept a new region.) If you'd like to import all of the regions into the Playlist, drag diagonally through the region list in the Contents Drawer, and drag the regions *en masse* into the Playlist where they'll assemble in the same order.

Peak Pro doesn't limit you to creating a Playlist from a single document. You can also assemble a Playlist from regions in several audio files as long as the files are all currently open. Although you could drag the regions from the various Contents Drawers for the different audio files, it's often more efficient to open the Contents window (Window > Contents). There you'll see a list of all the currently active Audio Documents (see **Figure 11-7**). Click the triangle before each name to reveal the associated list of regions. You can then drag the regions that you want into the Playlist window as before.

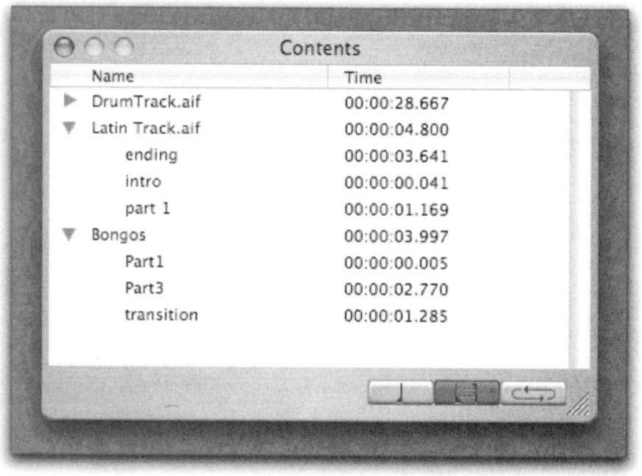

Figure 11-7
The Contents window shows all of the regions in the currently active Audio Documents.

For an even faster way to build a Playlist, set up your regions and then open the Playlist window. Click the Add Region button (the one with the large "+" symbol) in the Playlist Toolbar. That opens a drop-down menu listing all of the available regions in all of the currently open audio files. Choose any one to instantly add it to the Playlist.

There are two factors to bear in mind when assembling a Playlist: You can't mix mono and stereo regions, and the recordings must all have the same resolution and sample rate. Otherwise, the Playlist window won't accept them.

Both of the above approaches to Playlist creation assume a certain level of preparation and premeditation. If you're not a premeditation kind of person, though, don't worry. Peak Pro also lets you take a more free-form approach to assembling Playlists.

> **Tool Tips:**
> **PLAYS WELL WITH OTHERS**
> When creating Playlists with regions from multiple audio files, remember that the regions must all come from files with the same sampling rate and resolution. Also, you can't create a Playlist that mixes mono and stereo regions.

First, open a new Playlist window, and set it aside where you can see it. Next, open the audio file that you'd like to work with. Drag through any part of the waveform, and choose Capture Region to Playlist from the Action menu, or simply hit Command-K. Your selection is instantly turned into a region, given a default name, and added to the Playlist. It can't get much easier than that! Of course, you can go back later and rename the regions (Events) in the Playlist and even change the boundaries if you need to; nothing in the Playlist is set in stone.

To remove an Event from the Playlist, select it and click the Delete (trash can) button in the Toolbar, or just hit the Delete key. Use the Duplicate Event button (third from the left) to add a copy of an existing Event (with the same crossfade and other parameters) to the Playlist.

The Playlist has its own unlimited Undo history, which you can access when the Playlist is active. Hit Command-Z to undo the last edit. You can view the Playlist's entire Undo history by choosing Edits from the Edit menu. (Make sure the Playlist is the active window.)

> **Tool Tips: QUICK STEPS**
> Once you have created a Playlist, you can move quickly from one Event to the next by hitting the Up Arrow and Down Arrow keys. These shortcuts work during playback or when playback is stopped.

Crossfades

As Events are added to the Playlist, the corresponding regions appear in the waveform display without any overlaps or crossfades. To create a crossfade, you must overlap two adjacent regions (to provide a transition area where the crossfade can occur).

Crossfades appear onscreen automatically when an overlap occurs. The type of crossfade is indicated by a set of graph lines superimposed on the transition between regions. The same line also appears in the List View under the I-XF (Crossfade-In) and O-XF (Crossfade-Out) columns. We'll take a closer look at creating crossfades later in the chapter.

List View Setup

The List View's drag-and-drop capabilities make it easy to arrange Events and their parameters to suit each project's needs. For starters, you can reorganize the parameter columns so that the most important information is always visible onscreen. That can improve your workflow by saving you a lot of unnecessary scrolling.

Click in the heading area at the top of any column. The cursor turns into a grab hand, and you can drag the column left or right to relocate it. Most of the columns have a fixed width, but you can make a modest adjustment to the Name column. Click the divider line at the right side of the Name column heading. When the cursor turns into a left/right arrow, drag to resize the column.

Try this: It's easy to rearrange the order of Events in a Playlist. Click on an Event to select it. (Let's call it Event A.) Drag the Event up or down through the Playlist, and notice that as you pass over the other Events, they become highlighted. Drag Event A until it hovers over another Event. (Let's call it Event B.) When you release the mouse button, Event A will jump into position above Event B. Remember, to move the first Event in a Playlist into the second position, you must drag it over the third Event in the list. (This will make sense once you've tried it.)

The first column on the far left of the List View (you can move it if you want) numbers the Events as they appear in the Playlist sequence. When you click on the heading, you'll see a small triangle to the right of the # symbol. Click the triangle to reverse the order of the Events. Click it again to return to the original sequence.

Waveform View

The Waveform View offers two display modes: a traditional-looking Linear display or a two-level Staggered display. You can switch between viewing modes with the two buttons in the upper-left corner of the Waveform View area. The three radio buttons to the right of the viewing mode buttons (L, R, and L+R) let you specify whether the left channel, right channel, or a blend of the two will appear in the mono-style display.

Tool Tips: EASY ZOOM
Peak Pro uses the same keyboard shortcuts for zooming in the Playlist window as it uses in an Audio Document window: Command-] (Zoom In) and Command-[(Zoom Out).

The Linear Waveform display (see **Figure 11-8**) provides a nice big view of the regions, especially when zoomed in using the Zoom buttons in the upper-right corner. In the overlapping areas that form the crossfades, you can see which part of one region's waveform overlaps the other's, because one waveform is superimposed on the other with enough transparency to allow both waveforms to be visible.

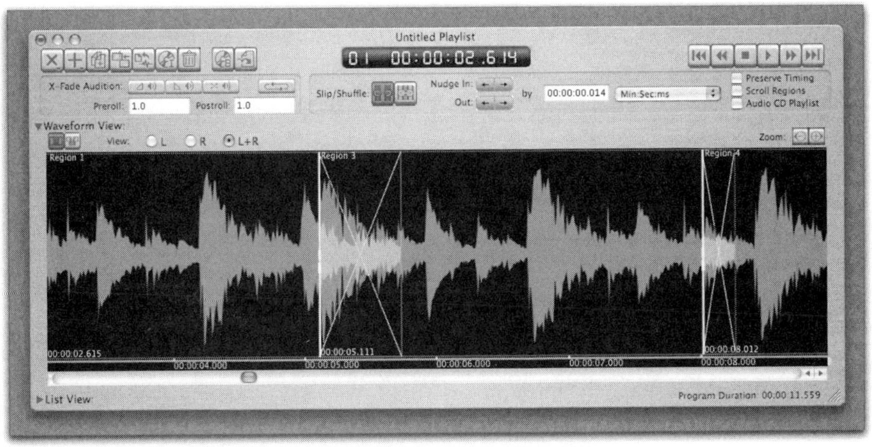

Figure 11-8
When the Waveform View presents regions in a standard monaural-style Linear display, overlapping sections appear as one waveform area superimposed on another.

In many cases, however, it's easier to see what's going on and to make adjustments when adjacent Events are not overlapping on the same plane. Peak Pro solves that problem by letting you stagger adjacent events between an upper and lower viewing level (see **Figure 11-9**). These are not separate tracks or channels as in a multitrack program. Splitting the waveform into an upper and lower level is strictly an onscreen device for improving visibility and editability.

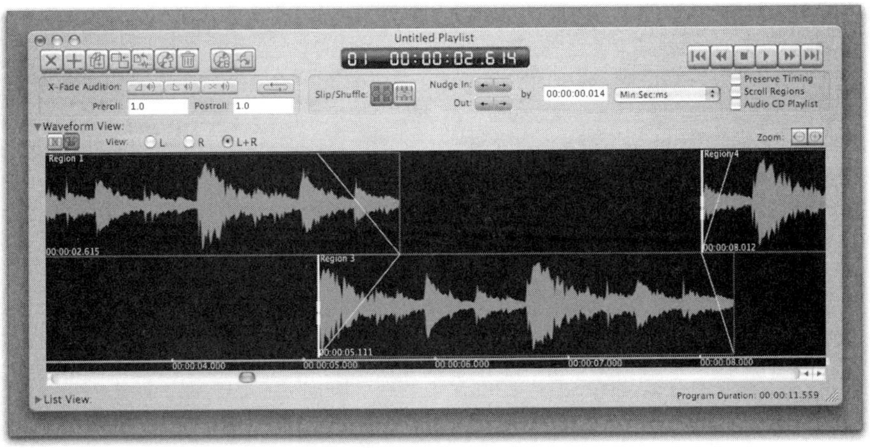

Figure 11-9
In the Waveform View's Staggered mode, adjacent regions alternate between an upper and lower display area, making it easier to see and edit region borders and crossfades.

Region Tools

Click any Event in the List View, and the corresponding waveform section becomes highlighted. When you move the cursor into a region in the Waveform View, the standard arrow cursor turns into a two-way arrow cursor. Grab any waveform

Tool Tips: HANDY OPTIONS
When using the Region Move tool to move a region in the Waveform View, hold down the Control key while dragging to move the region in 1ms increments.

Tool Tips: BORDER CROSSING
When using the Region Resize tool, hold down the Control key while dragging to move the region border in 1ms increments. Also with the Region Resize tool, click the edge of any region with a crossfade to show the crossfade's duration. Clicking and dragging gives a continuous readout of the crossfade's length (lower right) as well as the region's overall length (upper left).

segment with this Region Move tool, and drag the segment left or right to change its timing in the Playlist. When you select a region in the Waveform View by clicking with the Region Move tool, numeric displays in the upper-left and lower-right corners of the region show its start and end times.

Position the cursor at any of the region borders, and it turns into a small arrow with a bracket—the Region Resize tool. With the cursor in that mode, you can drag the edge of a region to shorten the Event (by cutting it off sooner) or to lengthen it (by revealing more of the original waveform). Notice that when you drag a region or border to a new position and let go, the List View instantly updates.

Track Start Offset & Pause Markers

As you import regions into the Playlist window, you'll notice two grab handles that appear at the left edge of each region. The upper handle is for the Track Start Offset marker, and the lower handle is for the Pause marker. Moving these markers has no effect on the sound of the Playlist if it's played straight through. They affect only the way the Playlist will be interpreted by an audio CD player after it's burned to a CD.

With the Track Start Offset marker, you can add a small offset to the start of each CD track. Some older CD players are a bit slower than new machines at unmuting the audio at the beginning of a new track when you use the CD player's controls to locate directly to the track. By setting the Track Start Offset marker to a slightly earlier point, you can ensure that the first fraction of a second of music won't be skipped by the CD player. By changing the time units to CD frames (Options > Time Units > CD Frames), you can add a precise offset in frames, as required by many record labels.

You can change a region's Track Start Offset by dragging the marker's grab handle in the Waveform View, or you can enter a number directly into the TS Offset column in the List View. Negative numbers move the marker to the area before the region start time. Positive numbers move it to the right of the start-time border. Because the List and Waveform Views are dynamically linked, any change made at one place is reflected in the other. You can choose whatever time unit (samples, seconds, bars/beats, etc.) is appropriate to the task at hand.

The lower grab handle is for the Pause marker. By dragging it to the left, you can add a pause (gap) *before* the event. When the Playlist is used to master a CD, the Pause marker will cause a CD player's time position meter to "count down" before the beginning of the next track. Pauses are also required for CD replication in some circumstances; if you're planning to turn your Playlist into a CD master, consult with the replicator to learn their requirements. As with the Track Start Offset marker, changes made to the marker are reflected in the corresponding List View column (Gap/Pause), where you can enter values directly.

Tool Tips: CURSOR CONFUSION

When the Playback cursor, Track Start Offset marker, and region start-time border all overlap (as they typically do in new regions that are selected), it can be a bit tricky to drag just the right item. Here's how to handle those left-side overlaps.

Drag the small triangle at the base of the Playback cursor to move it to another location. With the cursor over the left border, click the Track Start Offset marker to drag it to another location. Move the cursor along the left border above or below the grab handle to change from Arrow mode to Region Resize mode (small arrow with bracket). Dragging in that mode moves the region border, but not the Offset marker.

Slip & Shuffle

In addition to its two viewing modes, the Waveform View also provides two Edit modes when regions are dragged with the Region Move tool. You can toggle between the two Edit modes with the Slip and Shuffle buttons (see **Figure 11-10**) in the recessed area beneath the Counter display.

Figure 11-10
You can toggle between Slip and Shuffle modes with the buttons in the recessed area, or use the tilde (~) key.

With the Slip button (on the left) active, you can independently drag any region back and forth without affecting the timing of the other regions. With the Shuffle button (on the right) active, the selected region and all subsequent regions move as a unit. In other words, all of the regions before the selected region stay where they are, while the selected region and all regions to the right of it slide back and forth together as you drag.

If the selected region has crossfades at its beginning and end, the beginning crossfade will be altered when you drag the region. The ending crossfade, however, will remain unchanged in Shuffle mode, because the two regions that are crossfading are locked together.

Creating Crossfades

Peak Pro's graphic editing capabilities enable you to produce crossfades in two ways: by overlapping the original region boundaries or by extending the regions beyond the original markers to provide material for the crossfade.

In the first approach, simply drag one of the regions left or right until it overlaps the neighboring region. The default crossfade graph lines automatically appear. The potential pitfall when using this type of crossfade is that the very beginning of the second region may be obscured as it fades in while the first region is fading out. Choosing a fast fade-in might help, but there could still be a problem. (The same sort of thing could also occur with the end of the first region being obscured by the beginning of the second region.)

In those cases, try the second approach of dragging the region borders to reveal more of the source waveform. (The mouse cursor will turn into the Region Resize tool, a vertical bracket with an arrow, when it's in position for this type of edit.) Use the additional material to form the overlap. You can then apply the crossfade in such a way that it's almost completed by the time it reaches the second region's original start point. You can extend the first region's ending and use it in the same way if necessary. Of course, this approach only works if the audio material outside of the original region markers is compatible in the context of the current Playlist. A combination of the two approaches sometimes yields the best results.

Changing Crossfade Shapes

To change a region's current fade-in or fade-out shape, select an Event in the Playlist and double-click on the miniature graph line in the I-XF or O-XF column. You can also double-click directly on a region's fade-in or fade-out graph in the Waveform View. Either approach opens the Region Crossfade-In or Region Crossfade-Out dialog box (see **Figure 11-11**) where you can choose from the available fade types. Or, you can create your own custom fade by starting with one of the presets and dragging on the envelope breakpoints. (Add more breakpoints by clicking anywhere on the line.)

To quickly change the fade-in and fade-out shapes together, select a region in the waveform display and click the Crossfade button (with the big "X" on it) in the Playlist Toolbar. It opens a drop-down menu where you can choose one of several common crossfade types. The crossfade is applied to the transition from the end of the preceding region to the beginning of the selected region.

Crossfade Times

You can change the duration of any crossfade by selecting the appropriate region and dragging it left or right. The new settings appear in the List View area and in

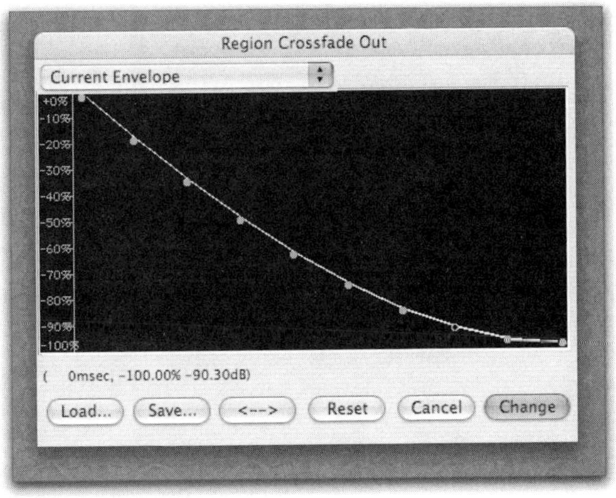

Figure 11-11
With the Region Crossfade-Out dialog box you can change a region's fade-out shape by choosing a standard preset or by creating a custom envelope graph.

the selected region's waveform display. Be careful, however, when using this approach in Slip mode with regions that have crossfades at both ends, because the durations of both crossfades will change at the same time. (One will increase as the other decreases.)

For the greatest precision in adjusting crossfade times, select an Event in the List View, and double-click the value in the Crossfade-In Time (I-XF-T) or Crossfade-Out Time (O-XF-T) column. In the dialog box that appears (see **Figure 11-12**), type the duration that you want, and click OK. This will move the selected Event to the left or right. If you're in Shuffle mode, editing the Crossfade-Out Time won't work. The event and all following events will be moved to the left or right, but the cross-fade time will remain the same.

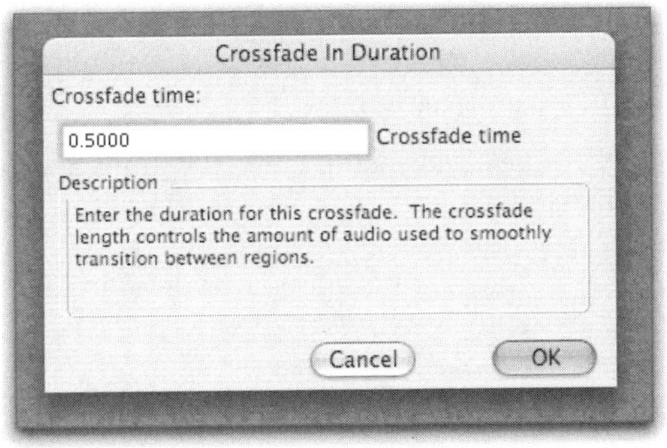

Figure 11-12
Use the Crossfade Duration dialog boxes to enter a precise fade-in or fade-out time for a crossfade.

Preserve Timing

If you want to move a crossfade along the Playlist's timeline, but you don't want to change the crossfade's duration, you can take advantage of Peak Pro's handy

Preserve Timing mode. With the Playlist in Slip mode, click the Preserve Timing checkbox in the recessed area beneath the Transport controls (see **Figure 11-13**). Select a region that has a crossfade into the following region. (Let's call them region A and region B.)

Figure 11-13
The Preserve Timing and Scroll Regions checkboxes change the contents of one or more regions without changing the overall timing of the Playlist.

Move the cursor to the end border of region A; the arrow should turn into the Region Resize tool (a small arrow with a bracket). Slowly drag region A's border to the left and right and notice what happens. The crossfade moves, but its duration stays the same, because region B's size will change.

The Preserve Timing mode maintains the overall duration of the two regions from which the crossfade was created. It does this by adding length to one region as it simultaneously subtracts from the other. In other words, the total duration of the two regions and their position on the timeline stay the same (as does the crossfade duration), even though the proportion of one region to the other changes.

Why would you want to use this feature? Suppose you were working with tempo-based music regions and you wanted to move the crossfade in an effort to find a more natural-sounding transition. In Preserve Timing mode, you could reposition the crossfade without losing the overall relationship of one region to the other.

By the way, Preserve Timing mode works even if there isn't a crossfade between the regions. In those cases, dragging the end border of a region adds or subtracts from the following region just as before, keeping the two regions anchored with the same overall duration. That's an especially handy feature for adjusting splice points when creating composite recordings from different takes.

> **Tool Tips:**
> **WELL PRESERVED**
> If you don't want to apply the Preserve Timing feature globally, you can also apply it on a case-by-case basis. Just hold down the Option key while dragging with the Region Resize tool. (This only works if the Preserve Timing checkbox is not active.)

Scroll Regions

In addition to Preserve Timing mode, Peak Pro offers another mode for modifying regions while maintaining the duration of the Playlist. With the Scroll Regions checkbox selected (see **Figure 11-13**), you can drag a waveform left and right within its region boundaries but without changing the duration or timing of the region.

Try this: Click the Scroll Regions checkbox and move the cursor over one of the region waveforms. When you see the Region Move tool, click-and-drag to the left or right. The waveform moves within the region borders, revealing a new area from the original source audio file. In other words, the region stays locked in place, but the *content* changes.

To activate the Scroll Regions mode temporarily (without using the checkbox), hold down the Option key as you drag the waveform with the Region Move tool. You can even "scroll" several regions at once by clicking on two or more regions while holding down the Shift key. With the regions selected, let go of the Shift key and hold down the Option key. Drag any one of the selected waveforms and all of the waveforms scroll together.

It's important to keep in mind that Scroll Regions mode only works if there is more waveform available in the source file than is visible in the Playlist region. If the region represents the entire audio document, there won't be any new waveform to reveal, and Scroll Regions mode won't work.

Synchronize Regions

Although it isn't always necessary, for many projects it makes sense to update the region markers in the source files so that they match the corresponding region borders in the Playlist window.

The Playlist regions may have started out the same as the source-file regions when you first created the Playlist, but after making various edits such as resizing the regions or scrolling the region waveforms, the original regions may be quite different from the Playlist versions.

That's because Peak Pro does not automatically update the source files every time you edit one of the Playlist regions. If it did, it could cause all kinds of trouble when you try to use one region in several Playlists. To keep things simple, Peak Pro lets you "synchronize" the source regions with their Playlist counterparts on a case-by-case basis.

To update the source regions, select one or more regions and click the Synchronize Regions button (fifth from the left) in the Playlist Toolbar. The source regions are repositioned to reflect the editing changes. Don't forget to save the source Audio Document to preserve the new marker positions.

Butt to Previous Event

The Playlist has another handy button, just to the left of the Synchronize Regions button in the Toolbar. The Butt to Previous Event button (fourth from the left) snaps any selected region's start border to the end border of the previous region.

Select any number of regions, and click the button. The regions jump together to form a tight contiguous group of Events without gaps or crossfades. (If you do this in the middle of a Playlist, and if the selected group of Events has crossfades, when the command gets rid of the internal crossfades it will quite likely create a new crossfade at the end of the selected area.) This is a great way to get back to a good starting place if your editing attempts have gone astray. Be careful though, the Butt to Previous Event command overrides Slip and Shuffle mode and may dramatically change the relative positions of the regions.

Crossfade Auditioning

To produce a professional-sounding Playlist, it's important to spend a little time fine-tuning your crossfades. Playing straight through the Playlist won't always reveal subtle problems at the transitions, because they usually go by too fast. To enable you to focus on just the crossfades, one at a time, Peak Pro includes the X-Fade Audition section beneath the Toolbar buttons (see **Figure 11-14**).

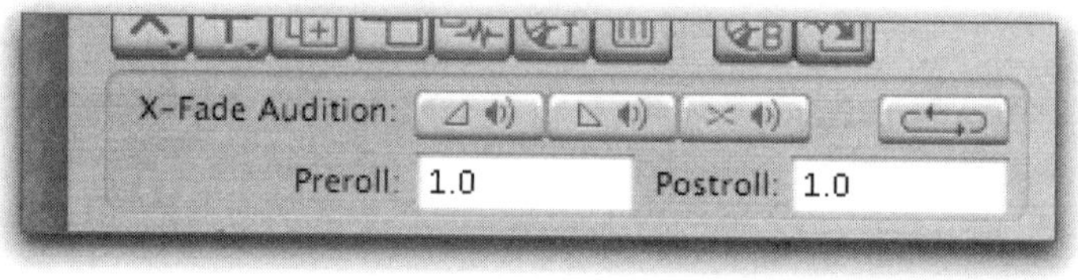

Figure 11-14
With the X-Fade Audition buttons, you can focus your attention on each part of the crossfade.

After selecting a region, you can use the buttons to play just the fade-in part of the crossfade, just the fade-out part, or both parts together. By switching from one button to another, you can scrutinize each part of the crossfade and make adjustments as needed. The Preroll and Postroll fields let you specify an amount of playback time preceding and following the audition. The Audition Loop button (on the right) lets you play the audition section repeatedly, so you don't have to keep clicking buttons to initiate playback.

The Nudge In and Out arrows (in the other recessed area) enable you to shift the regions to fine-tune the crossfades. You can specify an increment for nudging in any of several time units provided in the drop-down menu.

Tool Tips: FADING FAST
Instead of using the Fade-In, Fade-Out, and Crossfade Audition buttons in the Waveform View, you can use the following keyboard shortcuts: I (Fade-In), O (Fade-Out), X (Crossfade). Hit the L key to toggle the Loop Audition button on and off.

Adding Effects

Peak Pro lets you use any of your BIAS, VST, and AU plug-ins to process the Events in a Playlist. In fact, you can have a different set of real-time effects for each Event. To add one or more effects to an Event, select an Event in the List View or Waveform View area, and then open the Vbox window (Plug-Ins > Vbox).

As described in Chapter 9, Vbox lets you combine effects plug-ins with complete flexibility. Add one or more effects to the Vbox Matrix and when you're satisfied with the arrangement, click the drop-down menu button in the Vbox column of the List View area (see **Figure 11-15**). If you don't have a large screen, you'll probably have to scroll horizontally to the far right to see it.

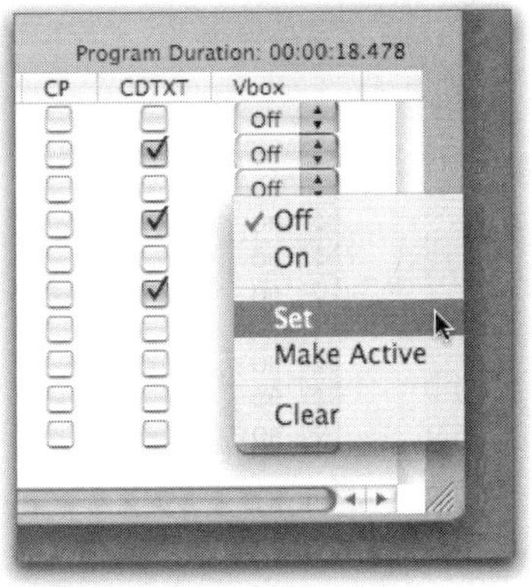

Figure 11-15
Use the List View's Vbox drop-down menus to apply plug-in effects to Events. You can use different combinations of effects for each of the Events in the Playlist.

In the Vbox drop-down menu, choose Set to apply the current Vbox configuration to the selected Event. You can follow the same procedure to add different Vbox setups (with the same or different effects) to the other Events.

Tool Tips: SMOOTH TRANSITIONS

You might hear a clicking sound between Playlist Events when using some plug-in effects with Vbox. That's because Vbox activates and deactivates the effects as needed. If you're using different effects for the various Events in a Playlist, and you experience this problem, here's a simple workaround.

Instead of creating a completely new Vbox setup for each Event, try loading all of the desired plug-ins for the whole Playlist into Vbox at once. Configure them in such a way that you can turn on the necessary effects by muting or bypassing the unwanted plug-ins. Then use a "snapshot" of each different muted/unmuted combination as needed for each Event.

Here's the procedure. With Vbox open and loaded with all of the effects that you'll need for the Playlist, create the first snapshot by muting or bypassing the unwanted effects. Click the Set command in the Playlist's drop-down Vbox menu to assign the current state to the first Event. Then select another Event, make the appropriate mute/unmute changes to Vbox, and select Set for that Event. Continue until all of the Events that need processing have appropriate configurations assigned to them. To review any setup, select an Event and choose Make Active to view that Event's current state.

Vbox doesn't automatically update the appearance of the Matrix display each time you click on an Event. So if you want to go back and review or edit one of the Vbox setups, select the Event, and choose Make Active in the Vbox drop-down menu at the right side of the Playlist. That updates the Matrix display to show the associated effects for the selected Event. If you make any changes, choose Set again from the Vbox menu. If necessary, you can choose Clear to remove all of the effects plug-ins from a selected Event.

Bouncing a Playlist

It's important to keep in mind that in order to open any Playlist document in the future, the original source audio documents, with all the original regions intact, must be available to properly reconstruct the playback. If you work with a lot of audio files and create a large library of Playlists, that can eventually get to be a problem. Fortunately, Peak Pro lets you record (bounce) any Playlist to disk, which makes it easy to archive various Playlist arrangements. It also lets you open them in a wide variety of other audio programs.

In effect, bouncing is like making a digital recording of the Playlist, complete with all of its crossfades and plug-in processing. Actually, it's even better than making a recording, because Peak Pro also saves the Events as markers, which it labels according to the original Event names.

The procedure is simple. Create a Playlist, and then with the Playlist window active, choose Select All from the Edit menu, or just hit Command-A. To bounce just part of a Playlist, select the starting Event, hold down the Shift key, and select the ending Event. You can bounce any part of a Playlist as long as the Events are contiguous.

Tool Tips:
PLAYING WITH WORDS
If you just want to keep a record of a Playlist, but you don't need to make an actual recording, you can create a text document with the basic Playlist information in it. With the Playlist window active, choose Export as Text from the File menu. That produces a generic text document with the Event list names, the Event timings, the crossfade timings, and several other useful parameter settings.

After making the necessary selections, click the Bounce Playlist button (first on the right) in the Toolbar to open the Bounce Playlist dialog box (see **Figure 11-16**). It lets you specify the audio-file resolution and whether to apply POW-r dithering if the audio will end up at a lower resolution than it started out. You can also specify the format of the resulting audio file: AIFF, Sound Designer II, Jam Image file (for opening directly in Roxio Jam), or Disc Description Protocol (DDP).

The DDP format is an industry standard that is used in the preparation of commercial CDs. It is employed by many major record labels, and is offered as an optional feature by BIAS. Check the BIAS Web site (www.bias-inc.com) for more information on adding DDP capability.

In the Bounce Playlist dialog box, you can use the set of radio buttons to specify whether the Events should be identified with region markers, with regular markers, or should be left without any indication. When you've made your selections, click the Bounce button to open a Save dialog box where you can name the new audio file. Click the Save button to bounce the Playlist.

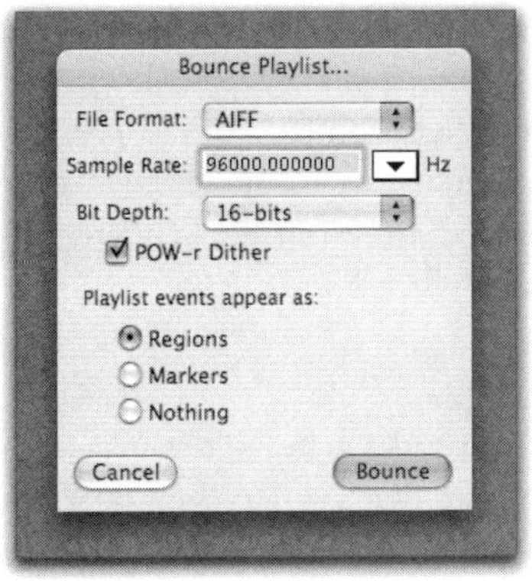

Figure 11-16
The Bounce Playlist dialog box lets you specify the resolution and format of the resulting audio file.

Mastering CDs

In Peak Pro you can burn an audio CD directly from any Audio Document window. Just create regions where you want the tracks to be (Shift-Command-R), and choose Burn Audio CD from the File menu. At the bottom of the Burn Audio CD dialog box that appears (see **Figure 11-17**), specify that the regions should be treated as tracks. Then click the Burn button. If you don't click the Regions Are Tracks option (or if there are no regions), Peak Pro will burn the entire audio document as a single track.

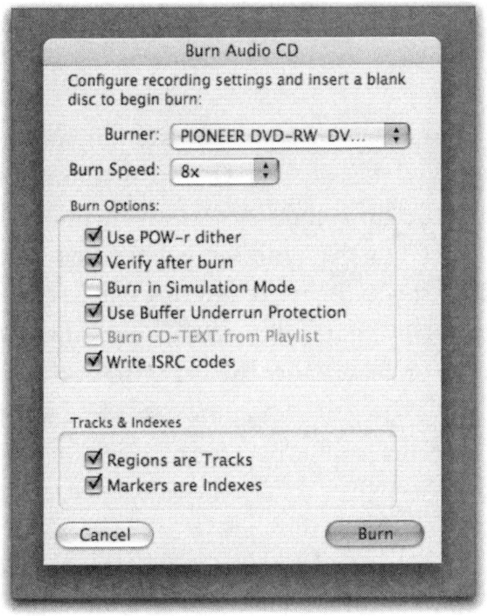

Figure 11-17
The Burn Audio CD dialog box lets you set the burn speed and other criteria before burning the disc.

This is a quick and easy way to archive an audio file or to simply save it for playback by other people. However, the process of mastering a fully Red Book-compatible audio CD involves several additional considerations and a few extra steps. Fortunately, Peak Pro's Playlist window is ideally set up to handle those tasks.

The first step, of course, is to create the Playlist that will eventually represent your finished CD. Organize the Events so that they flow logically (or at least artistically) from one to another. Audition the entire Playlist while paying special attention to how each Event relates to its neighbors. You can rearrange Events by dragging them to different locations in the List View.

Mind the Gap

In the Gap column, you can add a pause (a period of silence) between tracks. Double-click an Event's gap number to open the Playlist Event Gap Time dialog box (see **Figure 11-18**). Enter a number of seconds, and click the OK button. The pause will be added just before the beginning of that track. (Naturally, this only applies where crossfades aren't being used between tracks.)

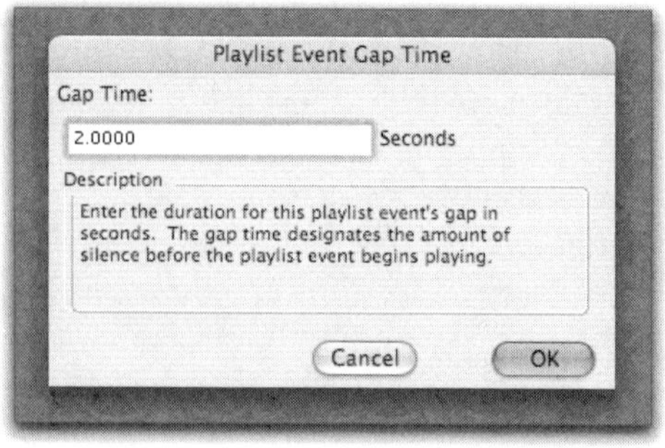

Figure 11-18
Use the Playlist Event Gap Time dialog box to specify how long a pause should be before each track.

If you aren't sure how much of a gap to use, start out with a two-second gap between tracks, and see how that sounds when you audition the Playlist. Setting the gap can often be tricky, because the listener's perception of how much time has elapsed is greatly influenced by the audio on either side of the pause. There's no scientific formula for success; you'll have to employ a little trial and error.

For example, a two-second gap following a long, slow fade-out will seem to be much longer than two seconds, because the very end of the fade may not be audible. (A slow fade-in following the gap can cause the same kind of problem.) Similar tracks with similar material can often get by with less of a gap than tracks that are radically different. The pause gives the listener a chance to digest the end of the previous track and prepare for something new.

On the other hand, having little or no gap between tracks is an effective way to keep the forward momentum going, which is an important technique when producing a demo CD with several tracks packed into a short space. In any case, always be sure to carefully edit the region boundaries so you'll be working with some level of consistency.

Gain No Pain

Another important area to consider is the individual gain setting for each track. Peak Pro lets you enter a gain offset to even out the level (real or perceived) of each track. You can't simply normalize your source documents and expect the various regions to work smoothly together. How loud or soft a track seems has a lot to do with how loud or soft the previous track was. One of the most important CD mastering tasks, therefore, is ensuring that no track suddenly jumps out (unless you want it to) or seems too quiet compared to the rest of the CD.

As you audition the Playlist, pay close attention to the perceived levels of the tracks. If any need adjustment, double-click the corresponding Event's setting in the Gain column to open the Playlist Event Gain dialog box (see **Figure 11-19**).

Figure 11-19
Double-click an Event's setting in the Gain column to open the Playlist Event Gain dialog box. It lets you raise or lower the overall level of an Event, so that it fits in better with the other tracks.

Enter a positive or negative value in decibels to raise or lower a track's overall level. Click the OK button, and audition the track again in context to see how well it fits with the other tracks. Be very careful when boosting the gain; it's easy to cause distortion. Try decreasing the level of the neighboring tracks if necessary. It's also easy to get into a chasing-your-tail situation, so for the best results, audition frequently and try not to lose sight of the big picture.

PQ Subcode

Except for the Vbox column at the very end, the remaining Playlist parameters after the Gain column fall into the category of PQ subcode data. The PQ subcode data includes additional bits that ensure the proper playback of the CD on any CD player. The P and Q subchannels provide information and parameter settings that are required for full Red Book (Compact Disc Digital Audio) compatibility.

For example, the P subchannel indicates the start and stop time for each track. The Q subchannel provides absolute and relative time information as well as the table of contents (TOC) information in the lead-in area of the disc. Much of the PQ subcode business is handled automatically by Peak Pro; the rest can be entered through the Playlist window.

For starters, click the Disc Info button (next to the trash can button) in the Playlist Toolbar. That opens a large dialog box where you can enter information about the CD as a whole (see **Figure 11-20**). This text-based information, such as the title, the performer's name, the composer's name, and the musical genre, is stored on the CD when it's burned and is viewable on some high-end CD players. It can also be accessed on home computers when audio CDs are played.

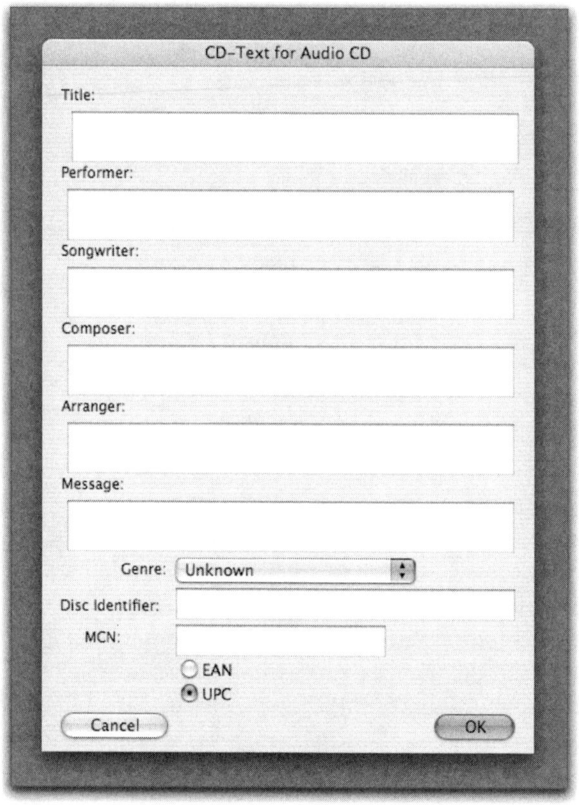

Figure 11-20
Click the Disc Info button in the Playlist Toolbar to open the CD Text dialog box. It provides fields for filling in important text-based information.

After filling out the necessary information for the disc, you can then move on to the individual tracks. In the CDTXT column in the List View, click on an Event's checkbox to add text info to the corresponding track (see **Figure 11-21**). Each track can have its own text information; click the OK button to add the info to the track.

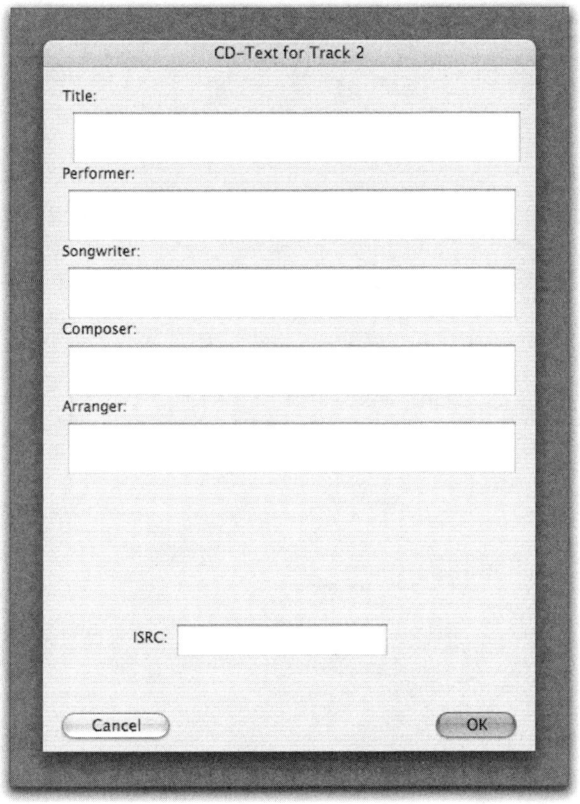

Figure 11-21
Each track can have its own text-based information, which is entered in a separate CD Text dialog box.

For many musicians, the most important part of the dialog box is the area where you enter the ISRC (International Standard Recording Code) number. This universally recognized 12-character "serial number" (part of the Q subcode) is assigned to commercially released compact discs to provide copyright identification and rights management capability. (Find out more about the ISRC at: www.ifpi.org/isrc.)

The ISRC number for each track (if added) appears in the ISRC column in the List View. You can also add the number directly in the list by double-clicking in the column and typing. The ISRC number does not become part of the subcode data (necessary for copyright tracking) unless you click the Write ISRC Codes checkbox in the Burn Audio CD dialog box (see below).

If you later change your mind about adding text to a track, uncheck the box in the CDTXT column. That removes the information when burning the disc, but you can bring the data back again by just clicking the box to activate it; the text is saved with the Playlist file.

The CP column (to the left of the CDTXT column) lets you activate the Copy Prohibit bit in the Q subcode channel. The Copy Prohibit option was added to the

> **Audio Lingo: RED BOOK**
> The Red Book standard developed by Sony and Philips in 1980 is a comprehensive manual (originally released in a red cover, hence the name) that defines the Compact Disc Digital Audio (CD-DA) format. Adhering to the Red Book standard ensures that CDs are playable on all commercial CD players. Among other things, Red Book audio must be in stereo and have a resolution of 16 bits and a sample rate of 44.1kHz.

Red Book specification primarily to prevent DAT recorders from making digital copies of CDs. Few CD players actually implement the Copy Prohibit feature, so is has become pretty much obsolete. Peak Pro includes it mainly because it's still a part of the Red Book standard.

The Emp column (next to the CP column) lets you activate a pre-emphasis feature that is part of the Q subcode. When you check the box for a track, the high frequencies are boosted (pre-emphasized) before they're burned to CD. This feature was added to the Red Book standard to prevent high-frequency loss, which is mainly a problem with older digital-to-analog converters. With the pre-emphasis turned on, the CD player automatically corrects for the boost during playback. As with the Copy Prohibit feature above, this feature has become obsolete and is rarely used.

Audio CD Playlist Mode

If you're using the Playlist window to create a Red Book-compliant CD, be sure to click on the Audio CD Playlist checkbox (see **Figure 11-13**). That puts the entire Playlist window into Audio CD mode.

With the checkbox selected, Peak Pro automatically takes care of several important parameters to ensure Red Book compatibility. A two-second gap is inserted before the first track; region-boundary edits automatically snap to the nearest CD frame; and if the total Playlist length exceeds 74 minutes, the Program Duration display (in the List View) turns red to warn you.

You can, of course, create slightly longer CDs (up to around 79 minutes) if you turn off Audio CD Playlist mode. If all else adheres to standard Red Book specs, most modern CD players can play them. But to ensure compatibility with all players, it's best to limit the length to the standard 74-minute duration.

Burning CDs

Once you've set all of the Playlist parameters and you've auditioned the Playlist to see how well the tracks work together, the remaining step is to record the tracks (and all of the other data) onto a compact disc.

Click the Burn CD button (second from the right) in the Playlist Toolbar or select Burn Audio CD in the File menu to open the Burn Audio CD dialog box (see **Figure 11-17**). Select the appropriate settings, and choose a CD burner and burn speed from the drop-down menus at the top.

At the bottom of the dialog, the Regions Are Tracks checkbox offers the option of burning the CD without creating separate tracks from the Events. The final recording should sound the same whether or not the box is checked. But with it unchecked, the track indications won't appear on the CD player's screen during playback.

For most CDs, having track indications greatly aids in navigating the disc, which is why this option is selected by default. In some cases, however, the track indications could be confusing. For example, if the Playlist is compiled from sound effects, dialog clips, or musical fragments that don't really represent bona fide tracks, you might want to uncheck the box.

By the same token, the Markers Are Indexes checkbox could be used to locate key places within a track for easier navigation (if your CD player recognizes indexes), but only if the markers are located at useful reference points. For example, because CDs are limited to 99 tracks, many sound effects and sample libraries use indexes to subdivide their large numbers of sounds.

Insert a blank CD-R in the computer's drive, and click the Burn button. Although the usual approach is to burn the entire Playlist, you can also burn just part of the Playlist by selecting a number of contiguous Events and then clicking the Burn CD button. The procedure is similar to bouncing part of a Playlist. Whether you burn some or all of the tracks, Peak Pro always burns in disc-at-once mode. In other words, the entire CD is burned in a single pass without turning off the laser between tracks. Disc-at-once mode is necessary for properly preparing CDs for commercial reproduction.

> **Audio Lingo:**
> **CD TRACKS**
> Audio CDs store their data in 2,352-byte chunks called *sectors. Tracks* are comprised of sectors (600 or more per track), and an audio compact disc can have up to 99 tracks. Some CD writers and players also support *index points,* which allow you to mark subdivisions of a track for more precise navigation. CDs are further divided into segments called *frames.* There are 75 frames per second.

What's Next?

In the next chapter, I'll take a look at using Peak Pro when working to picture. Peak Pro integrates well with Apple's QuickTime format and provides the ability to sync an audio file to a video clip with audio/video scrubbing and other powerful features. These features can be used for film and video scoring or soundtrack development for games and multimedia.

Chapter 12

Screen Gems: Soundtracks for Video and Multimedia

For many years, the standard practice in the TV and movie industry was to create workprints on ¾-inch videotape for composers and sound effects editors to use as a reference. The video workprints always had *SMPTE timecode* on one of the audio tracks and a visual timecode display called a *window burn* that appeared somewhere onscreen. The audio timecode was used to synchronize the tape with other hardware; the window burn made it possible to visually locate and identify specific frames within the movie.

Working with ¾-inch videotape was often awkward and cumbersome, and the tape decks were bulky and expensive. As movie budgets diminished and as more independent films began to appear, ½-inch VHS tape gained in popularity as a workprint medium.

The problem with all videotape workprints, however, is that they must be synchronized with your other equipment. Locking a video tape deck to an audio tape deck requires an expensive piece of hardware called a synchronizer. Locking a video tape to a computer running audio software requires a SMPTE-to-MIDI-timecode converter. (MIDI timecode—MTC—is essentially a version of SMPTE timecode that a computer can understand.) In either case, you're still stuck with a system that requires frequent tape shuttling, starting, stopping, and time-consuming rewinding.

Although many film composers and sound effects editors still use video workprints, a newer medium has recently gained considerable popularity: QuickTime. In fact, the trend in many studios is to provide the workprint on disc in the form of a QuickTime movie with a timecode window burn, just as in the videotape counterpart.

The advantages of using QuickTime are numerous. You don't need any special hardware (except your computer) to run the movie, and by opening the movie inside an audio program such as Peak Pro, you can gain subframe-accurate synchronization as well as full access to any point in the film with no rewind or fast-forward time. When you start, stop, or rewind in Peak Pro's Transport window, the movie does the same thing at precisely the same time. What's more, as you scrub forward and back through a waveform display in Peak Pro, the movie follows along, never losing sync.

Tool Tips: PASSING TIME

Peak Pro's elapsed time and SMPTE timecode displays are very similar. They both indicate the passing of time in hours:minutes:seconds and subdivisions of a second. For elapsed time, the subdivisions are milliseconds; for SMPTE timecode, they're either film or video frames.

The different SMPTE timecode types are for different media and their associated frame rates: 24 fps (frames per second) is the standard for film, 25 fps is the European standard for video, 29.97 fps is the American standard for color video, and 30 fps is used mainly for audio-only synchronization, multimedia, and black-and-white video. In addition, Peak Pro version 5 can also display SMPTE timecode rates for High Definition video.

As computers become faster and multiple-monitor systems become commonplace, videotape workprints will likely disappear in favor of QuickTime workprints distributed on disc or through the Internet. Video editors and multimedia developers have already discovered the power of integrating Peak Pro with Final Cut Pro, Apple's blockbuster video editing and DVD authoring software. Beginning film score composers and jingle writers can try their hand at editing new music and combining it with existing QuickTime movies.

Movie Window

Although you can't use Peak Pro to edit the video part of a QuickTime movie, you can open a movie's soundtrack and apply any of Peak Pro's editing and processing tools to the audio part of the file. Peak Pro automatically opens the QuickTime movie in a dedicated Movie window, extracts the soundtrack, and opens it in a separate Audio Document window (see **Figure 12-1**).

If you don't want the Movie window taking up space onscreen, go to the Window menu and click on Movie to deselect it. To resize the window, go to the Options menu and select Movie to open a cascading submenu with three window-size options: Half Size, Original Size, and Double Size. These are relative sizes based on the movie's original dimensions (not on any specific settings), so the actual sizes may vary from file to file. You don't have to stop the movie playback to change from one size to another.

Tool Tips: GROWING PANES

You can change the size of the Movie window with the green "Grow" button in the upper-left corner. With the window at original size, click the button to expand the window to double size. Click it again to jump back to original size. Control-Option-click the button to shrink the window to half size. Click the button again—but without any keys down—to jump back to original size. With the Control-Option-click combination, you can jump directly from double size to half size. All of these changes can be made as the movie plays.

Figure 12-1
When you open a QuickTime movie, Peak Pro extracts the audio track and displays the video and audio in separate windows.

Editing Soundtracks

To edit a QuickTime soundtrack, begin by opening the movie within Peak Pro. Choose the Open command in the File menu, use the dialog box to navigate to the movie that you want, and click the Open button. The soundtrack appears in its own window ready for editing.

When you place the Insertion Point in the waveform by clicking with the mouse, the movie jumps to the corresponding movie frame. Scrubbing through the waveform scrubs the movie as well; the Movie and Audio Document windows remain in tight sync. That makes it possible to perform all of the usual kinds of edits while observing the relationship between audio and video.

When you're through editing the audio file, choose the Save As command from Peak Pro's File menu to save the QuickTime movie with its new soundtrack.

Keep in mind, however, that the original audio/video relationship can only remain intact if you don't change the length of the audio track. In other words, be careful when using editing commands such as cut, paste, insert, or delete that typically alter the length of the audio file. Instead of using Copy and Paste, for example, try using Copy and Replace (where appropriate) to avoid extending the waveform's length.

Removing Unwanted Sounds

The above caveat is especially relevant when you're trying to remove sudden unwanted noises from a recording. If a narrator coughs between words, the drummer drops a stick during a pause, the guitarist bumps the mic stand, or a car horn beeps in the distance during a take, it's easy to remove these problems (if they're in the clear) by cutting them out in Peak Pro.

But simply deleting the unwanted sounds will throw off the picture-to-soundtrack relationship from the edit point on. Lip movements won't match the spoken words, sound effects won't match onscreen actions, and music hits won't arrive at exactly the right place. In general, if the soundtrack becomes shorter after editing, the movie will continue at the end without sound. If the soundtrack becomes longer, the movie will display blank frames (beyond the original ending) until the soundtrack ends.

The typical strategy, therefore, is to replace the bad sound with an equal length of good sound. For example, let's take the cough from the aforementioned narrator. If the recording was made in a quiet studio, the fastest and easiest solution is to use Peak Pro's Silence command.

Scrub through the waveform to locate the cough, and select it by dragging through it (see **Figure 12-2**). Audition the cough by hitting the Spacebar to make sure that all of the cough is selected. With the cough still selected, choose Silence from the Edit menu. Peak Pro replaces the cough with pure silence (see **Figure 12-3**).

In many cases the Silence command doesn't provide a seamless match with the rest of the waveform, because unless the recording was made in a soundproof anechoic chamber, there's always some ambient sound in the room. This *room tone* is often subtle, but it can be important. If you use the Silence command and you notice a drop-off in the background sound (it's particularly noticeable with outdoor recordings), you'll have to use the next approach.

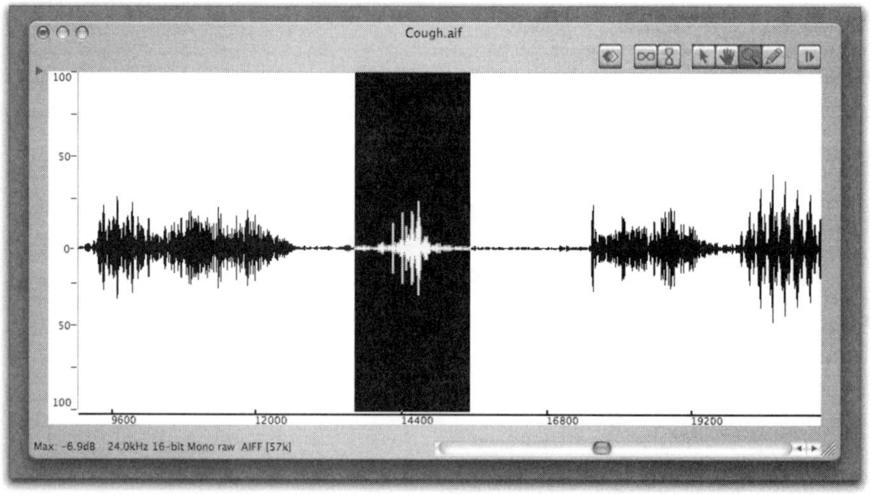

Figure 12-2
Locate the cough (or other unwanted noise) and select it.

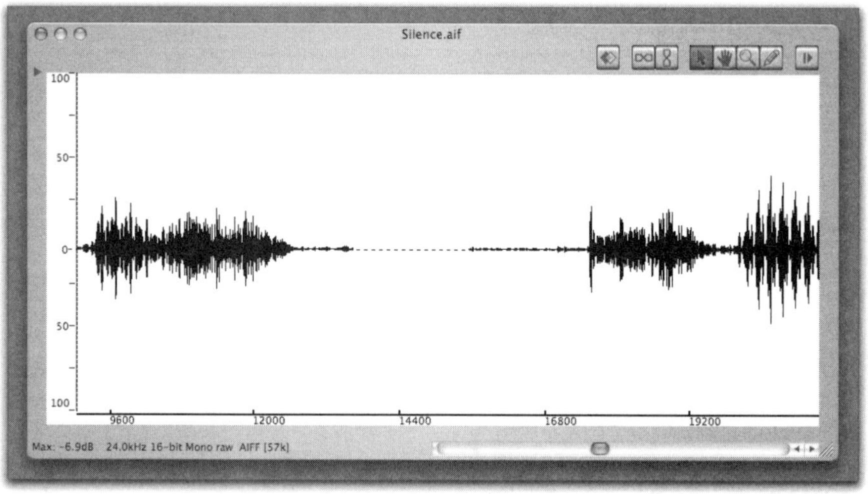

Figure 12-3
The Silence command replaces the selected audio with the same length of complete silence.

Patching with Ambience.
The best way to remove a sound without any tell-tale sign is to replace it with a piece of "silence" from the recording itself. In other words, capture a piece of good, clean room tone and press it into service. The trick is to make sure that the unwanted noise and the replacement background sound are exactly the same length. Here's one approach.

Locate the cough and drag through it to select it. Choose New Region from the Action menu (Shift-Command-R) to mark the boundaries of the selection (see **Figure 12-4**). You can adjust the beginning and end of the region by dragging each marker. When you're sure that the entire cough is selected, hit Shift-Command-R again to generate a second set of region markers on top of the first set.

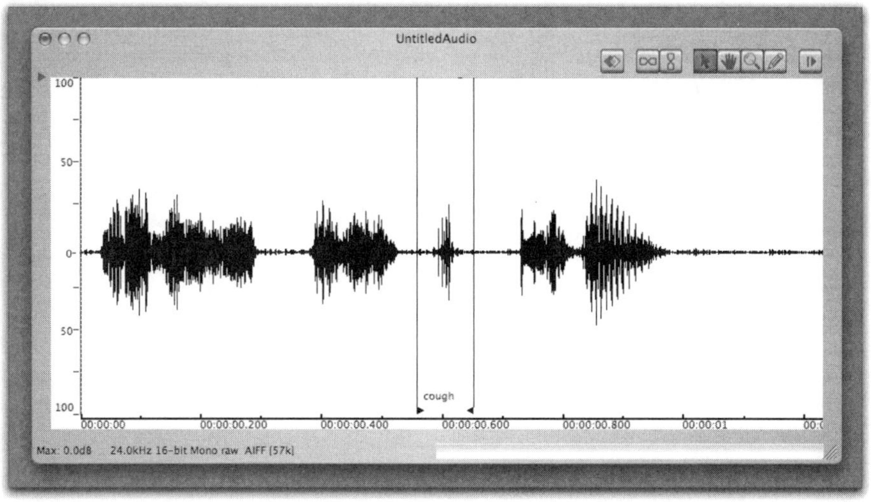

Figure 12-4
Select the cough or other unwanted sound and use the New Region command to mark its boundaries. Repeat the command a second time to generate an overlapping set of markers.

Next, locate a place in the recording where no one is speaking or playing an instrument—a place with clean room tone. The usual places are at the beginning or end of the recording and during pauses, especially between takes.

After finding some good background sound, return to the overlapping regions. Click the Horizontal Lock button at the top of the Audio Document window (or just hold down the Option key), and drag one of the End markers (see **Figure 12-5**). The Start marker that corresponds to that marker should follow in parallel as you drag. The other set of markers should stay where they are, surrounding the cough. Continue dragging until the region outlines a useable section of room tone. If you've followed these steps accurately, both regions will still be the same length (see **Figure 12-6**).

Command-click between the room-tone markers to select the audio in the region, and choose Copy from the Edit menu (Command-C). Then, Command-click between the other markers to select that region, and choose Paste from the Edit menu (Command-V). The room tone completely replaces the cough, and because the two regions are exactly the same length, the soundtrack remains in sync with the picture.

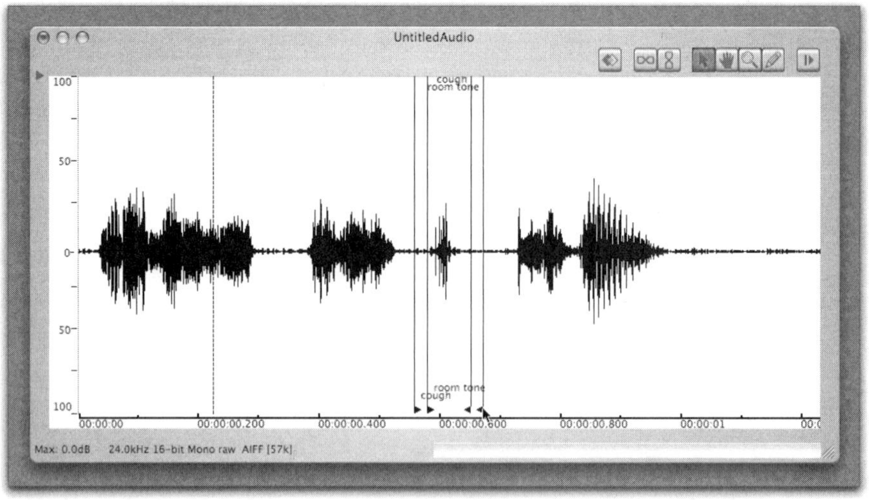

Figure 12-5
While holding the Option key, drag one of the End markers to separate one set of region markers from the other without changing its size.

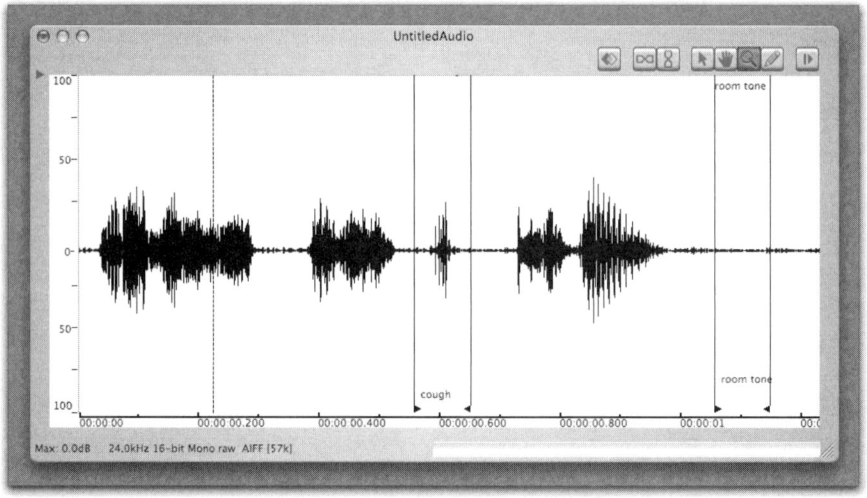

Figure 12-6
Drag one of the regions onto a useable section of room tone. Both regions should still be the same length.

Multitrack QuickTime

Although most QuickTime movies have only a single mono or stereo soundtrack, QuickTime actually lets you combine several different audio and video tracks in a movie. You can even include MIDI tracks (called Music Tracks) that use Quick-Time's built-in QuickTime Musical Instrument samples for playback. Adding tracks to a QuickTime movie is very simple, but you must first upgrade from the free (and rather limited) QuickTime Player to the much more powerful QuickTime Pro. (You can purchase the upgrade online at www.apple.com/quicktime.)

In QuickTime Pro, open the movie that you'd like to work with and choose Enable Tracks in QuickTime's Edit menu. That opens the Enable Tracks dialog box where you can view all of the tracks that comprise the movie (see **Figure 12-7**). The On/Off button in front of each track lets you enable or disable the track during playback. If you want to remove a track completely, choose Delete Tracks in the Edit menu, select a track to eliminate, and click the Delete button. Use the Extract Tracks command in the same menu to copy a selected track into a separate QuickTime window.

Figure 12-7
In QuickTime Pro's Enable Tracks dialog box you can view all of the tracks in a movie.

Combining audio tracks in QuickTime offers a number of creative possibilities. For example, you could record and edit a drum track, a background music track, and a voice-over track in Peak Pro and save them as separate files. Then import them into a movie with QuickTime Pro. Or you could have narration tracks in several languages and enable the appropriate one as needed according to where the movie is being sent. In both cases, by keeping the tracks as separate files and combining them in QuickTime Pro, you can edit individual tracks without affecting the others.

After preparing and saving your audio files in Peak Pro, open the movie in QuickTime Pro that you want to add the tracks to. Choose Import from the File menu and select one of your audio files; it will appear in its own QuickTime window (see **Figure 12-8**).

Figure 12-8
An audio-only QuickTime movie looks like this.

With this audio-only QuickTime window active, choose Select All (Command-A) and then Copy (Command-C) from the Edit menu. Click on the movie window where you want to add the tracks (to make the window active), move the playback indicator (the little sliding triangle) to the place where you want the audio track to begin, and choose the Add command (Option-Command-V) from the Edit menu. Repeat the same process to add other audio files to the movie. When you're done, choose Enable Tracks from the Edit menu to verify that all the tracks are present.

Peak Pro can open and play back QuickTime movies with multiple audio tracks, but because Peak Pro only lets you work on one audio file at a time, you must decide in advance which track to edit. When you open a multitrack QuickTime movie (choose Open from the File menu), Peak Pro first presents the QuickTime Document Sound Tracks dialog box (see **Figure 12-9**). It lists the audio tracks present in the movie and lets you select one. When you click the Edit button, the audio track appears in an Audio Document window, and the movie appears in its own Movie window.

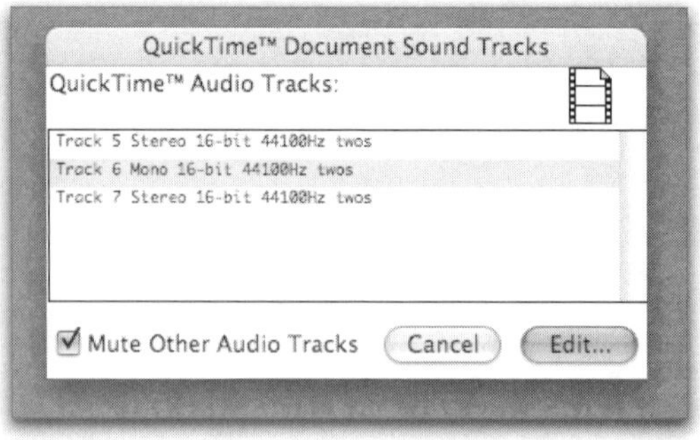

Figure 12-9
For multitrack QuickTime movies, Peak Pro presents a dialog box where you select which audio track to open in the Audio Document window.

The Mute Other Audio Tracks checkbox lets you turn off the audio tracks that aren't being edited, so you can hear what you're doing as you work on the file. If you need to maintain a sense of context as you edit, uncheck the box.

The Movie Soundtracks command in Peak Pro's Movie submenu (Options > Movie > Movie Soundtracks) opens the QuickTime Audio Tracks dialog box (see **Figure 12-10**). It lists all of the soundtracks in the movie. If the movie you're working on has two or more tracks, you can enable or disable each one by selecting it and clicking the appropriate button. You can also simply double-click a track to toggle it between the enabled and disabled state. When it's enabled, the track name jumps slightly to the left; when it's disabled, the name moves slightly to the right.

The QuickTime Audio Tracks dialog box offers an easy way to solo tracks or experiment with different submixes. When you have the combination of tracks that you want, click the Set button to accept the changes and close the dialog box.

Figure 12-10
The Movie Soundtracks command in the Movie menu shows all of the soundtracks in the current QuickTime file. You can use the dialog box to enable or disable audio tracks or to experiment with submixes.

Fixing the Mix

Working with multilayer QuickTime soundtracks enables you to create a fuller and more realistic sound field by carefully panning the sounds in each of the tracks. In the real world, however, the recordings that you have to work with may not always be ideal. For example, the dialog may have been recorded in mono with a lapel mic. Or the location sound may have been recorded on a single channel of a stereo track.

These kinds of problems make it difficult to properly place the sounds where you want them, because neither Peak Pro (which focuses on one document at a time) nor QuickTime Pro includes a mixing board utility. Fortunately, Peak Pro has the necessary tools for individually preparing the audio files as well as for adjusting the positions of the sounds in each track.

Proper Place

Let's say you have a movie in which two people are having a conversation and each was recorded separately with a mono lapel mic. Ideally, you would want to pan one person to the left and one person to the right. But with two mono files, you're stuck, because both sounds will be centered in the mix.

The quickest and easiest solution is to convert each of the mono files into a stereo file. Open one of the mono files and choose Mono To Stereo in the DSP menu. Move the Pan slider to the left (perhaps around 80 percent), and click the OK button (see **Figure 12-11**). This yields a stereo file with strong emphasis on the left. Repeat the process for the other audio file, but move the Pan slider to the right by the same amount.

Figure 12-11
To pan mono sounds to the right or left you must first convert them to stereo using the Mono To Stereo dialog box.

When combined in QuickTime Pro, your two dialog tracks will be spread decisively to the left and right. Make sure that you correlate the pan position of each track with the onscreen position of the corresponding actor. Keeping the two dialog tracks as separate files enables you to edit them independently at a later date if the need should arise.

Moveable Feast

For a more sophisticated solution, use Peak Pro's Panner command. Convert each file from mono to stereo as before, but this time leave the Pan slider in the center (zero percent) position. When you click the OK button, you'll get a "stereo" file with the same waveform in each channel.

Now open the Panner command in the DSP menu (see **Figure 12-12**). Using the customizable graph, you can control the sound's left/right position and have it change over time. For example, if the actor starts on the left side of the screen and walks from left to right while talking, you can have the audio move across the stereo field as well. (For more on the Panner command, see Chapter 7.)

With separate Panner graphs for the two dialog tracks, you can create some realistic audio movement as the actors change position. The Panner command is especially effective with sound effects. For example, you could use it to make the sound of a motorcycle move across the stereo field as it zooms across the screen.

On Location

The case with the stereo location sound file in which most or all of the audio was recorded on only one channel is a bit trickier. Open the file and choose Stereo to Mono in the DSP menu. In the Stereo To Mono Conversion dialog box (see **Figure 12-13**), drag the Pan slider all the way toward the side that corresponds to the good channel. (You're essentially throwing out the bad channel and keeping all of the good channel.) Then click the OK button. You should now have a mono audio file containing only the good channel's contents.

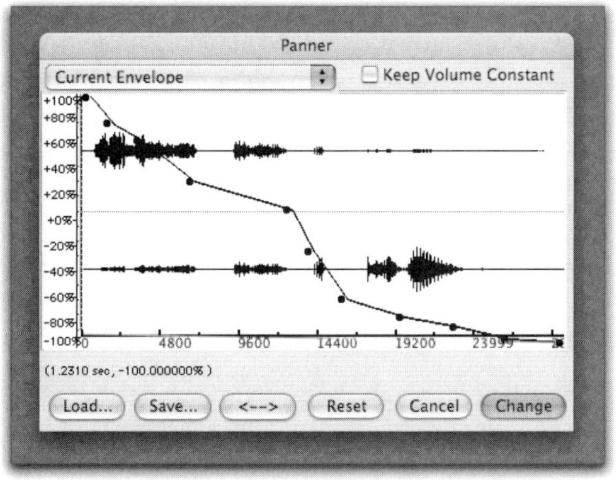

Figure 12-12
The Panner command's customizable graph lets you change panning positions over time.

Figure 12-13
You can eliminate a bad channel in a stereo file by moving the slider all the way to one side in the Stereo To Mono dialog box.

Having discarded the unwanted channel, you can convert back to stereo. Choose the Mono To Stereo command in the DSP menu and leave the Pan slider in the center (zero percent). When you click the OK button, Peak Pro converts the file to "stereo." You can now use the Panner command as described above to adjust the sound and even have it change over time if necessary. When you have the audio processed the way you want, save the file and add it to your QuickTime movie.

Other Edits

Some of the other typical problems that occur in soundtracks have already been covered in earlier chapters. For example, clicks and pops commonly appear in soundtracks, not only from the recording process, but also as a result of edits made in a program that isn't a specialized audio application.

High-end video editing programs, such as Apple's Final Cut Pro, typically offer subframe editing resolutions down to around 1/100 of a frame. That's pretty good for working with video, but it's not good enough for the kinds of microsurgery that audio files often require.

> **Tool Tips:**
> **CONVERSION POINT**
> You can use Peak Pro as a handy converter if you're working with standard minutes and seconds and want to know what the SMPTE equivalent is (or vice versa). Go to Options > Time Units and choose Min:Sec:ms. Click to set the Insertion Point anywhere in the waveform to get an elapsed time reading in the Transport window for that spot. Now return to Options > Time Units and choose one of the SMPTE rates. The Transport window display instantly changes to the SMPTE equivalent.

Because Peak Pro can function at the single-sample level, it can offer an editing resolution that is around 16 times more precise (for a 30 frame-per-second video with a 48kHz soundtrack). That means you can zoom in on a single spike in the soundtrack's waveform and zap it with the Magic Pencil tool. It also means that edits can always be restricted to zero-crossing points to avoid adding clicks and pops from the editing process itself. See Chapter 6 for more on using the Pencil and Magic Pencil tools as well as other tools, such as the DC Offset command, for fixing problems in audio files.

Another common soundtrack problem is the need to change the overall duration of the recording to accommodate last-minute cuts in the video. Cutting one or two seconds from a 60-second video spot can cause some serious headaches for the audio producer, who must create a new soundtrack that starts and stops precisely with the visuals. Fortunately, Peak Pro's Change Duration command can solve many such problems by letting you stretch or shrink the audio without changing the pitch. For a close look at the Change Duration command, see Chapter 7.

And finally, don't forget the value of a good EQ in taming many kinds of noise. For example, if your vocal soundtrack is marred by an intermittent low-frequency rumble, such as the wind noise that often occurs during outdoor recordings, open Freq in Vbox or in one of Peak Pro's inserts.

Using Freq, you can create a highpass filter that rolls off the frequencies below the range of human speech (see **Figure 12-14**). For high-pitched mechanical or electrical noises, create a lowpass filter that targets the annoying high-frequency sounds. With careful adjustment (you can listen to the changes in real time as you make them), it's often possible to reduce the distracting noise without causing deterioration to sounds in the rest of the frequency range. See Chapter 7 for a closer look at Freq.

Final Cut Pro

One of the most popular ways in which Peak Pro is used is as an integrated audio editor for Final Cut Pro. If you set up Peak Pro as the program's dedicated audio

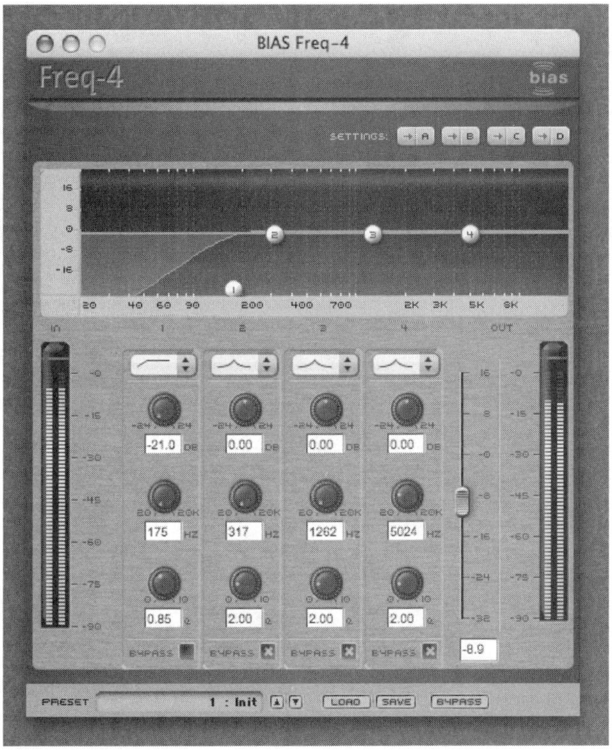

Figure 12-14
You can use Freq to create a highpass filter that selectively targets low-frequency noise.

editor, you can quickly send audio tracks from Final Cut Pro to Peak Pro and back again. Here's how to set it up.

After launching Final Cut Pro, choose System Settings from the Final Cut Pro menu and click the External Editors tab in the System Settings dialog box (see **Figure 12-15**). In the External Editors section, click the Set button in the Audio Files category. Use the dialog box to navigate to the Applications folder, and locate and highlight the Peak Pro application icon. Click the Choose button to designate Peak Pro as the external audio editor.

Repeat the same process for the Video Files category to designate Peak Pro as the external video editor, and then close the System Settings window. Why choose Peak Pro as the external video editor too? Because Final Cut Pro can use several kinds of files in a project, and some kinds of video files, such as QuickTime movies, include their own audio tracks.

With Peak Pro designated as the external video editor, you can open QuickTime movies in Peak Pro and edit the soundtracks as described earlier in this chapter. The QuickTime audio and video tracks remain in sync as you edit the soundtrack, and when you're through, you can send the video clip back to Final Cut Pro.

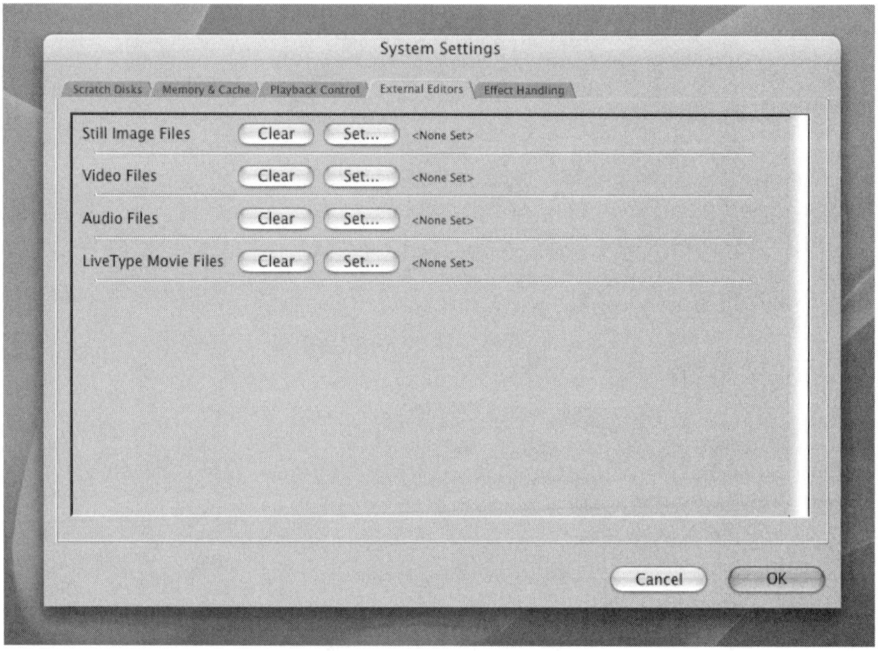

Figure 12-15
The External Editors tab in Final Cut Pro's System Settings dialog box opens a page where you can assign Peak Pro as the program's audio editor.

What's Next?

In the next chapter, we'll take a look at Peak Pro's powerful batch processing capabilities and examine how they can speed up your workflow. We'll also look at how Peak Pro's support for Apple Events can help you manage your growing library of sound files by integrating Peak Pro with database programs such as FileMaker Pro.

Chapter 13

Piles of Files: Batch Processing and Apple Events

Whether you're working with snippets of dialog, compiling a sound effects library, or creating the ultimate sampled instrument, before long you'll find yourself buried in a virtual mountain of audio clips. Fortunately, Peak Pro offers two powerful features to help you manage large collections of files: a versatile Batch File Processor and support for Apple Events.

The Batch File Processor automates the task of processing piles of files and supports almost three dozen of Peak Pro's DSP tools and editing commands. Peak Pro's support for Apple Events makes it possible to organize and manage entire libraries of audio files, and it enables the program to work in tandem with a database program, such as File-Maker Pro, providing rapid access to your recordings when you need them.

Batch File Processor

When it comes to improving your workflow, nothing speeds things up like a powerful batch processor. Peak Pro's easy-to-use Batch File Processor lets you create a list of tasks (a batch script) and apply the processes in the list to any number of files that you want. Once you set up and activate the Batch File Processor, you can drag-and-drop audio files onto the Peak Pro icon (or alias) and have them automatically processed by the batch script that you have created. You can even drop entire folders onto the Peak Pro icon, and the program will process all of the specified types of files, including the ones inside subfolders.

Choose Batch Processor in the File menu to open the Batch File Processor dialog box (see **Figure 13-1**). The dialog box consists of three parts labeled Input, Process, and Save Changes. To begin using the Batch File Processor you must create a batch script, so turn your attention first to the Process section in the middle.

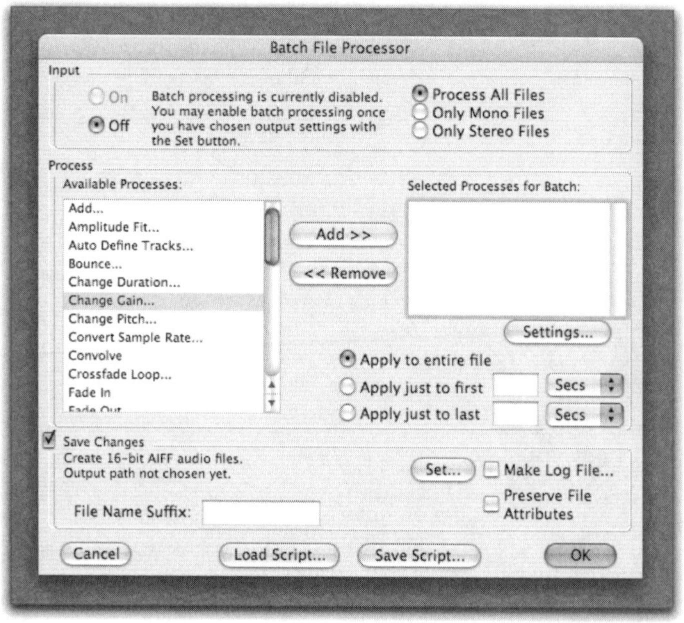

Figure 13-1
The three-part Batch File Processor dialog box has sections labeled Input, Process, and Save Changes. Begin by creating a batch script in the Process section.

Process Section

From the list on the left, select the DSP or editing commands that you want to apply to your audio documents. Click one of the items to highlight it, and then click the Add button to add it to the Batch list on the right. Or if you prefer, simply double-click an item on the left to automatically add it to the list on the right.

You can add several commands to the Batch list, and Peak Pro will apply them in the order in which they appear. You can even add the same process more than once with different settings. For example, you might normalize the file to 85 percent, apply Rappify and Phase Vocoder, and then normalize again to 95 percent before applying a fade-out (see **Figure 13-2**).

Speaking of fade-outs, a set of radio buttons beneath the Batch list lets you apply each command to only the first or last part of the audio file. In this example, you wouldn't have to fade out the entire file from beginning to end, you could fade out just the last few seconds of the file by selecting Fade Out in the Batch list and then clicking the "Apply just to last" radio button. You specify how much of the file is to be affected by entering an amount in seconds or as a percentage of the whole document.

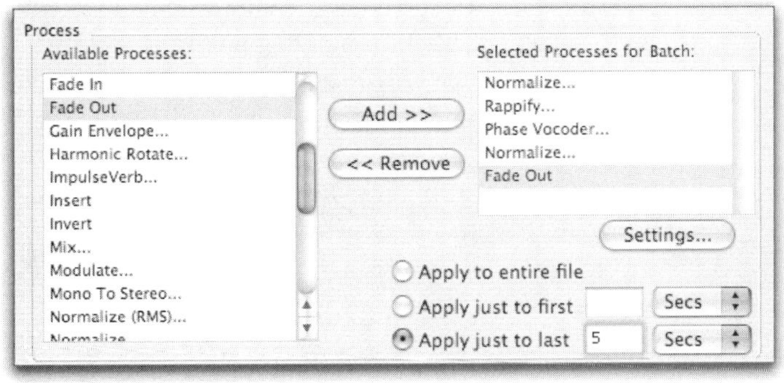

Figure 13-2
Commands added to the Batch list are applied in the order in which they appear.

The "Apply to entire file" option is selected by default, but you can individually aim any of the commands in the Batch list to the area in the audio file that you want to process (except for commands, such as Mono To Stereo, that must be applied to the document as a whole).

Many of the DSP commands in the list on the left have parameters that must be set before you use them. When one of those commands is added to the Batch list, the appropriate dialog box pops up automatically, allowing you to enter the settings that you want. If you change your mind, just select the command in the Batch list and click the Settings button to reopen the dialog box.

A few of the commands, such as Harmonic Rotate, include a Preview button in the dialog box. Peak Pro uses the current (front-most) Audio Document or selection for previewing. If you're planning on processing a lot of files, it's a good idea to open a representative file ahead of time, so it can serve as a preview file. To delete any item in the Batch list, simply select it and click the Remove button.

The Batch File Processor supports AU and VST plug-ins. To apply a plug-in effect to multiple files, open the plug-in first and configure it as needed. Then add the Bounce command to the batch script in the Process section.

Save Changes Section

Once you've set up your batch script in the Process section, turn your attention to the Save Changes area at the bottom (see **Figure 13-3**). In the Save Changes area you can specify how and where the processed files will be stored.

Figure 13-3
Use the Save Changes section to specify how and where you want the processed files stored.

Tool Tips: STICKY LOOP
When using the Batch File Processor, avoid choosing the input folder as the output folder, because Peak Pro might get stuck in a loop that could cause the processor to malfunction.

First, click the Save Changes box and then click the Set button to open the Save Audio Document dialog box. Navigate to the folder or drive where you want your processed files to end up. Click the New Folder button if you don't already have a folder for the files.

At the bottom of the Save Audio Document dialog box, three drop-down menus provide options for the final output format (see **Figure 13-4**). The File Type menu offers all of the file types that Peak Pro supports: AIFF (Peak Pro's native file format), Sound Designer II, WAV, QuickTime, raw, Jam Image, and several others.

The Bit Depth menu lets you specify a resolution for the files: 8-, 16-, 24-, or 32-bits. If you're reducing the resolution (such as going from 24 to 16 bits), you'll get the best results if you check the Pow-r dithering box. (For more on Pow-r dithering, see Chapter 4.)

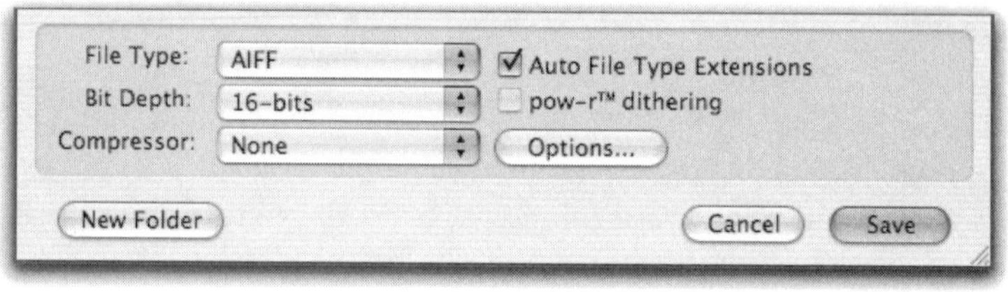

Figure 13-4
The Save Audio Document dialog box provides drop-down menus for specifying the final output resolution and format.

The Compressor menu enables you to apply a data compression algorithm to the files. Peak Pro supports more than a dozen compression schemes that include a variety of lossy and lossless options. Keep in mind that not all of the compression schemes are available for all of the file types. For example, MPEG-4 is available for QuickTime files, but not for AIFF. Apple Lossless compression is available for AIFF, but not for Sound Designer II. In fact, only AIFF and QuickTime allow for compression; the options differ between the two.

Tool Tips: NAME BLAME
When using the Batch File Processor in versions of Peak before version 5, generating file names longer than 32 characters could cause the process to act improperly or fail. In Peak Pro 5 and later, support for longer file names has solved the problem.

When you're finished with the Save Audio Document dialog, click the Save button to return to the Batch File Processor. If you'd like to generate a Log File text document, click the Log File checkbox. That opens the Batch Processor Log File dialog box, where you can name the file and choose a destination to save it. Log Files are useful for keeping track of which processes you've applied to your files, and for diagnosing problems if the processing fails for some reason. (You can read the log files with TextEdit or any program, such as Microsoft Word, that reads TXT files.)

If you want to add a suffix to the names of the processed files, enter it in the File Name Suffix box. As a general rule, it's best to keep the suffix as short as possible to keep the total file-name length from becoming unwieldy.

When processing a group of files with different sampling rates or formats, you can retain their original file characteristics by clicking the Preserve File Attributes checkbox in the lower-right corner of the Batch File Processor.

Once the Save Changes section has been set up, turn to the Input area at the top of the dialog box (see **Figure 13-5**). Click the On button to activate the Batch File Processor. The three radio buttons on the right let you specify which kinds of files will be affected: all files (the default setting), only mono files, or only stereo files. If you'll be processing both mono and stereo files, it's a good idea to open a stereo document and make a selection before opening the Batch File Processor. That will help most of the DSP commands make the appropriate decisions about how to handle both types of input files.

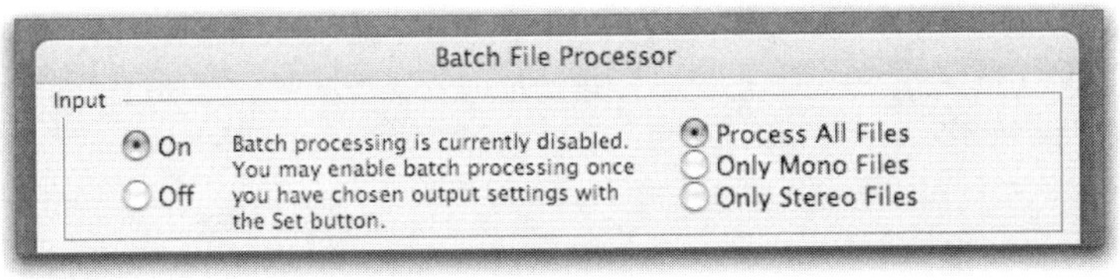

Figure 13-5
Click the On button at the top of the Batch File Processor dialog box to activate the processor.

Processing

With everything configured in the Batch File Processor dialog box and the On button active, click the OK button in the lower-right corner. That closes the dialog box and places a checkmark in front of the Batch Processor command in the File menu. You can now drag any file or folder (or even a disk full of files) and drop it onto the Peak Pro program icon (or an alias or Dock icon), and it will automatically be processed with the commands that you have set up. If the input folder has subfolders in it, Peak Pro reproduces the hierarchical structure of the original folder in the output folder. Although any file dropped onto the Peak Pro icon will be processed, files opened with the Open command in the File menu will not.

When you're through processing your files, remember to immediately turn off the Batch File Processor; otherwise, any Peak Pro file that you double-click or drag-and-drop will be sent to the processor. To turn off the Batch File Processor, go to the File menu and choose Batch Processor to reopen the dialog box. Click the Off button to deactivate the processor. To stop the batch processing in the middle of a run, hit Command-period. Peak Pro will finish up the current file and stop. It will also turn off the Batch File Processor.

If you find yourself using the same configuration over and over, you can save the Batch Script by clicking the Save Script button at the bottom of the dialog box (see **Figure 13-3**). Use the Load Script button to open existing configurations.

Apple Events

Peak Pro's other great tool for automating tasks is its support for Apple Events. The Mac's operating system includes a built-in scripting language called AppleScript, which has been a part of the Mac environment since 1990. AppleScript enables you to combine Apple Events into a sequence of actions called a *script,* which can perform a variety of tasks. Each Apple Event carries out a single action, such as opening a file, closing a window, or saving a document. By combining Apple Events into a script, you can create customized operations to greatly improve your efficiency when hunting for and auditioning audio files.

Peak Pro's support for Apple Events makes it possible to integrate the program with a database application, such as FileMaker Pro. You can then use the database to catalog, organize, and audition your audio files. To combine the two programs, both must have a *dictionary* of common Apple Events that they can receive and respond to.

You can view a program's dictionary by opening Script Editor (Hard Drive > Applications > AppleScript > Script Editor) and choosing Open Dictionary in the File menu. The dialog box that appears presents a list of applications; choose one and click the Open button, or browse to one that is not on the list. Script Editor then opens the selected program and displays its dictionary of supported Apple Events with their associated programming syntax (see **Figure 13-6**).

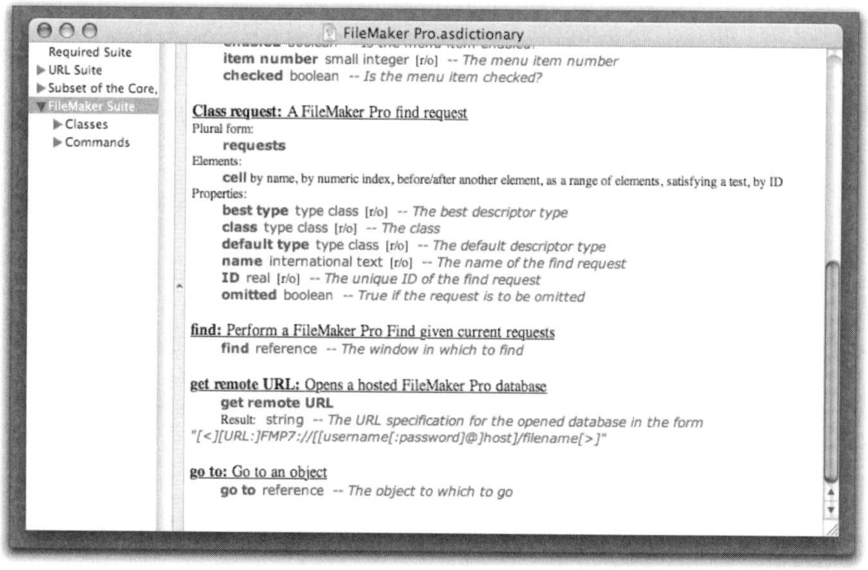

Figure 13-6
Use Script Editor to view a program's dictionary of supported Apple Events.

Although Peak Pro doesn't fully support AppleScript, its Core Suite of Apple Events includes the ODOC event (instructs Peak Pro to open an Audio Document) and QUIT (to quit the program). Peak Pro also has its own special class of events that it understands. These are all preceded by the FURP identification, which must be present for the program to understand the events. The FURP events include:

SFFV (set the FindFile Volume)
SFFF (set the FindFile file)
OFFF (open the FindFile file)
STOP (stop audio playback)
CLOS (close the front-most window)
PLAY (play the front-most window)

To demonstrate what you can do with these events, Peak Pro includes a couple of example FileMaker Pro scripts to try out. They offer a simple way to find and audition your audio documents. To use one, open it in FileMaker Pro after you have opened Peak Pro. The first example provides several categories for organizing sounds and an Audition button to play the located audio files (see **Figure 13-7**).

The second example has a simpler interface with Play and Stop buttons (see **Figure 13-8**). Just indicate the drive and file names to locate and audition the sound. A complete discussion of programming with Apple Events is beyond the scope of this book. But if you'd like to explore the subject further, you can learn a lot by analyzing existing scripts. I'd suggest starting with the two examples that come with Peak Pro.

Tool Tips: AN APPLE A DAY

If you would like to explore AppleScript and Apple Events in more detail, you can find much more information at the following Web sites:

www.apple.com/applescript
www.apple.com/applescript/studio
www.apple.com/applescript/resources
www.applescriptsourcebook.com

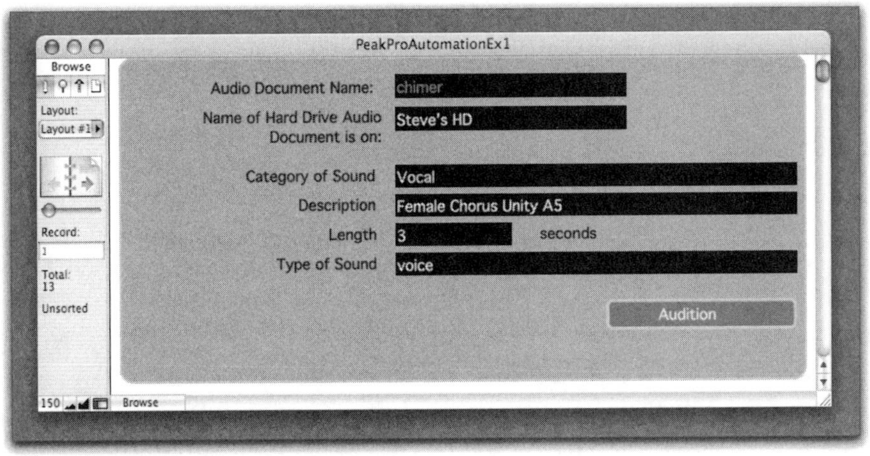

Figure 13-7
Peak Pro includes an example FileMaker Pro script for finding and auditioning files.

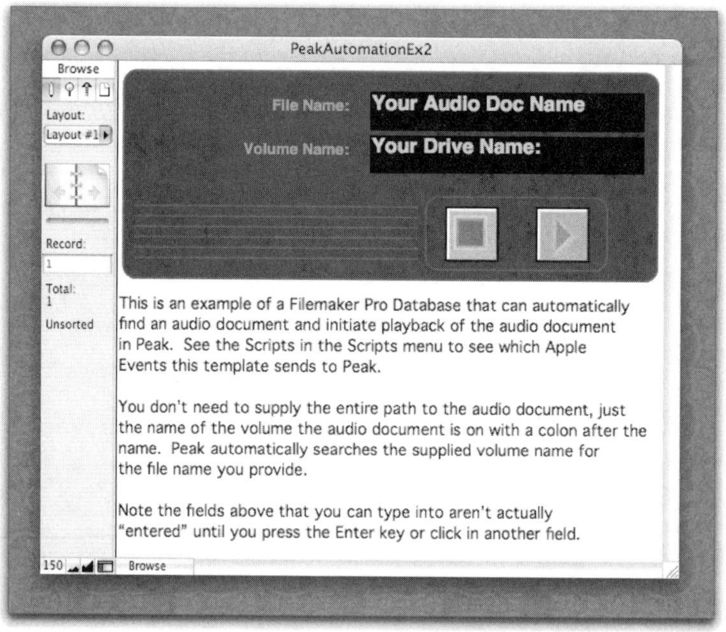

Figure 13-8
This is another example script template for finding and playing audio files with FileMaker Pro.

Open one of the example files in FileMaker Pro, and then choose ScriptMaker in the Scripts menu. In the dialog box that appears, choose one of the actions from the list, and click the Edit button to view the script. You'll see how the Apple Events were combined into a script and what additional information must be included (see **Figure 13-9**).

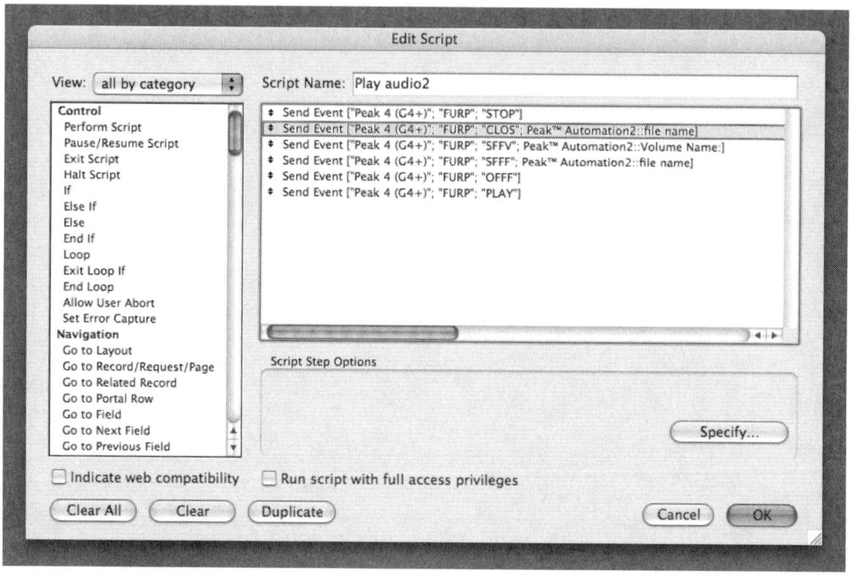

Figure 13-9
You can use FileMaker Pro's ScriptMaker to see how the Apple Events in Peak Pro's examples were combined into a script.

That's a Wrap!

Using Peak Pro's Batch File Processor to process large numbers of files will definitely speed up your productivity. And using Apple Events to integrate Peak Pro with a database program can help you manage your growing library of audio clips and recordings. Putting these two power tools together with the rest of Peak Pro's high-end features yields a more streamlined workflow, which is especially important if you're working in a high-pressure, high-stakes environment.

Appendix I

Keyboard Shortcuts

Peak Pro comes with a large collection of preset keyboard shortcuts to help speed up your workflow. You can, however, create your own shortcuts to replace the default combinations if you have some personal preferences or if you want to match the shortcuts in another program. Here are Peak Pro's keyboard shortcuts as they appear from left to right in the menu bar. See the appropriate chapters in the book for more details on how to use these commands.

Peak

Help	Command-/
Hide Peak Pro	Command-H
Hide Others	Command-Option-H
Quit Peak Pro	Command-Q

File

New Mono Document	Command-N
New Stereo Document	Command-Shift-N
New Document from Selection	Control-N
New Playlist Document	Command-Shift-P
New Document from Playlist	Command-Shift-B
Open...	Command-O
Close	Command-W

File *(continued)*

Close All	Command-Option-W
Save	Command-S
Save As…	Command-Shift-S
Save a Copy As	Command-Option-S

Edit

Undo	Command-Z
Redo	Command-Y
Cut	Command-X
Copy	Command-C
Paste	Command-V
Insert	Command-D
Silence	Command-E
Delete	Delete
Delete Except Audio	Option-Delete
Crop	Command-'
Select All	Command-A
Insertion Point at Selection Start	Up Arrow
Insertion Point at Selection End	Down Arrow
Select Loop	Command-- (Command-Hyphen)
Previous Selection	Command-Shift-Left Arrow
Next Selection	Command-Shift-Right Arrow

Action

Zoom Out	Command-[
Zoom In	Command-]
Increase Vertical Zoom	Control-Up Arrow
Decrease Vertical Zoom	Control-Down Arrow
Fit Selection	Command-Shift-]
Zoom Out All the Way	Command-Shift-[
Zoom to Just Before the Sample Level (start)	Shift-Left Arrow
Zoom to Just Before the Sample Level (end)	Shift-Right Arrow
Loop This Selection	Command-Shift-- (Command-Shift-Hyphen)
Nudge Loop Backward	Option-Left Arrow
Nudge Loop Forward	Option-Right Arrow
New Marker	Command-M

Action *(continued)*

New Region	Command-Shift-R
Capture Region to Playlist	Command-K
Go to Selection Start	Left Arrow
Go to Selection End	Right Arrow
Go to Time…	Command-G
Loop Surfer	Command-J

Audio

Stop/Rewind	Return
Play/Pause	Spacebar
Play Selection	Spacebar
Play With Auditioning	Command-Spacebar
Stop and Extend Selection	Shift-Return
Record	Command-R
Record Settings	Option-R

Options

Use Loop in Playback	Command-L
Show Overview	Command-,
Show Cursor Info	Command-Shift-T
Audio Info…	Command-I

Window

New Playlist	Command-Shift-P
Tile Windows	Command-T
Toggle Contents Drawer	Command-F
Plug-In Effect 1 to Front	Command-Option-1
Plug-In Effect 2 to Front	Command-Option-2
Plug-In Effect 3 to Front	Command-Option-3
Plug-In Effect 4 to Front	Command-Option-4
Plug-In Effect 5 to Front	Command-Option-5

Other Shortcuts

Bring Audio Document Windows to Front in Order	Command-1, -2, -3, and so on

Appendix II

File Formats Supported by Peak Pro 5

AAC The Advanced Audio Coding format uses a lossy data compression scheme that is optimized for audio streaming. It was designed to offer better performance than the popular MP3 format, and has now gained widespread acceptance as the native format for Apple's highly successful iPod product line.

AIFC This is the compressed variant of the AIFF format (see below).

AIFF The Audio Interchange File Format was co-developed by Apple Computer based on the Interchange File Format from Electronic Arts. It is designed to be a universal audio format that stores data in uncompressed form. AIFF is currently supported by virtually all Macintosh audio software and many Windows programs as well. Peak Pro uses AIFF as its native format.

AU The AU format (also known as Audio/Basic) was developed in the early 1990s by NeXT Computer and Sun Microsystems. It is a popular format on the Internet and is supported internally by many Web browsers, especially Unix-based programs. (Don't confuse this with the AU abbreviation used to designate Apple's Audio Units plug-in format.)

Jam Image File This is the file format used by Roxio Jam for burning audio CDs, including those that are destined for replication and commercial use.

MP3 The MPEG-1 Audio Layer 3 format, popularly referred to as MP3, achieves significant reductions in file size through the use of a lossy compression scheme based in part on psychoacoustic modeling. MP3's appeal is that it maintains reasonably good audio fidelity while reducing file sizes enough for downloading over the Internet or for storing and playing with personal music players.

MP4 The MPEG-1 Audio Layer 4 format is also known as AAC (see above). As with MP3, it uses psychoacoustic-based lossy compression to reduce file sizes. However, MP4 provides better audio quality than MP3, and many people feel that it approaches the quality of compact disc audio.

PAF This is the native format for the E-mu/Ensoniq PARIS (Professional Audio Recording Integrated System) digital audio workstation. Peak Pro supports 8- and 16-bit mono or stereo PAF files.

QuickTime Apple released the original version of QuickTime in 1991 as a multimedia addition to System 7. (In 1994, Apple also introduced QuickTime for Windows.) Aside from various graphics and video formats, QuickTime supports a number of audio file types along with several kinds of audio compression schemes (codecs). Apple's iTunes jukebox software uses QuickTime for its playback engine. The QuickTime file format eventually became the basis of the MPEG-4 standard, and Peak Pro now supports the MP4 format (and several others) through QuickTime.

Raw This is a simple nonproprietary audio data file without a header. It may be of use to game, multimedia, and audio software developers.

Sonic AIFF This is the native format used in Sonic Solutions digital audio workstations. Peak Pro supports Sonic AIFF resolutions from 16 to 32 bits.

Sound Designer II Developed by Digidesign for its Mac-based DAWs, the uncompressed SDII (also abbreviated SD2) format is the native format for Pro Tools and other Digidesign products. Now supported on both platforms, SDII files can be mono or stereo in a range of sampling rates and resolutions. As with WAV and AIFF, the SDII format has become a popular standard for transferring audio files between applications.

System 7 Sounds This legacy format is for saving sounds in the native audio format for Mac OS 7.

WAV This format, also known as WAVE, is the Waveform Audio format. It's the standard universal format for Microsoft Windows and is most often employed as an uncompressed method for storing audio data. It is supported by virtually all Windows-based audio software as well as many Macintosh programs.

Index

T

U